Taste of Home

Make it!

TAKE IT

TASTE OF HOME BOOKS • RDA ENTHUSIAST BRANDS, LLC • MILWAUKEE, WI

PAGE 26

PAGE 109

PAGE 18

PAGE 62

CONTENTS

CHAPTERS

REFERENCE

PAGE 116

PAGE 217

PAGE 198

PAGE 83

Visit us at tasteofhome.com for other
Taste of Home books and products.

Executive Editor: Mark Hagen
Senior Art Director: Raeann Thompson
Senior Editor: Christine Rukavena
Art Director: Maggie Conners
Assistant Art Director: Julianne Petrasko
Designers: Arielle Jardine, Maggie Roethle
Deputy Editor, Copy Desk: Dulcie Shoener
Copy Editor: Sara Strauss

Cover:
Photographer: Mark Derse
Set Stylist: Stacey Genaw
Food Stylist: Shannon Norris

Pictured on front cover:
Potluck Fried Chicken, p. 90
No-Bake Mango Strawberry Cheesecake, p. 252
Super Italian Chopped Salad, p. 119

Pictured on title page:
Grilled Angel Food Cake with Strawberries, p. 232

Pictured on back cover:
Cheddar-Ham Oven Omelet, p. 41
Muffuletta Pasta, p. 79
Hearty Meatball Sub Sandwiches, p. 83
7-Layer Gelatin Salad, p. 250

International Standard Book Numbers:
D 978-1-62145-763-3
U 978-1-62145-764-0
International Standard Serial Number:
2166-0522
Component Numbers:
D 118100104H
U 118100106H

Printed in USA
1 3 5 7 9 10 8 6 4 2

More ways to connect with us:

BRING OUT THE BEST
OUR TOP RECIPES & TIPS MAKE THE GATHERING JOYFUL!

Share the dishes folks love when you prepare a recipe from *Make It, Take It*. This edition is packed with hundreds of party-sized, crowd-pleasing foods, plus tips for potluck success and make-ahead ideas.

From choosing a dish to packing and serving it, you'll savor every moment with reader-submitted recipes and Test Kitchen pointers all approved by *Taste of Home*.

Inside, you'll discover 255 delightful dishes. Also watch for these useful features throughout the book.

TRIFLES & NO-BAKE DESSERTS: Nothing beats the summertime ease and wow factor at a sweets table more than a beautiful no-bake trifle, gelatin or cheesecake (as is on the cover!). Find 26 ideas in this special chapter.

MAKE AHEAD dishes let you do most of the work ahead and then pop the dish in the fridge or freezer for easy serving on a moment's notice. Simple!

BRING IT
These tips sprinkled throughout the book provide insights for organizing the buffet, keeping foods hot or cold, and making sure your contribution is the belle of the ball.

PACK LIKE A PRO
These tips and tricks will have you hitting the road with confidence.

1 Build a DIY Multilevel Tote
If you have more dishes than hands, reach for a cooling rack with folding legs. Fold out the legs and use the rack to create sturdy, stable levels inside a carrying tote without crushing what's below. Get creative. You can also build layers by propping up a sheet pan with ring molds or cans.

2 Ensure a No-Slip Trip
Place grippy drawer liners or silicone baking mats in the car before loading your food. The lining will keep dishes from sliding and contain any errant spills. An old yoga mat works well for this, too.

3 Keep a Lid on It
Use a bungee cord, painter's tape or thick ribbon to keep the lid for your slow cooker or Dutch oven in place. Secure the cord around the handles and over the top. Now you're ready to transport without risk of a mess.

4 Bring a Salad
Yes, you can serve a crisp, freshly tossed salad when you're far from home. Just bring the fixings in a serving bowl, along with the utensils. Toss the salad at your destination. Voila! Remember to bring a grocery bag to corral the leftovers and dirty dishes.

5 Frosting Is Good Glue
If you're transporting cake to a special event, make it easier to tote with this little tip. Secure the cake (or cardboard cake circle if you're using one) onto the presentation plate with a dab of frosting. This makes the cake less likely to slide around, even if you have to brake suddenly. And you're the only one who'll know the frosting is there!

6 Pack a Touch-Up Kit
Make a little touch-up kit of decorations and frosting (just in case) to take with your decorated cake. Pack the items with a clean dish towel and offset spatula. Transport the frosting in its pastry bag if you used one.

7 Tailgate Grill Skills
Place the grill on a solid surface, away from any activities so no one bumps into it. Don't set the grill near shrubs, grass, overhangs or fences. Keep coolers away from the grill. Set the coolers out of direct sunlight and replenish the ice if possible.

8 Tailgate Kit
Store all your tailgate needs (such as linens, serveware, games and sunblock) in a plastic bin inside a cooler. You'll be ready to go at a moment's notice.

Apricot Turkey
Pinwheels
page 23

Appetizers & Dips

Time to gather around the good stuff! Dig into tiny sandwiches, creamy dips, spicy wings and dozens of other irresistible party dishes. Folks will love these make-and-take wonders.

AVOCADO SALSA

I first made this recipe for a party, and it was an absolute success. People love the garlic, corn and avocado combination.
—Susan Vandermeer, Ogden, UT

- -

Prep: 20 min. + chilling
Makes: about 7 cups

1⅔	cups (about 8¼ oz.) frozen corn, thawed
2	cans (2¼ oz. each) sliced ripe olives, drained
1	medium sweet red pepper, chopped
1	small onion, chopped
5	garlic cloves, minced
⅓	cup olive oil
¼	cup lemon juice
3	Tbsp. cider vinegar
1	tsp. dried oregano
½	tsp. salt
½	tsp. pepper
4	medium ripe avocados, peeled
	Tortilla chips

1. Combine the corn, olives, red pepper and onion. In another bowl, mix the next 7 ingredients. Pour over corn mixture; toss to coat. Refrigerate, covered, overnight.
2. Just before serving, chop avocados; stir into salsa. Serve with tortilla chips.
¼ cup: 82 cal., 7g fat (1g sat. fat), 0 chol., 85mg sod., 5g carb. (1g sugars, 2g fiber), 1g pro. **Diabetic exchanges:** 1½ fat.

DILLY CHEESE BALL

My whole family devours this herby cheese spread—even my son, the chef. Serve it with your favorite crackers.
—Jane Vince, London, ON

- -

Prep: 10 min. + chilling • **Makes:** 2½ cups

- 1 pkg. (8 oz.) cream cheese, softened
- 1 cup dill pickle relish, drained
- ¼ cup finely chopped onion
- 1½ cups shredded cheddar cheese
- 1 Tbsp. Worcestershire sauce
- 2 Tbsp. mayonnaise
- 2 Tbsp. minced fresh parsley
  Assorted crackers

Beat the first 6 ingredients until smooth. Shape into a ball; wrap and refrigerate several hours. Sprinkle with parsley; serve with crackers.
2 Tbsp.: 100 cal., 8g fat (4g sat. fat), 22mg chol., 244mg sod., 5g carb. (1g sugars, 0 fiber), 3g pro.

BRIE PHYLLO CUPS

Mini phyllo shells from the freezer section make quick work of these elegant appetizers. They look fancy and taste delicious, but they're a snap to put together for a special occasion.
—Brenda Little, Boise, ID

- -

Takes: 20 min. • **Makes:** 15 appetizers

- 1 pkg. (1.9 oz.) frozen
     miniature phyllo tart shells
- 3 Tbsp. crushed gingersnaps
- 6 oz. Brie cheese, rind removed, cubed
- ¼ cup spreadable fruit of your choice

Preheat oven to 325°. Place the tart shells on an ungreased baking sheet. Sprinkle about ½ tsp. gingersnap crumbs into each shell; top with Brie and spreadable fruit. Bake 5 minutes or until cheese is melted.
1 serving: 83 cal., 4g fat (2g sat. fat), 11mg chol., 100mg sod., 7g carb. (3g sugars, 0 fiber), 3g pro.

DEVILED EGGS WITH BACON

These yummy deviled eggs went over so well at our summer cookouts, I started making them for holiday dinners as well. Everyone likes the flavorful addition of crumbled bacon.

—Barbara Reid, Mounds, OK

Takes: 30 min. • **Makes:** 2 dozen

12   **hard-boiled large eggs**
⅓   **cup mayonnaise**
3   **bacon strips, cooked and crumbled**
3   **Tbsp. finely chopped red onion**
3   **Tbsp. sweet pickle relish**
¼   **tsp. smoked paprika**

Cut eggs in half lengthwise. Remove yolks; set whites aside. In a small bowl, mash yolks. Add the mayonnaise, bacon, onion and relish; mix well. Stuff into egg whites. Refrigerate until serving. Sprinkle eggs with paprika.

1 stuffed egg half: 68 cal., 5g fat (1g sat. fat), 108mg chol., 82mg sod., 1g carb. (1g sugars, 0 fiber), 3g pro.

MAMMA'S CAPONATA

This is fabulous as an appetizer, but you can easily turn it into a meal. Instead of having it on bread, serve it over warm pasta.
—Georgette Stubin, Canton, MI

Prep: 30 min. • **Cook:** 40 min.
Makes: 6 cups

- 1   large eggplant, peeled and chopped
- ¼   cup plus 2 Tbsp. olive oil, divided
- 2   medium onions, chopped
- 2   celery ribs, chopped
- 2   cans (14½ oz. each) diced tomatoes, undrained
- ⅓   cup chopped ripe olives
- ¼   cup red wine vinegar
- 2   Tbsp. sugar
- 2   Tbsp. capers, drained
- ½   tsp. salt
- ½   tsp. pepper
   French bread baguettes, sliced and toasted

1. In a Dutch oven, saute eggplant in ¼ cup oil until tender. Remove from the pan and set aside. In the same pan, saute onions and celery in remaining oil until tender. Stir in tomatoes and eggplant. Bring to a boil. Reduce heat; simmer, uncovered, for 15 minutes.

2. Add the olives, vinegar, sugar, capers, salt and pepper. Return to a boil. Reduce heat; simmer, uncovered, for 20 minutes or until thickened. Serve warm or at room temperature with baguettes.

¼ cup: 57 cal., 4g fat (1g sat. fat), 0 chol., 134mg sod., 6g carb. (4g sugars, 2g fiber), 1g pro. **Diabetic exchanges:** 1 vegetable, ½ fat.

PIZZA PUFFS

What's more fun than a pizza puff? Skip the kind sold in the freezer section and sample this homemade version. You can substitute any meat or vegetable for the pepperoni and any cheese for the mozzarella.
—Vivi Taylor, Middleburg, FL

- -

Takes: 30 min. • **Makes:** 20 servings

    1   loaf (1 lb.) frozen pizza dough,
        thawed
   20   slices pepperoni
    8   oz. part-skim mozzarella cheese,
        cut into 20 cubes
   ¼   cup butter
    2   small garlic cloves, minced
        Dash salt
        Marinara sauce, warmed
        Optional: Crushed red pepper flakes
        and grated Parmesan cheese

1. Preheat oven to 400°. Shape dough into 1½-in. balls; flatten into ⅛-in. thick circles. Place 1 pepperoni slice and 1 cheese cube in center of each circle; wrap dough around pepperoni and cheese. Pinch edges to seal; shape into a ball. Repeat with remaining dough, cheese and pepperoni. Place seam side down on greased baking sheets; bake until light golden brown, 10-15 minutes. Cool slightly.

2. Meanwhile, in a small saucepan, melt butter over low heat. Add garlic and salt, taking care not to brown butter or garlic; brush over puffs. Serve with marinara sauce; if desired, sprinkle with red pepper flakes and Parmesan.

Freeze option: Cover and freeze unbaked pizza puffs on waxed paper-lined baking sheets until firm. Transfer to a freezer container; seal and return to freezer. To use, preheat oven to 325°; bake pizza puffs on greased baking sheets as directed, increasing the time as necessary to heat through.

1 pizza puff: 120 cal., 6g fat (3g sat. fat), 15mg chol., 189mg sod., 11g carb. (1g sugars, 0 fiber), 5g pro.

BUTTERSCOTCH MULLED CIDER

Five minutes of preparation result in this dynamite spiced drink. You'll love the sweet taste of butterscotch and cinnamon in this hot apple cider.
—Karen Mack, Webster, NY

- -

Takes: 30 min. • **Makes:** 18 servings

    1   gallon apple cider or juice
    2   cups butterscotch schnapps liqueur
    8   cinnamon sticks (3 in.)

Optional: Apple pieces and additional cinnamon sticks

In a Dutch oven, combine the first 3 ingredients. Cook, stirring occasionally, until heated through and the flavors are blended, 25-30 minutes. If desired, garnish with apple pieces and additional cinnamon sticks.

1 cup: 128 cal., 0 fat (0 sat. fat), 0 chol., 22mg sod., 27g carb. (23g sugars, 0 fiber), 0 pro.

FIG & GOAT CHEESE MEATBALLS

Around the holidays, saucy cocktail meatballs are always the first appetizer to go. In this dish, the sweet flavor of the fig glaze goes perfectly with the pork and tangy goat cheese. Serve them hot from the skillet or freeze and gently reheat them.
—Kim Banick, Turner, OR

Prep: 45 min. • **Bake:** 25 min.
Makes: 3 dozen

- 1 **cup panko bread crumbs**
- 2 **large eggs, lightly beaten**
- 2 **lbs. bulk Italian sausage**
- 1 **log (4 oz.) fresh goat cheese**
- 1 **cup red wine vinegar**
- ½ **cup sugar**
- 1 **cinnamon stick (3 in.)**
- 4 **whole cloves**
- 1 **whole star anise**
- 1 **cup dried figs, chopped**
- 1 **cup water**
  Chopped fresh chives, optional

1. Preheat oven to 350°. In a large bowl, combine bread crumbs and eggs. Add sausage; mix lightly but thoroughly. Divide into 36 portions. Shape each portion around ½ tsp. cheese to cover completely. Place meatballs on a greased rack in a 15x10x1-in. baking pan. Bake until cooked through, 25-30 minutes.
2. Meanwhile, in a large saucepan, bring vinegar, sugar, cinnamon, cloves and star anise to a boil. Reduce heat; simmer 5 minutes. Discard cinnamon, cloves and star anise. Add figs; cook until softened, 8-10 minutes. Remove from heat; cool slightly. Transfer to a blender. Add 1 cup water; process until almost smooth. Serve with meatballs. If desired, top meatballs with chopped chives.
Freeze option: Freeze cooled meatballs and sauce in freezer containers. To use, partially thaw in refrigerator overnight. Heat through in a covered saucepan, stirring gently; add a little water if necessary.
1 meatball: 97 cal., 6g fat (2g sat. fat), 26mg chol., 175mg sod., 7g carb. (5g sugars, 0 fiber), 4g pro.

MINI GRILLED CHEESE

If you're looking for a fantastic make-ahead snack, try these. They're nice to have in the freezer for lunch with soup or a salad. My family loves to nibble on them anytime.
—Anita Curtis, Camarillo, CA

Takes: 30 min. • **Makes:** 8 dozen

- 1 **cup butter, softened**
- 2 **jars (5 oz. each) sharp American cheese spread, softened**
- 1 **large egg**
- 1 **can (4 oz.) chopped green chiles, drained**
- ¼ **cup salsa**
- 2 **cups shredded cheddar cheese**
- 2 **loaves (1½ lbs. each) thinly sliced sandwich bread, crusts removed**

1. Preheat oven to 350°. Cream butter, cheese spread and egg until smooth. Stir in chiles, salsa and cheddar cheese. Spread about 1 Tbsp. cheese mixture on each slice of 1 loaf of bread.
2. Top with remaining bread; spread with more cheese mixture. Cut each sandwich into 4 squares or triangles; place on a baking sheet lined with parchment. Bake until cheese is melted, 10-15 minutes.
Freeze option: Place cooled appetizers in a single layer on a baking sheet. Freeze 1 hour. Transfer to an airtight container and store in the freezer. Bake frozen appetizers as directed until bubbly and browned, about 15-20 minutes.
1 piece: 77 cal., 4g fat (2g sat. fat), 10mg chol., 168mg sod., 7g carb. (1g sugars, 0 fiber), 2g pro.

PROSCIUTTO-WRAPPED ASPARAGUS WITH RASPBERRY SAUCE

Grilling the prosciutto with the asparagus gives this dish a salty crunch that's perfect for dipping into a sweet glaze. When a delicious appetizer is this easy to prepare, you owe it to yourself to try it!
—Noelle Myers, Grand Forks, ND

Takes: 30 min. • **Makes:** 16 appetizers

- ⅓ lb. thinly sliced prosciutto or deli ham
- 16 fresh asparagus spears, trimmed
- ½ cup seedless raspberry jam
- 2 Tbsp. balsamic vinegar

1. Cut prosciutto slices in half. Wrap a prosciutto piece around each asparagus spear; secure ends with toothpicks.
2. Grill asparagus, covered, on an oiled rack over medium heat for 6-8 minutes or until prosciutto is crisp, turning once. Discard the toothpicks.
3. In a small microwave-safe bowl, microwave jam and vinegar on high for 15-20 seconds or until jam is melted. Serve with asparagus.

1 asparagus spear with 1½ tsp. sauce: 50 cal., 1g fat (0 sat. fat), 8mg chol., 184mg sod., 7g carb. (7g sugars, 0 fiber), 3g pro. **Diabetic exchanges:** ½ starch.

MAKE AHEAD
GOUGERES

I brought the recipe for these gougeres back from a trip to Nice, France. The original called for Gruyere cheese, but I found that Gouda is a more budget-friendly alternative. These puffs are a wonderful bite-sized treat. If you have leftovers, float a few of these gems on a bowl of soup in place of croutons.
—Lily Julow, Lawrenceville, GA

Prep: 40 min. • **Bake:** 20 min.
Makes: about 3 dozen

- 1 cup water
- 6 Tbsp. unsalted butter, cubed
- ½ tsp. sea salt
- ¼ tsp. pepper
- ¾ cup all-purpose flour
- 4 large eggs
- 1 cup (4 oz.) shredded regular or smoked Gouda cheese
- ⅓ cup minced fresh chives
- ⅛ tsp. ground nutmeg

TOPPING
- 1 large egg
- 1 tsp. water
- ⅓ cup shredded regular or smoked Gouda cheese

1. Preheat oven to 425°. In a large heavy saucepan, bring the first 4 ingredients to a rolling boil. Remove from heat; add all flour and beat until blended. Cook over medium-low heat, stirring vigorously until mixture pulls away from sides of pan and forms a ball, about 3 minutes.
2. Transfer to large bowl; beat 1 minute to cool slightly. Add eggs, 1 at a time, beating well after each addition until smooth. Continue beating until shiny. Beat in cheese, chives and nutmeg. Drop dough by tablespoonfuls 2 in. apart onto parchment-lined baking sheets.
3. For topping, whisk together egg and water; brush lightly over tops. Sprinkle with cheese. Bake until puffed, firm and golden brown, 20-25 minutes. Serve warm.
Freeze option: Freeze unbaked puffs on parchment-lined baking sheets until firm; transfer to resealable freezer containers and return to freezer. To use, place frozen puffs on parchment-lined baking sheets. Top and bake as directed, increasing time by 2-3 minutes.
1 appetizer: 52 cal., 4g fat (2g sat. fat), 36mg chol., 71mg sod., 2g carb. (0 sugars, 0 fiber), 2g pro.

STRAWBERRY & CREAM BRUSCHETTA

This is a dessert take on bruschetta. Sweet, cinnamony toast slices are topped with a cream cheese mixture, strawberries and almonds. They are like miniature cheesecakes and so yummy!
—Christi Meixner, Aurora, IL

- -

Takes: 25 min. • **Makes:** 2 dozen

- 1 **French bread baguette (8 oz.),
  cut into 24 slices**
- ¼ **cup butter, melted**
- 3 **Tbsp. sugar**
- ½ **tsp. ground cinnamon**
- 1 **pkg. (8 oz.) cream cheese, softened**
- ¼ **cup confectioners' sugar**
- 2 **tsp. lemon juice**
- 1 **tsp. grated lemon zest**
- 2½ **cups fresh strawberries, chopped**
- ⅓ **cup slivered almonds, toasted**

1. Preheat oven to 375°. Place bread on an ungreased baking sheet; brush with butter. Combine sugar and cinnamon; sprinkle over bread. Bake 4-5 minutes on each side or until lightly crisp.

2. In a small bowl, beat cream cheese, confectioners' sugar, and lemon juice and zest until blended; spread over toast. Top with strawberries; sprinkle with almonds.

1 appetizer: 94 cal., 6g fat (3g sat. fat), 15mg chol., 70mg sod., 8g carb. (4g sugars, 1g fiber), 2g pro.

FRIED CINNAMON STRIPS

These sweet chips are a must for your next party. You can use holiday cookie cutters to shape the tortillas into fun shapes. Kids just love them.
—Nancy Johnson, Laverne, OK

Takes: 25 min. • **Makes:** 5 dozen

- 1 **cup sugar**
- 1 **tsp. ground cinnamon**
- ¼ **tsp. ground nutmeg**
- 10 **flour tortillas (8 in.)**
  Canola oil

1. In a large bowl, combine sugar, cinnamon and nutmeg; set aside.

2. Cut tortillas into 3x2-in. strips. Heat 1 in. oil in a cast-iron or other heavy skillet to 375°, fry 4-5 strips at a time until golden brown, 30 seconds on each side. Drain on paper towels.

3. While still warm, place strips in bowl with sugar mixture; shake gently to coat. Serve them immediately or store them in an airtight container.

1 piece: 44 cal., 1g fat (0 sat. fat), 0 chol., 39mg sod., 8g carb. (3g sugars, 0 fiber), 1g pro.

TEST KITCHEN TIP
Serve these versatile chips with a fun fruit salsa or tropical fruit salad or even with fresh fruit and a chocolate or caramel dip.

SKINNY QUINOA VEGGIE DIP

Don't let the name fool you. This good-for-you recipe may appeal to an athlete in training, but it has plenty of flavor to satisfy everyone. We use crunchy cucumber slices for dippers.
—Jennifer Gizzi, Green Bay, WI

Prep: 20 min. • **Cook:** 15 min.
Makes: 32 servings

2	cans (15 oz.) black beans, rinsed and drained
1½	tsp. ground cumin
1½	tsp. paprika
½	tsp. cayenne pepper
1⅔	cups water, divided
	Salt and pepper to taste
⅔	cup quinoa, rinsed
5	Tbsp. lime juice, divided
2	medium ripe avocados, peeled and coarsely chopped
2	Tbsp. plus ¾ cup sour cream, divided
¼	cup minced fresh cilantro
3	plum tomatoes, chopped
¾	cup peeled, seeded and finely chopped cucumber
¾	cup finely chopped zucchini
¼	cup finely chopped red onion
	Cucumber slices

1. Pulse beans, cumin, paprika, cayenne and ⅓ cup water in food processor until smooth. Add salt and pepper to taste.
2. In a small saucepan, cook the quinoa with remaining 1⅓ cups water according to package directions. Fluff with fork; sprinkle with 2 Tbsp. lime juice. Set aside. Meanwhile, mash together avocados, 2 Tbsp. sour cream, cilantro and the remaining lime juice.
3. In a 2½-qt. dish, layer bean mixture, quinoa, avocado mixture, remaining sour cream, tomatoes, chopped cucumber, zucchini and onion. Serve immediately with cucumber slices for dipping or refrigerate.
¼ cup: 65 cal., 3g fat (1g sat. fat), 4mg chol., 54mg sod., 8g carb. (1g sugars, 2g fiber), 2g pro. **Diabetic exchanges:** ½ starch, ½ fat.

TOMATO-WALNUT PESTO SPREAD

Whenever I bring this popular spread to parties, I know to bring copies of the recipe. Once people taste it, they always ask how I make it. The red, green and white layers make it especially festive for Christmastime.
—Marsha Dawson, Appleton, WI

Prep: 15 min. + chilling • **Makes:** 2⅓ cups

- 3 Tbsp. chopped oil-packed sun-dried tomatoes, patted dry
- 1 pkg. (8 oz.) cream cheese, softened
- ½ cup grated Parmesan cheese
- ¼ cup sour cream
- 2 Tbsp. butter, softened
- ½ cup finely chopped walnuts
- ½ cup prepared pesto
  Assorted crackers

1. Line a 4-cup mold with plastic wrap; coat with cooking spray. Place tomatoes in bottom of mold; set aside.
2. In a large bowl, beat the cheeses, sour cream and butter until blended. In another bowl, combine walnuts and pesto. Spread cheese mixture over tomatoes in prepared mold; top with walnut mixture.
3. Bring edges of plastic wrap together over pesto; press down gently to seal. Refrigerate for at least 4 hours or until firm. Open plastic wrap; invert mold onto a serving plate. Serve with crackers.

2 Tbsp.: 129 cal., 12g fat (5g sat. fat), 24mg chol., 137mg sod., 2g carb. (0 sugars, 0 fiber), 4g pro.

CHICKARITOS

After our son grew fond of a fast-food restaurant's burritos, I created this recipe by substituting chicken for beef and omitting the frying. It's been a big hit with our whole family ever since!
—Nancy Coates, Oro Valley, AZ

- -

Prep: 30 min. • **Bake:** 20 min.
Makes: 3 dozen

  3 **cups finely chopped cooked chicken**
1½ **cups shredded sharp cheddar cheese**
  1 **can (4 oz.) chopped green chiles**
  4 **green onions, finely chopped**
  1 **tsp. hot pepper sauce**

  1 **tsp. garlic salt**
¼ **tsp. paprika**
¼ **tsp. ground cumin**
¼ **tsp. pepper**
  2 **pkg. (17.3 oz. each) frozen puff pastry, thawed**
  1 **large egg, beaten**
     Salsa and guacamole

1. Preheat oven to 425°. In a large bowl, combine chicken, cheese, chiles, onions, pepper sauce and seasonings.

2. Unfold 1 sheet of puff pastry onto a lightly floured surface. Roll into a 12x9-in. rectangle. Cut into 9 rectangles.

3. Place 2 Tbsp. filling across the center of each rectangle. Brush edges of pastry with water and roll up pastry around filling. Press edges with a fork to seal. Repeat with remaining pastry and filling. Refrigerate, covered, until ready to bake.

4. Place pastries on a lightly greased baking sheet, seam sides down. Brush the tops with egg. Bake 20-25 minutes or until golden brown. Serve warm with salsa and guacamole.

1 appetizer: 213 cal., 12g fat (4g sat. fat), 31mg chol., 294mg sod., 16g carb. (0 sugars, 2g fiber), 11g pro.

APRICOT TURKEY PINWHEELS

I created these unique pinwheels for a football game snack using ingredients I had on hand. They were a huge hit! I appreciate how quick and easy they are to prepare.
—Melanie Foster, Blaine, MN

- -

Takes: 30 min. • **Makes:** 16 pinwheels

1	sheet frozen puff pastry, thawed
¼	cup apricot preserves
½	tsp. ground mustard
½	cup shredded Monterey Jack cheese
¼	lb. sliced deli turkey

Unfold the pastry; layer with preserves, mustard, cheese and turkey. Roll up jelly-roll style. Cut into 16 slices. Place cut side down on a parchment-lined baking sheet. Bake at 400° for 15-20 minutes or until golden brown.

Freeze option: Freeze cooled appetizers in a resealable freezer container. To use, reheat appetizers on a parchment-lined baking sheet in a preheated 400° oven until crisp and heated through.

1 appetizer: 108 cal., 5g fat (2g sat. fat), 6mg chol., 135mg sod., 12g carb. (2g sugars, 1g fiber), 3g pro.

★ ★ ★ ★ ★ **READER REVIEW**

"We loved these yummy pinwheels. Be sure to use parchment so they don't stick."

DVHENNING TASTEOFHOME.COM

BACON & SUN-DRIED TOMATO PHYLLO TARTS

Frozen mini phyllo tart shells are so convenient. Just add a savory filling featuring sun-dried tomatoes and bacon, then pop them in the oven.
—Patricia Quinn, Omaha, NE

Prep: 40 min. • **Bake:** 10 min.
Makes: 45 tartlets

- 2 tsp. olive oil
- ¾ cup chopped onion (about 1 medium)
- ¾ cup chopped green pepper (about 1 small)
- ¾ cup chopped sweet red pepper (about 1 small)
- 1 garlic clove, minced
  Dash dried oregano
- 3 pkg. (1.9 oz. each) frozen miniature phyllo tart shells
- 1 pkg. (8 oz.) cream cheese, softened
- 1½ tsp. lemon juice
- ⅛ tsp. salt
- 1 large egg, lightly beaten
- ½ cup oil-packed sun-dried tomatoes, chopped and patted dry
- 2 bacon strips, cooked and crumbled
- 1 Tbsp. minced fresh basil or 1 tsp. dried basil
- ½ cup crushed butter-flavored crackers
- ½ cup shredded cheddar cheese

1. Preheat oven to 350°. In a large skillet, heat oil over medium-high heat. Add onion and peppers; cook and stir 6-8 minutes or until tender. Add garlic and oregano; cook 1 minute longer. Cool completely.
2. Place tart shells on ungreased baking sheets. In a large bowl, beat cream cheese, lemon juice and salt until smooth. Add egg; beat on low speed just until blended. Stir in tomatoes, bacon, basil and onion mixture.
3. Spoon 2 tsp. filling into each tart shell. Top each with ½ tsp. crushed crackers and ½ tsp. cheddar cheese. Bake 10-12 minutes or until set. Serve warm.

Freeze option: Freeze cooled baked pastries in resealable freezer containers. To use, reheat on a baking sheet in a preheated 350° oven 15-18 minutes or until heated through.
1 tartlet: 58 cal., 4g fat (1g sat. fat), 11mg chol., 59mg sod., 4g carb. (1g sugars, 0 fiber), 2g pro.

SAUSAGE CHEESE PUFFS

People are always surprised when I tell them there are only four ingredients in these tasty bite-sized puffs. Cheesy and spicy, the golden morsels are a fun novelty at a breakfast or brunch, and they also make yummy party appetizers.
—Della Moore, Troy, NY

Takes: 25 min. • **Makes:** about 4 dozen

- 1 lb. bulk Italian sausage
- 3 cups biscuit/baking mix
- 4 cups shredded cheddar cheese
- ¾ cup water

1. Preheat oven to 400°. In a large skillet, cook sausage over medium heat until no longer pink, 5-7 minutes, breaking into crumbles; drain.
2. In a large bowl, combine the biscuit mix and cheese; stir in sausage. Add water and toss with a fork until moistened. Shape into 1½-in. balls. Place 2 in. apart on ungreased baking sheets.
3. Bake until puffed and golden brown, 12-15 minutes. Cool on wire racks.
1 appetizer: 89 cal., 6g fat (3g sat. fat), 14mg chol., 197mg sod., 6g carb. (0 sugars, 0 fiber), 4g pro.

TEST KITCHEN TIPS
- Baked puffs may be frozen; reheat at 400° for 7-9 minutes or until heated through (they do not need to thaw first).
- Serve with your favorite jam, jelly or flavored maple syrup.

SPICY MAPLE CHICKEN WINGS

My girls and I often ask my husband to make his famous chicken wings. They're sweet yet spicy, and we love 'em.
—Dona Hoffman, Addison, IL

Prep: 20 min. • **Cook:** 10 min./batch
Makes: about 2½ dozen

- 3 lbs. chicken wings
  Oil for deep-fat frying
- ½ cup butter, cubed
- ½ cup maple syrup
- ½ cup Louisiana-style hot sauce
- ¼ cup packed brown sugar
- ½ tsp. salt
- ¼ tsp. pepper
- 2 Tbsp. water
- 1½ tsp. cornstarch

1. Cut each chicken wing into 3 sections; discard wing tip sections.
2. In an electric skillet or deep-fat fryer, heat oil to 375°. Fry chicken, a few pieces at a time, for 8 minutes or until golden brown and juices run clear, turning occasionally. Drain on paper towels.
3. In a small saucepan, melt butter. Stir in the syrup, hot sauce, brown sugar, salt and pepper. Combine water and cornstarch; stir into sauce. Bring to a boil; cook and stir for 2 minutes or until thickened.
4. Place wings in a large bowl; pour sauce over wings and toss to coat.
Note: Uncooked chicken wing sections (wingettes) may be substituted for whole chicken wings.
1 piece: 140 cal., 11g fat (3g sat. fat), 23mg chol., 213mg sod., 6g carb. (5g sugars, 0 fiber), 5g pro.

GROUND BEEF TACO DIP

What's a football party without taco dip? This version made with spicy ground beef and fresh toppings does not disappoint the die-hards. It is full of classic flavors and is a little extra filling for game day appetites.
—Errika Perry, Green Bay, WI

Takes: 25 min. • **Makes:** 24 servings

- 1 lb. lean ground beef (90% lean)
- ¾ cup water
- 2 envelopes taco seasoning, divided
- 2 cups fat-free sour cream
- 1 pkg. (8 oz.) cream cheese, softened
- 2 cups shredded iceberg lettuce
- 1 cup shredded cheddar cheese
- 3 medium tomatoes, finely chopped
- 1 medium green pepper, finely chopped
- 1 can (2¼ oz.) sliced ripe olives, drained

1. In a large skillet, cook and crumble beef over medium heat until no longer pink, 4-6 minutes; drain. Add water and 1 envelope taco seasoning; cook until thickened. Cool slightly.
2. Beat sour cream, cream cheese and remaining taco seasoning until blended. Spread in a 3-qt. dish; add ground beef. Top with lettuce, cheddar, tomatoes, pepper and olives.
½ cup: 116 cal., 7g fat (3g sat. fat), 30mg chol., 378mg sod., 7g carb. (2g sugars, 0 fiber), 7g pro.

SALMON APPETIZERS

As a cook for a commercial salmon fishing crew, I found this recipe to be an innovative use of salmon. The roll-ups are a terrific addition to a Mexican meal or a marvelous prelude to a steak dinner.
—Evelyn Gebhardt, Kasilof, AK

- -

Prep: 15 min. + chilling
Makes: about 4 dozen

1	can (15 oz.) salmon or 2 cups flaked cooked salmon
1	pkg. (8 oz.) cream cheese, softened
4	Tbsp. salsa
2	Tbsp. chopped fresh parsley
1	tsp. dried cilantro
¼	tsp. ground cumin, optional
8	flour tortillas (8 in.)

1. Drain salmon; remove any bones. In a small bowl, combine salmon, cream cheese, salsa, parsley and cilantro. Add cumin if desired. Spread about 2 Tbsp. salmon mixture over each tortilla.
2. Roll up each tortilla tightly and wrap individually. Refrigerate for 2-3 hours. Slice each tortilla into bite-sized pieces.
1 piece: 58 cal., 3g fat (1g sat. fat), 12mg chol., 95mg sod., 5g carb. (0 sugars, 0 fiber), 3g pro.

MEATBALLS IN PLUM SAUCE

A topping made of plum jam and chili sauce beautifully coats these tender meatballs. You'll want to have these delightful appetizers at every party.
—Mary Poninski, Whittington, IL

- -

Prep: 50 min. + standing • **Bake:** 30 min.
Makes: about 3 dozen

½	cup 2% milk
1	cup soft bread crumbs
1	large egg, lightly beaten
1	Tbsp. Worcestershire sauce
1	medium onion, finely chopped
¼	tsp. salt
¼	tsp. pepper
⅛	tsp. ground cloves
½	lb. lean ground beef
½	lb. ground pork
½	lb. ground veal
2	Tbsp. canola oil
½	tsp. beef bouillon granules
½	cup boiling water
3	Tbsp. all-purpose flour
1	cup plum jam
½	cup chili sauce

1. In a large bowl, pour milk over bread crumbs; let stand for 10 minutes. Add egg, Worcestershire sauce, onion, salt, pepper and cloves. Crumble beef, pork and veal over mixture and mix well (mixture will be soft). Shape into 1-in. balls.
2. In a large skillet, brown meatballs in oil in batches. Drain on paper towels. Place in a greased 13x9-in. baking dish.
3. In a small bowl, dissolve bouillon in water. Stir flour into pan drippings until blended; add the bouillon mixture, jam and chili sauce. Bring to a boil; cook and stir for 1-2 minutes or until thickened. Pour over the meatballs.
4. Cover; bake at 350° for 30-45 minutes or until meat is no longer pink and sauce is bubbly.
1 meatball: 77 cal., 3g fat (1g sat. fat), 19mg chol., 105mg sod., 8g carb. (6g sugars, 0 fiber), 4g pro.

CHEESY MEATBALL SLIDERS

These meatball sliders are a fun way to serve meatballs at your party without using a slow cooker. Made on mini Hawaiian rolls, they have a hint of sweetness to balance out all the wonderful Italian seasonings.
—*Taste of Home* Test Kitchen

Prep: 1 hour • **Bake:** 30 min.
Makes: 12 servings

- 2 lbs. lean ground beef (90% lean)
- 1 cup Italian-style bread crumbs
- 3 Tbsp. prepared pesto
- 1 large egg, lightly beaten
- 1 jar (24 oz.) pasta sauce
- 1 pkg. (18 oz.) Hawaiian sweet rolls
- 12 slices part-skim mozzarella cheese
- ½ tsp. dried oregano
- ¼ cup melted butter
- 1 Tbsp. olive oil
- 3 garlic cloves, minced
- 1 tsp. Italian seasoning
- ½ tsp. crushed red pepper flakes
- 2 Tbsp. grated Parmesan cheese
- 1 cup shredded part-skim mozzarella cheese or shredded Italian cheese blend
  Minced fresh basil

1. Preheat oven to 350°. Combine ground beef, bread crumbs, pesto and egg; mix lightly. Shape into 12 meatballs; place on a greased rack in a 15x10x1-in. baking pan. Bake until browned and a thermometer reads 160°, about 35 minutes. Toss meatballs with sauce; set aside.
2. Meanwhile, without separating rolls, cut horizontally in half; arrange bottom halves in a greased 13x9-in. baking dish. Place half the cheese slices over roll bottoms; sprinkle with oregano. Add meatballs and sauce. Top with remaining cheese slices and bun tops.
3. Combine butter, oil, garlic, Italian seasoning and pepper flakes; brush over buns. Bake, covered, for 20 minutes. Uncover; sprinkle with Parmesan and shredded mozzarella.

4. Bake, uncovered, until cheese is melted, 10-15 minutes longer. Sprinkle with basil before serving.
1 slider: 514 cal., 25g fat (12g sat. fat), 120mg chol., 856mg sod., 39g carb. (15g sugars, 3g fiber), 33g pro.

MAKE AHEAD
SANTA FE CHEESECAKE

All of my favorite southwestern ingredients are combined in this clever appetizer. It looks and tastes superb!
—Jean Ecos, Hartland, WI

Prep: 25 min. • **Bake:** 30 min. + chilling
Makes: 20 servings

- 1 cup crushed tortilla chips
- 3 Tbsp. butter, melted
- 2 pkg. (8 oz. each) cream cheese, softened
- 2 large eggs, lightly beaten
- 2 cups shredded Monterey Jack cheese
- 1 can (4 oz.) chopped green chiles, drained
- 1 cup sour cream
- 1 cup chopped sweet yellow pepper
- ½ cup chopped green onions
- ⅓ cup chopped tomato

1. In a small bowl, combine tortilla chips and butter; press onto the bottom of a greased 9-in. springform pan. Place on a baking sheet. Bake at 325° for 15 minutes or until lightly browned.
2. In a large bowl, beat cream cheese until smooth. Add eggs; beat on low speed just until combined. Stir in the Monterey Jack cheese and chiles; pour into crust.
3. Bake for 30-35 minutes or until the center is almost set. Cool on a wire rack for 10 minutes. Spread sour cream over cheesecake. Carefully run a knife around edge of pan to loosen; cool for 1 hour. Refrigerate overnight.
4. Remove sides of pan. Sprinkle the top with yellow pepper, onions and tomato.
1 slice: 137 cal., 12g fat (7g sat. fat), 56mg chol., 151mg sod., 3g carb. (1g sugars, 0 fiber), 5g pro.

CHICKEN CRESCENT WREATH

Here's an impressive-looking dish that is a snap to prepare. Even when my cooking time is limited, I can still serve this delicious crescent wreath. The colorful red pepper and green broccoli add a festive touch.

—Marlene Denissen, Saint Croix Falls, WI

- -

Prep: 15 min. • **Bake:** 20 min.
Makes: 16 servings

- 2 tubes (8 oz. each) refrigerated crescent rolls
- 1 cup shredded Colby-Monterey Jack cheese
- ⅔ cup condensed cream of chicken soup, undiluted
- ½ cup chopped fresh broccoli
- ½ cup chopped sweet red pepper
- ¼ cup chopped water chestnuts
- 1 can (5 oz.) white chicken, drained, or ¾ cup cubed cooked chicken
- 2 Tbsp. chopped onion

1. Arrange crescent rolls on a 12-in. pizza pan, forming a ring with the pointed ends facing the outer edge of the pan and wide ends overlapping.
2. Combine the remaining ingredients; spoon over wide ends of rolls. Fold points over filling and tuck them under wide ends (filling will be visible). Bake at 375° for 20-25 minutes or until golden brown.

Freeze option: Securely wrap cooled wreath in foil before freezing. To use, remove from freezer 30 minutes before reheating. Remove wreath from foil; reheat on a greased baking sheet in a preheated 325° oven until heated through.

1 piece: 151 cal., 8g fat (2g sat. fat), 11mg chol., 357mg sod., 14g carb. (3g sugars, 0 fiber), 6g pro.

SAVORY CUCUMBER SANDWICHES

Italian salad dressing easily flavors this simple spread. Serve it as a dip with crackers and veggies, or use it as a sandwich filling.
—Carol Henderson, Chagrin Falls, OH

Prep: 15 min. + chilling • **Makes:** 3 dozen

- 1   pkg. (8 oz.) cream cheese, softened
- ½   cup mayonnaise
- 1   envelope Italian salad dressing mix
- 36   slices snack rye bread
- 1   medium cucumber, sliced
     Snipped fresh dill, optional

1. In a small bowl, combine the cream cheese, mayonnaise and salad dressing mix. Refrigerate for 1 hour.

2. Just before serving, spread over each slice of rye bread; top each with a cucumber slice. If desired, sprinkle with dill.

1 sandwich: 62 cal., 5g fat (2g sat. fat), 7mg chol., 149mg sod., 4g carb. (1g sugars, 0 fiber), 1g pro.

BRING IT

These zesty sandwiches are easy to tote and assemble fresh on-site. They require just a little refrigerator space for the spread and sliced cucumber, and you can easily replenish them as needed. If you prefer to make them all ahead of time, gently layer sandwiches with parchment in a large covered container and store in a cooler or fridge.

Mini
Ham Quiches
page 57

Breakfast for a Bunch

From candied bacon and overnight bakes to giant cinnamon rolls and iced coffee for a crowd, good mornings are made of these.

CARAMELIZED BACON TWISTS

Whenever my grandchildren come over, these sweet chewy bacon strips are a big hit. Lining the pan with foil before baking helps cut down on cleanup.
—Jane Paschke, University Park, FL

Takes: 30 min. • **Makes:** about 3 dozen

½ **cup packed brown sugar**
2 **tsp. ground cinnamon**
1 **lb. bacon strips**

1. Preheat oven to 350°. Line a 15x10x1-in. pan with foil.

2. In a shallow bowl, mix brown sugar and cinnamon. Cut bacon strips crosswise in half; dip in sugar mixture to coat. Twist 2 or 3 times, then place in prepared pan. Bake until browned and crisp, 15-20 minutes.

Freeze option: Freeze cooled bacon twists in freezer containers, separating layers with waxed paper. If desired, reheat in a microwave oven or on a foil-lined baking sheet in a preheated 350° oven before serving.

1 bacon twist: 35 cal., 2g fat (1g sat. fat), 5mg chol., 81mg sod., 3g carb. (3g sugars, 0 fiber), 2g pro.

BRING IT

Candied bacon tastes wonderful at room temperature, so it's a smart potluck pick. It's equally good with egg dishes or a sweet entree like French toast, or even gracing the Bloody Mary bar.

COFFEE CAKE MUFFINS

 I combine the dry ingredients for these muffins the night before baking. In the morning, I add the remaining items, fill the muffin cups and pop them in the oven. Brown sugar, cinnamon and pecans give them coffee cakelike flavor.
—Margaret McNeil, Germantown, TN

Prep: 20 min. • **Bake:** 25 min.
Makes: 1 dozen

- ¼ cup packed brown sugar
- ¼ cup chopped pecans
- 1 tsp. ground cinnamon
- 1½ cups all-purpose flour
- ½ cup sugar
- 2 tsp. baking powder
- ¼ tsp. baking soda
- ¼ tsp. salt
- 1 large egg, room temperature
- ¾ cup 2% milk
- ⅓ cup canola oil

GLAZE
- ½ cup confectioners' sugar
- 1 Tbsp. 2% milk
- 1 tsp. vanilla extract

1. Preheat oven to 400°. In a small bowl, combine the brown sugar, pecans and cinnamon; set aside. In a large bowl, whisk flour, sugar, baking powder, baking soda and salt. In another bowl, whisk egg, milk and oil until blended. Add to flour mixture; stir just until moistened.

2. Spoon 1 Tbsp. batter into each of 12 paper-lined muffin cups. Top each with 1 tsp. nut mixture and about 2 Tbsp. batter. Sprinkle with the remaining nut mixture.

3. Bake until a toothpick inserted in center comes out clean, 22-24 minutes. Cool for 5 minutes before removing from pan to a wire rack. Combine glaze ingredients; spoon over muffins. Serve warm.

1 muffin: 215 cal., 9g fat (1g sat. fat), 17mg chol., 170mg sod., 31g carb. (19g sugars, 1g fiber), 3g pro.

APPLE BUTTER BREAD PUDDING

This is one of my mother's best recipes! I'm sure your family will be delighted with it, too. Serve it as a dessert or a marvelous breakfast treat.

—Jerri Gradert, Lincoln, NE

Prep: 20 min. + standing • **Bake:** 50 min.
Makes: 12 servings

- ⅓ cup raisins
- 1 cup apple butter
- 6 croissants, split

CUSTARD
- 8 large eggs
- 3 cups 2% milk
- 1½ cups sugar
- 2 tsp. vanilla extract
- ¼ tsp. salt

STREUSEL
- ½ cup all-purpose flour
- ½ cup packed brown sugar
- ¼ tsp. salt
- ¼ cup cold butter

1. Place raisins in a small bowl. Cover with boiling water; let stand for 5 minutes. Drain and set aside.
2. Combine the apple butter and raisins. Spread over croissant bottoms; replace tops. Cut each croissant into 3 pieces; place in a greased 13x9-in. baking dish.
3. In a bowl, combine eggs, milk, sugar, vanilla and salt. Pour over croissants; let stand 30 minutes or until bread is softened.
4. In a small bowl, combine flour, brown sugar and salt. Cut in butter until mixture resembles coarse crumbs. Sprinkle over top.
5. Bake, uncovered, at 350° until a knife inserted in the center comes out clean, 50-60 minutes. Serve warm. Refrigerate the leftovers.
Note: This recipe was tested with a commercially prepared apple butter.
1 serving: 433 cal., 14g fat (7g sat. fat), 175mg chol., 422mg sod., 68g carb. (51g sugars, 1g fiber), 9g pro.

CHEDDAR BACON GRITS

In the South, grits are served plain with a little butter or loaded with extras, as is my recipe with bacon, cheddar and green chiles.
—Amanda Reed, Nashville, TN

Takes: 30 min. • **Makes:** 12 servings

- 8 cups water
- 2 cups uncooked old-fashioned grits
- 1 tsp. salt
- ¼ tsp. paprika
- 2 cups shredded white cheddar cheese
- 5 bacon strips, cooked and crumbled
- 1 can (4 oz.) chopped green chiles
  Sliced green onions, optional

1. In a 6-qt. stockpot, bring water to a boil. Slowly stir in grits, salt and paprika. Reduce heat; cook, covered, 15-20 minutes or until thickened, stirring occasionally.
2. Reduce heat to low. Stir in cheese, bacon and chiles until cheese is melted. If desired, sprinkle with green onions.
¾ cup: 199 cal., 8g fat (4g sat. fat), 22mg chol., 418mg sod., 24g carb. (0 sugars, 1g fiber), 7g pro.

WILD BLUEBERRY MUFFINS

Nothing is better than a warm blueberry muffin in the morning. These muffins are the best I have ever made. The wild blueberries make them extra special.
—Dewey Grindle, Blue Hill, ME

Prep: 15 min. • **Bake:** 20 min.
Makes: 1 dozen

- ¼ cup butter, softened
- ⅓ cup sugar
- 1 large egg, room temperature
- 2⅓ cups all-purpose flour
- 4 tsp. baking powder
- ½ tsp. salt
- 1 cup 2% milk
- 1 tsp. vanilla extract
- 1½ cups fresh or frozen wild blueberries or 1 can (15 oz.) water-packed wild blueberries, well drained

STREUSEL TOPPING

- ½ cup sugar
- ⅓ cup all-purpose flour
- ½ tsp. ground cinnamon
- ¼ cup cold butter, cubed

1. In a bowl, cream butter and sugar until light and fluffy, 5-7 minutes. Add egg; mix well. Combine dry ingredients; add to creamed mixture alternately with milk. Stir in vanilla. Gently fold in blueberries.

2. Fill greased or paper-lined muffin cups two-thirds full. In a small bowl, combine the sugar, flour and cinnamon; cut in the butter until crumbly. Sprinkle over muffins. Bake at 375° until a toothpick comes out clean, 20-25 minutes.

1 muffin: 252 cal., 9g fat (5g sat. fat), 41mg chol., 325mg sod., 39g carb. (17g sugars, 1g fiber), 4g pro.

POTATO & BACON FRITTATA

This frittata is so versatile. You can serve it with pesto or fresh salsa, and it's tasty with almost any type of cheese.
—Mariela Petroski, Helena, MT

- -

Prep: 30 min. • **Bake:** 20 min. + standing
Makes: 8 servings

10	large eggs
¼	cup minced fresh parsley
3	Tbsp. 2% milk
¼	tsp. salt
⅛	tsp. pepper
8	bacon strips, chopped
2	medium potatoes, peeled and thinly sliced
2	green onions, finely chopped
4	fresh sage leaves, thinly sliced
1	cup shredded pepper jack cheese
2	plum tomatoes, sliced

1. Preheat oven to 400°. In a large bowl, whisk eggs, parsley, milk, salt and pepper; set aside. In a 10-in. ovenproof skillet, cook bacon over medium heat until partially cooked but not crisp.
2. Add potatoes, onions and sage; cook until potatoes are tender. Reduce heat; sprinkle with cheese. Top with the egg mixture and tomato slices.
3. Bake, uncovered, 20-25 minutes or until the eggs are completely set. Let stand 15 minutes. Cut into wedges.
1 slice: 287 cal., 21g fat (8g sat. fat), 295mg chol., 441mg sod., 10g carb. (2g sugars, 1g fiber), 15g pro.

BACON & EGG PIZZA

Pizza for breakfast? You bet! Kids especially will enjoy eating the bacon, cheese, hash browns and eggs layered on an easy-to-cut pizza crust.
—Georgiann Franklin, Canfield, OH

- -

Prep: 10 min. • **Bake:** 25 min.
Makes: 8 servings

1	tube (8 oz.) refrigerated crescent rolls
12	bacon strips, cooked and crumbled
1	cup frozen shredded hash brown potatoes
¾	cup shredded cheddar cheese
4	large eggs
2	Tbsp. 2% milk
½	cup grated Parmesan cheese

1. Unroll the crescent dough into 1 long rectangle. Press onto the bottom and ½ in. up the sides of a greased 13x9-in. baking pan. Seal seams and perforations. Sprinkle with bacon, potatoes and cheddar cheese.
2. In a large bowl, beat eggs and milk. Pour over cheddar cheese. Sprinkle with Parmesan cheese. Bake, uncovered, at 375° for 25-30 minutes or until a knife inserted in the center comes out clean.
1 serving: 273 cal., 18g fat (7g sat. fat), 130mg chol., 566mg sod., 14g carb. (3g sugars, 0 fiber), 13g pro.

★ ★ ★ ★ ★ **READER REVIEW**

"I made this for our youth group breakfast. I added sausage and extra cheese. It was an absolute hit for all 55 kids and adults."

HUNTER6295 TASTEOFHOME.COM

MAKE AHEAD
CHUNKY BREAKFAST COOKIES

Who says cookies aren't for breakfast? We devour these hearty oatmeal cookies, especially on the run. Add any dried fruits and nuts you have on hand.
—Lea Langhoff, Round Lake, IL

- -

Prep: 20 min. • **Bake:** 15 min./batch
Makes: 16 cookies

⅔   **cup butter, softened**
⅔   **cup packed brown sugar**
1   **large egg, room temperature**
1   **large egg yolk, room temperature**
1½   **cups old-fashioned oats**
¾   **cup all-purpose flour**
¾   **cup whole wheat flour**
1   **tsp. baking soda**
½   **tsp. salt**
1   **cup semisweet chocolate chunks**
1   **cup chopped dates**
½   **cup sweetened shredded coconut**

1. Preheat oven to 350°. In a large bowl, cream butter and brown sugar until light and fluffy, 5-7 minutes. Beat in egg and egg yolk. In another bowl, mix the oats, flours, baking soda and salt; gradually beat into creamed mixture. Stir in the remaining ingredients.
2. Shape dough by ¼ cupfuls into balls; flatten to ¾-in. thickness. Place 2 in. apart on ungreased baking sheets.
3. Bake 13-15 minutes or until golden brown. Cool on pans 2 minutes. Remove to wire racks to cool. Serve warm or at room temperature. To reheat, microwave each cookie on high for 15-20 seconds or just until warmed.
Freeze option: Freeze unbaked cookies in a freezer container, separating layers with waxed paper. To use, place dough portions 2 in. apart on ungreased baking sheets; let stand at room temperature 30 minutes before baking. Bake as directed, increasing time by 1-2 minutes.

1 cookie: 291 cal., 15g fat (9g sat. fat), 44mg chol., 239mg sod., 40g carb. (24g sugars, 3g fiber), 4g pro.

CHEDDAR-HAM OVEN OMELET

We had a family reunion for 50 relatives from the U.S. and Canada, and it took four pans of this hearty, five-ingredient omelet to feed the crowd. Fresh fruit and an assortment of muffins helped round out our brunch menu.
—Betty Abrey, Imperial, SK

- -

Prep: 15 min. • **Bake:** 40 min. + standing
Makes: 12 servings

16   **large eggs**
2   **cups whole milk**
2   **cups shredded cheddar cheese**
¾   **cup cubed fully cooked ham**
6   **green onions, chopped**

1. Preheat oven to 350°. In a large bowl, whisk eggs and milk. Stir in cheese, ham and onions. Pour into a greased 13x9-in. baking dish.
2. Bake, uncovered, until a knife inserted in the center comes out clean, 40-45 minutes. Let stand 10 minutes before cutting.
1 piece: 208 cal., 14g fat (7g sat. fat), 314mg chol., 330mg sod., 4g carb. (3g sugars, 0 fiber), 15g pro.

CHAMPAGNE JELLY

When I hosted a Christmas open house, each guest left with a batch of my blush-colored jelly. It was a hit! Plus, it's made with just three ingredients: pink champagne, sugar and fruit pectin.
—Gail Sheppard, Somerville, AL

Prep: 15 min. • **Process:** 10 min.
Makes: about 3 half-pints

- 3 **cups sugar**
- 2 **cups pink champagne**
- 1 **pouch (3 oz.) liquid fruit pectin**

1. In a Dutch oven, combine the sugar and champagne. Bring to a full rolling boil over high heat, stirring often. Stir in pectin. Boil for 1 minute, stirring constantly.
2. Remove from the heat; skim off foam if necessary. Carefully ladle hot mixture into hot half-pint jars, leaving ¼-in. headspace. Wipe rims. Center lids on jars; screw on bands until fingertip tight.
3. Place jars into canner with simmering water, ensuring that they are completely covered with water. Bring to a boil; process for 10 minutes. Remove jars and cool.
2 Tbsp: 111 cal., 0 fat (0 sat. fat), 0 chol., 0 sod., 26g carb. (25g sugars, 0 fiber), 0 pro.

ELEGANT SMOKED SALMON STRATA

This fancy overnight bake is ideal for company. In the morning, you can simply let it come to room temperature and whip up side dishes as it bakes. So easy!
—Lisa Speer, Palm Beach, FL

Prep: 30 min. + chilling
Bake: 55 min. + standing
Makes: 12 servings

- 4 **cups cubed ciabatta bread**
- 2 **Tbsp. butter, melted**
- 2 **Tbsp. olive oil**
- 2 **cups shredded Gruyere or Swiss cheese**
- 2 **cups shredded white cheddar cheese**
- 10 **green onions, sliced**
- ½ **lb. smoked salmon or lox, coarsely chopped**
- 8 **large eggs**
- 4 **cups 2% milk**
- 4 **tsp. Dijon mustard**
- ¼ **tsp. salt**
- ¼ **tsp. pepper**
  Creme fraiche or sour cream and minced chives

1. In a large bowl, toss bread cubes with butter and oil; transfer to a greased 13x9-in. baking dish. Sprinkle with cheeses, onions and salmon. In another bowl, whisk the eggs, milk, mustard, salt and pepper; pour over top. Cover and refrigerate overnight.
2. Remove from refrigerator 30 minutes before baking. Preheat oven to 350°. Cover and bake for 30 minutes. Uncover; bake until a knife inserted in the center comes out clean, 25-30 minutes longer. Let stand for 10 minutes before serving. Serve with creme fraiche and chives.
1 piece: 359 cal., 21g fat (11g sat. fat), 194mg chol., 845mg sod., 21g carb. (6g sugars, 1g fiber), 22g pro.

SCRAMBLED EGG MUFFINS

After enjoying scrambled egg muffins at a local restaurant, I came up with this savory version that my husband likes even better. Freeze the extras to reheat on busy mornings.
—Cathy Larkins, Marshfield, MO

- -

Takes: 30 min. • **Makes:** 1 dozen

½ **lb. bulk pork sausage**
12 **large eggs**
½ **cup chopped onion**
¼ **cup chopped green pepper**
½ **tsp. salt**
¼ **tsp. garlic powder**
¼ **tsp. pepper**
½ **cup shredded cheddar cheese**

1. Preheat oven to 350°. In a large skillet, cook sausage over medium heat until no longer pink, breaking it into crumbles; drain.
2. In a large bowl, beat eggs. Add onion, green pepper, salt, garlic powder and pepper. Stir in sausage and cheese. Spoon by ⅓ cupfuls into greased muffin cups. Bake until a knife inserted in center comes out clean, 20-25 minutes.
Freeze option: Cool baked egg muffins. Place on waxed paper-lined baking sheets, cover and freeze until firm. Transfer to freezer container; return to freezer. To use, place in greased muffin pan, cover loosely with foil and reheat in a preheated 350° oven until heated through. Or microwave each muffin on high for 30-60 seconds or until heated through.
1 muffin: 133 cal., 10g fat (4g sat. fat), 224mg chol., 268mg sod., 2g carb. (1g sugars, 0 fiber), 9g pro.

CRANBERRY-APPLE FRENCH TOAST

My husband's breakfast club at work raves about this make-ahead French toast. Pop it in the oven in the morning to get your day off to a sweet, bubbly start.
—Mara Faulkner, Martinsburg, WV

- -

Prep: 25 min. + chilling
Bake: 40 min. + standing
Makes: 12 servings

⅔ **cup packed light brown sugar**
¼ **cup maple syrup**
¼ **cup unsalted butter, melted**
¼ **tsp. ground nutmeg**
3 **tsp. ground cinnamon, divided**
3 **medium Granny Smith apples, peeled and thinly sliced**
½ **cup dried cranberries**
6 **large eggs**
1½ **cups whole milk**
1 **tsp. vanilla extract**
1 **loaf (1 lb.) challah or egg bread, cut into 1-in. slices**

1. Mix the first 4 ingredients and 2 tsp. cinnamon; toss with apples and cranberries. Transfer to a greased 13x9-in. baking dish.
2. In a large bowl, whisk together eggs, milk, vanilla and remaining cinnamon. Dip bread in egg mixture to moisten; place over fruit, overlapping or trimming slices to fit. Pour the remaining egg mixture over bread. Refrigerate, covered, overnight.
3. Preheat the oven to 375°. Remove baking dish from refrigerator while the oven heats. Bake, covered, 30 minutes. Uncover; bake until bubbly and lightly browned, 10-15 minutes. Let stand for 10 minutes before serving.
1 serving: 295 cal., 10g fat (4g sat. fat), 126mg chol., 197mg sod., 45g carb. (25g sugars, 2g fiber), 8g pro.

GLAZED FRUIT MEDLEY

The orange dressing on this salad complements the fresh fruit flavors beautifully. It's perfect for a spring or summer brunch.
—Karen Bourne, Magrath, AB

Prep: 20 min. + chilling • **Makes:** 10 servings

- 2   **cups orange juice**
- 1   **cup sugar**
- 2   **Tbsp. cornstarch**
- 3   **cups cubed honeydew melon**
- 3   **medium firm bananas, sliced**
- 2   **cups green grapes**
- 2   **cups halved fresh strawberries**

1. In a small saucepan, mix the orange juice, sugar and cornstarch until smooth. Bring to a boil, stirring constantly; cook and stir for 2 minutes or until thickened. Transfer to a small bowl; cool slightly. Refrigerate, covered, for at least 2 hours.

2. Just before serving, combine the fruit in a large serving bowl. Drizzle with orange juice mixture; toss gently to coat.

¾ cup: 188 cal., 1g fat (0 sat. fat), 0 chol., 7mg sod., 47g carb. (41g sugars, 2g fiber), 1g pro.

Apple-Ginger Glazed Fruit: Omit first 3 ingredients. In a small saucepan, mix 2 cups unsweetened apple juice, ¼ cup honey, 2 Tbsp. finely chopped crystallized ginger and 2 Tbsp. lemon juice. Bring to a boil over medium-high heat. Cook and stir 2 minutes or until mixture is reduced to 1½ cups. Remove from heat. Cool. Mix 4 tsp. chopped fresh mint into fruit and drizzle with the cooled glaze.

ICED COFFEE LATTE

This amazing alternative to regular hot coffee is much more economical than store-bought coffee drinks. Sweetened condensed milk and a hint of chocolate lend a special touch.
—Heather Nandell, Johnston, IA

Takes: 10 min. • **Makes:** 8 servings

- ½   **cup instant coffee granules**
- ½   **cup boiling water**
- 4   **cups chocolate milk**
- 2   **cups cold water**
- 1   **can (14 oz.) sweetened condensed milk**
      Ice cubes

In a large bowl, dissolve coffee in boiling water. Stir in chocolate milk, cold water and condensed milk. Serve over ice.

1 cup: 270 cal., 9g fat (5g sat. fat), 32mg chol., 139mg sod., 41g carb. (39g sugars, 1g fiber), 8g pro.

TEST KITCHEN TIP
The perfect partner for this drink is coffee-flavored ice cubes. Freeze trays of brewed coffee, then combine the cubes with your coffee beverage in a large pitcher.

MAKE AHEAD

OVERNIGHT PANCAKES

Our kids love waking up to these golden, fluffy pancakes. The buttermilk batter is refrigerated overnight, making them perfect for busy mornings and special occasion breakfasts alike.
—Lisa Sammons, Cut Bank, MT

- -

Prep: 10 min. + chilling • **Cook:** 10 min.
Makes: 30 pancakes

- 1 pkg. (¼ oz.) active dry yeast
- ¼ cup warm water (110° to 115°)
- 4 cups all-purpose flour
- 1 Tbsp. baking powder
- 2 tsp. baking soda
- 2 tsp. sugar
- 1 tsp. salt
- 6 large eggs, room temperature
- 4 cups buttermilk
- ¼ cup canola oil

1. Dissolve yeast in warm water; let stand for 5 minutes. Meanwhile, in another bowl, combine the next 5 ingredients. Whisk eggs, buttermilk and oil; stir into flour mixture just until moistened. Stir in yeast mixture. Refrigerate, covered, for 8 hours or overnight.

2. To make pancakes, lightly grease griddle and preheat over medium heat. Pour the batter by ¼ cupfuls onto griddle; cook until bubbles on top begin to pop and bottoms are golden brown. Turn; cook until second side is golden brown.

Note: To substitute for each cup of buttermilk, use 1 Tbsp. white vinegar or lemon juice plus enough milk to measure 1 cup. Stir, then let stand 5 min. Or use 1 cup plain yogurt or 1¾ tsp. cream of tartar plus 1 cup milk.

3 pancakes: 319 cal., 10g fat (2g sat. fat), 116mg chol., 862mg sod., 44g carb. (6g sugars, 2g fiber), 12g pro.

PANCAKE SYRUP

My husband has fond memories of this recipe. Every Sunday, his dad would get up early to make the family pancakes and syrup. They didn't have much money, but the kids never knew that. What they do remember is that their dad always had time to make their Sundays extra special.
—Lorrie McCurdy, Farmington, NM

- -

Takes: 10 min. • **Makes:** 2 cups

- 1 cup packed brown sugar
- 1 cup sugar
- 1 cup water
- 1 tsp. maple flavoring

In a small saucepan, combine the sugars and water. Bring to a boil; cook and stir for 2 minutes. Remove from the heat; stir in maple flavoring. Refrigerate leftovers.

2 Tbsp.: 102 cal., 0 fat (0 sat. fat), 0 chol., 4mg sod., 26g carb. (26g sugars, 0 fiber), 0 pro.

CINNAMON CREAM SYRUP

The sugar and spice flavor of this syrup enhances waffles, griddle cakes, even cooked oatmeal. I often fix it for brunches.
—Vera Reid, Laramie, WY

- -

Takes: 15 min. • **Makes:** about 1⅔ cups

- 1 cup sugar
- ½ cup light corn syrup
- ¼ cup water
- ¾ tsp. ground cinnamon
- 1 can (5 oz.) evaporated milk

In a saucepan, combine the first 4 ingredients. Bring to a boil over medium heat; boil and stir for 2 minutes. Cool for 5 minutes. Stir in milk. Serve over pancakes, waffles or French toast.

2 Tbsp.: 109 cal., 1g fat (1g sat. fat), 3mg chol., 26mg sod., 26g carb. (22g sugars, 0 fiber), 1g pro.

RAISIN BREAD & SAUSAGE MORNING CASSEROLE

When we used to have Sunday breakfasts with my grandparents, Mom often made this for Grandpa because he enjoyed it so much. Pork sausage and cinnamon bread taste surprisingly good together.
—Carolyn Levan, Dixon, IL

- -

Prep: 25 min. + chilling • **Bake:** 35 min.
Makes: 12 servings

- ½ lb. bulk pork sausage
- 1 loaf (1 lb.) cinnamon-raisin bread, cubed
- 6 large eggs
- 1½ cups 2% milk
- 1½ cups half-and-half cream
- 1 tsp. vanilla extract
- ¼ tsp. ground cinnamon
- ¼ tsp. ground nutmeg

TOPPING
- 1 cup chopped pecans
- 1 cup packed brown sugar
- ½ cup butter, softened
- 2 Tbsp. maple syrup

1. In a large skillet, cook the sausage over medium heat 4-6 minutes or until no longer pink, breaking it into crumbles; drain. In a greased 13x9-in. baking dish, combine bread and sausage.
2. In a large bowl, whisk eggs, milk, cream, vanilla, cinnamon and nutmeg until blended; pour over the bread. Refrigerate, covered, several hours or overnight.
3. Preheat oven to 350°. Remove casserole from refrigerator while oven heats. In a small bowl, beat the topping ingredients until blended. Drop by tablespoonfuls over casserole.
4. Bake, uncovered, 35-45 minutes or until golden brown and a knife inserted in center comes out clean. Let stand 5-10 minutes before serving.
1 piece: 425 cal., 25g fat (10g sat. fat), 141mg chol., 324mg sod., 41g carb. (26g sugars, 3g fiber), 11g pro.

MUSTARD HAM STRATA

I had this at a bed-and-breakfast years ago. The innkeepers were kind enough to give me the recipe, and I've made it many times since.
—Dolores Zornow, Poynette, WI

- -

Prep: 15 min. + chilling • **Bake:** 45 min.
Makes: 12 servings

- 12 slices day-old bread, crusts removed, cubed
- 1½ cups cubed fully cooked ham
- 1 cup chopped green pepper
- ¾ cup shredded cheddar cheese
- ¾ cup shredded Monterey Jack cheese
- ⅓ cup chopped onion
- 7 large eggs
- 3 cups whole milk
- 3 tsp. ground mustard
- 1 tsp. salt

1. In a 13x9-in. baking dish coated with cooking spray, layer bread cubes, ham, green pepper, cheeses and onion. Combine eggs, milk, mustard and salt. Pour over top. Cover and refrigerate overnight.
2. Remove from refrigerator 30 minutes before baking. Preheat oven to 325°. Bake, uncovered, 45-50 minutes or until a knife inserted in the center comes out clean. Let stand 5 minutes before cutting.
1 piece: 198 cal., 11g fat (5g sat. fat), 153mg chol., 648mg sod., 11g carb. (4g sugars, 1g fiber), 13g pro. **Diabetic exchanges:** 2 medium-fat meat, 1 starch.

GOLDEN GRANOLA

This crunchy granola—which may be eaten as cereal or used to top ice cream or fruit—makes a welcome gift. Package it in a tin or jar decked with a festive bow.
—Maxine Smith, Owanka, SD

Prep: 15 min. • **Bake:** 1 hour
Makes: 18 servings

- 4 cups old-fashioned oats
- 1 cup sweetened shredded coconut
- ½ cup toasted wheat germ
- ½ cup sesame seeds
- ½ cup sunflower kernels
- ½ cup slivered almonds
- 1½ tsp. salt
- 1½ tsp. ground cinnamon
- ½ cup canola oil
- ¼ cup packed brown sugar
- ⅓ cup honey
- ⅓ cup water
- 1 Tbsp. vanilla extract
- ½ cup golden raisins or chopped dried apricots

1. In a large bowl, combine the first 8 ingredients. In a saucepan, cook and stir the oil, brown sugar, honey, water and vanilla until sugar is dissolved. Pour over dry ingredients and mix well.
2. Transfer to a greased 13x9-in. baking pan. Bake at 275° for 1 hour or until golden brown, stirring every 15 minutes. Cool completely. Stir in raisins or apricots.
½ cup: 258 cal., 15g fat (3g sat. fat), 0 chol., 237mg sod., 29g carb. (13g sugars, 3g fiber), 6g pro.

MAKE AHEAD

NIGHT BEFORE CASSEROLE

My family has a big farm appetite. To be extra sure I don't get caught short at breakfast, I make this casserole as a backup the evening before. It could be a meal in itself! It comes out of the oven light and puffy, but there's enough egg, cheese and meat to be hearty.
—Marion Kirst, Troy, MI

Prep: 10 min. + chilling
Bake: 50 min.
Makes: 12 servings

- 12 slices white bread, crusts removed
- 6 to 8 Tbsp. butter, softened
- 6 slices deluxe American cheese
- 6 slices boiled or baked ham
  Prepared mustard
- 4 large eggs, beaten
- 3 cups whole milk

MUSHROOM SAUCE
- 1 can (10¾ oz.) condensed cream of mushroom soup, undiluted
- ⅓ cup whole milk
  Dash Worcestershire sauce
  Chopped fresh parsley

1. Spread bread with butter. Place 6 slices in a greased 13x9-in. baking dish. Top each bread slice with a slice of cheese and ham. Brush with mustard. Place remaining bread slices, buttered side up, over mustard. Beat the eggs and milk; pour over all. Cover and refrigerate overnight.
2. Remove from refrigerator 30 minutes before baking. Bake at 325° 50-60 minutes or until a knife comes out clean. Let stand 5 minutes before serving. Meanwhile, heat sauce ingredients; keep warm. Serve with the mushroom sauce; garnish with parsley.
1 serving: 276 cal., 15g fat (7g sat. fat), 101mg chol., 745mg sod., 20g carb. (6g sugars, 1g fiber), 14g pro.

BEST CINNAMON ROLLS

Surprise a neighbor with a batch of oven-fresh cinnamon rolls slathered in cream cheese frosting. These breakfast treats make Christmas morning or any special occasion even more memorable.
—Shenai Fisher, Topeka, KS

- -

Prep: 40 min. + rising
Bake: 20 min. + cooling • **Makes:** 16 rolls

1   pkg. (¼ oz.) active dry yeast
1   cup warm whole milk (110° to 115°)
½   cup sugar
⅓   cup butter, melted
2   large eggs, room temperature
1   tsp. salt
4   to 4½ cups all-purpose flour

FILLING
¾   cup packed brown sugar
2   Tbsp. ground cinnamon
¼   cup butter, melted, divided

FROSTING
½   cup butter, softened
¼   cup cream cheese, softened
½   tsp. vanilla extract
⅛   tsp. salt
1½   cups confectioners' sugar

1. Dissolve yeast in warm milk. In another bowl, combine sugar, butter, eggs, salt, yeast mixture and 2 cups flour; beat on medium speed until smooth. Stir in enough remaining flour to form a soft dough (dough will be sticky).
2. Turn the dough onto a floured surface; knead until smooth and elastic, 6-8 minutes. Place in a greased bowl, turning once to grease the top. Cover and let rise in a warm place until doubled, about 1 hour.
3. Mix brown sugar and cinnamon. Punch down dough; divide in half. On a lightly floured surface, roll 1 portion into an 11x8-in. rectangle. Brush with 2 Tbsp. butter; sprinkle with half the brown sugar mixture to within ½ in. of edges. Roll up

jelly-roll style, starting with a long side; pinch seam to seal. Cut into 8 slices; place in a greased 13x9-in. pan, cut side down. Cover with a kitchen towel. Repeat with remaining dough and filling. Let rise in a warm place until doubled, about 1 hour. Preheat oven to 350°.
4. Bake until golden brown, 20-25 minutes. Cool on wire racks.
5. For frosting, beat butter, cream cheese, vanilla and salt until blended; gradually beat in confectioners' sugar. Spread over tops. Refrigerate leftovers.

1 roll: 364 cal., 15g fat (9g sat. fat), 66mg chol., 323mg sod., 53g carb. (28g sugars, 1g fiber), 5g pro.

HOW TO FROST CINNAMON ROLLS
Get the timing just right for a rich and melty cream cheese frosting. Cool the rolls at least 15 minutes before icing. If the frosting melts into the roll or slides off, wait a bit longer. Slather frosting on generously with a small spatula or spoon.

COLORFUL FRUIT KABOBS

These luscious fruit kabobs are perfect as a summer appetizer, snack or side dish. The citrus glaze clings well and keeps the fruit looking fresh.
—Ruth Ann Stelfox, Raymond, AB

Takes: 15 min. • **Makes:** 1 cup glaze

Assorted fruit of your choice: Strawberries, seedless red grapes, sliced kiwifruit, sliced star fruit, kumquats, and cubes of cantaloupe, honeydew or pineapple

⅓   cup sugar
2   Tbsp. cornstarch
1   cup orange juice
2   tsp. lemon juice

Alternately thread fruit onto skewers; set aside. In a saucepan, combine sugar, cornstarch and juices until smooth. Bring to a boil; cook and stir for 1-2 minutes or until thickened. Brush over fruit. Refrigerate until serving.

2 tsp. glaze: 54 cal., 0 fat (0 sat. fat), 0 chol., 0 sod., 14g carb. (11g sugars, 0 fiber), 0 pro.

★ ★ ★ ★ ★   **READER REVIEW**

"These were delightful and colorful for a party tray. I used cantaloupe, watermelon, honeydew, strawberries and pineapple on medium skewers. The glaze added a wonderful, subtle flavor."

JUSTMBETH TASTEOFHOME.COM

ITALIAN SAUSAGE EGG BAKE

This hearty entree warms up any breakfast or brunch menu with its herb-seasoned flavor.
—Darlene Markham, Rochester, NY

Prep: 20 min. + chilling • **Bake:** 50 min.
Makes: 12 servings

8   slices white bread, cubed
1   lb. Italian sausage links, casings removed, sliced
2   cups shredded sharp cheddar cheese
2   cups shredded part-skim mozzarella cheese
9   large eggs, lightly beaten
3   cups 2% milk
1   tsp. dried basil
1   tsp. dried oregano
1   tsp. fennel seed, crushed

1. Place bread cubes in a greased 13x9-in. baking dish; set aside. In a large skillet, cook sausage over medium heat until no longer pink; drain. Spoon sausage over bread; sprinkle with cheeses.

2. In a large bowl, whisk the eggs, milk and seasonings; pour over casserole. Cover and refrigerate overnight.

3. Remove from refrigerator 30 minutes before baking. Bake, uncovered, at 350° until a knife inserted in the center comes out clean, 50-55 minutes. Let stand for 5 minutes before cutting.

1 piece: 316 cal., 20g fat (10g sat. fat), 214mg chol., 546mg sod., 13g carb. (5g sugars, 1g fiber), 21g pro.

EASY CHEESY LOADED GRITS

A tasty bowl of grits inspired me to develop my own recipe with sausage, green chiles and cheeses. It just might be better than the original.
—Joan Hallford, North Richland Hills, TX

Prep: 35 min. • **Bake:** 50 min. + standing
Makes: 8 servings

- 1 lb. mild or spicy bulk pork sausage
- 1 small onion, chopped
- 4 cups water
- ½ tsp. salt
- 1 cup quick-cooking grits
- 3 cans (4 oz. each) chopped green chiles
- 1½ cups shredded sharp cheddar cheese, divided
- 1½ cups shredded Monterey Jack cheese, divided
- 2 Tbsp. butter
- ¼ tsp. hot pepper sauce
- 2 large eggs, lightly beaten
- ¼ tsp. paprika
  Chopped fresh cilantro

1. Preheat oven to 325°. In a large skillet, cook sausage and onion over medium heat for 6-8 minutes or until meat is no longer pink, breaking meat into crumbles; drain.
2. In a large saucepan, bring water and salt to a boil. Slowly stir in grits. Reduce heat to medium-low; cook, covered, about 5 minutes or until thickened, stirring occasionally. Remove from heat.
3. Add green chiles, ¾ cup cheddar cheese, ¾ cup Monterey Jack cheese, butter and pepper sauce; stir until cheese is melted. Stir in eggs, then sausage mixture.
4. Transfer to a greased 13x9-in. baking dish. Sprinkle with remaining cheeses and the paprika. Bake, uncovered, until golden brown and set, 50-60 minutes. Let stand 10 minutes before serving. Top with cilantro.
1 cup: 399 cal., 28g fat (15g sat. fat), 116mg chol., 839mg sod., 19g carb. (2g sugars, 2g fiber), 18g pro.

MINI HAM QUICHES

These adorable quiches are perfect for an after-church brunch when you don't want to fuss. Replace the ham with bacon, sausage, chicken or shrimp, or substitute chopped onion, red pepper or zucchini for the olives if you'd like.
—Marilou Robinson, Portland, OR

Prep: 15 min. • **Bake:** 20 min.
Makes: 1 dozen

- ¾ cup diced fully cooked ham
- ½ cup shredded sharp cheddar cheese
- ½ cup chopped ripe olives
- 3 large eggs, lightly beaten
- 1 cup half-and-half cream
- ¼ cup butter, melted
- 3 drops hot pepper sauce
- ½ cup biscuit/baking mix
- 2 Tbsp. grated Parmesan cheese
- ½ tsp. ground mustard

1. In a large bowl, combine the ham, cheddar cheese and olives; divide among 12 greased muffin cups. In another bowl, combine the remaining ingredients just until blended.
2. Pour over ham mixture. Bake at 375° until a knife inserted in the center comes out clean, 20-25 minutes. Let stand for 5 minutes before serving.
1 serving: 141 cal., 11g fat (6g sat. fat), 84mg chol., 332mg sod., 5g carb. (1g sugars, 0 fiber), 6g pro.

MAKE AHEAD

MAPLE-WALNUT STICKY BUNS

Mmm! These ooey-gooey goodies will have everyone licking maple syrup from their fingers—and reaching for seconds. The yeast dough chills overnight.
—Nancy Foust, Stoneboro, PA

- -

Prep: 45 min. + rising • **Bake:** 30 min.
Makes: 2 dozen

- 1 pkg. (¼ oz.) active dry yeast
- 1 cup warm water (110° to 115°)
- ½ cup mashed potatoes (without added milk and butter)
- 1 large egg, room temperature
- 2 Tbsp. shortening
- 2 Tbsp. sugar
- 1 tsp. salt
- 3 to 3½ cups all-purpose flour

TOPPING
- 1 cup maple syrup
- ¾ cup coarsely chopped walnuts

FILLING
- ⅓ cup sugar
- 1½ tsp. ground cinnamon
- 3 Tbsp. butter, softened

1. In a small bowl, dissolve yeast in warm water. In a large bowl, combine potatoes, egg, shortening, sugar, salt, yeast mixture and 1 cup flour; beat on medium speed until smooth. Stir in enough remaining flour to form a soft dough.
2. Turn dough onto a floured surface; knead until smooth and elastic, 6-8 minutes. Place in a greased bowl, turning once to grease the top. Cover and refrigerate overnight.
3. Pour syrup into a greased 13x9-in. baking dish; sprinkle with walnuts. In a small bowl, mix sugar and cinnamon. Punch down dough; turn onto a lightly floured surface. Roll into a 24x8-in. rectangle. Spread with butter to within ½ in. of edges; sprinkle with the cinnamon sugar. Roll up jelly-roll style, starting with a long side; pinch seam to seal. Cut into 24 slices.
4. Place in prepared baking dish, cut side down. Cover with a kitchen towel; let rise in a warm place until doubled, about 30 minutes. Preheat oven to 350°.
5. Bake 30-35 minutes or until golden brown. Cool 5 minutes before inverting buns onto a platter.
1 bun: 159 cal., 5g fat (1g sat. fat), 13mg chol., 114mg sod., 26g carb. (12g sugars, 1g fiber), 3g pro.

MAKE AHEAD

PHILLY BEEF & PEPPER STRATA

Here's a mouthwatering entree for brunch, lunch or dinner that's quick to fix. It combines several convenient ingredients for a large casserole that's pleasing to all who try it.
—Betty Claycomb, Alverton, PA

- -

Prep: 15 min. + chilling
Bake: 1¼ hours + standing
Makes: 12 servings

- 7 cups cubed Italian bread
- 3¾ cups julienned sweet red, yellow and/or green peppers
- ¼ cup chopped onion
- ¾ lb. cooked roast beef, cut into thin strips
- 2 cups shredded Monterey Jack cheese
- 8 large eggs
- 2¼ cups milk
- 2 Tbsp. Dijon mustard
- ½ tsp. salt
- ½ tsp. pepper

1. Place a third of the bread cubes in a greased 13x9-in. baking dish. Layer with a third of the peppers, onion, roast beef and cheese. Repeat layers twice. In a large bowl, whisk the eggs, milk, mustard, salt and pepper; pour over top. Cover and refrigerate for 8 hours or overnight.
2. Remove from refrigerator 30 minutes before baking. Bake, covered, at 325° for 1 hour. Uncover; bake 15-20 minutes longer or until a knife inserted in the center comes out clean. Let stand for 10 minutes before serving.
1 slice: 268 cal., 13g fat (6g sat. fat), 188mg chol., 477mg sod., 15g carb. (5g sugars, 1g fiber), 22g pro.

BRUNCH HAM ENCHILADAS

When I have company for brunch, this tried-and-true casserole is usually on the menu. With ham, eggs and plenty of cheese, the enchiladas are hearty and fun. I love being able to make them the day before.

—Gail Sykora, Menomonee Falls, WI

Prep: 15 min. + chilling
Bake: 40 min. + standing
Makes: 10 servings

- 2 cups cubed fully cooked ham
- ½ cup chopped green onions
- 10 flour tortillas (8 in.)
- 2 cups shredded cheddar cheese, divided
- 1 Tbsp. all-purpose flour
- 2 cups half-and-half cream
- 6 large eggs, lightly beaten
- ¼ tsp. salt, optional

1. In a large bowl, combine ham and onions; place about ¼ cup down the center of each tortilla. Top with 2 Tbsp. cheese. Roll up and place seam side down in a greased 13x9-in. baking dish.

2. In another large bowl, combine flour, cream, eggs and, if desired, salt until smooth. Pour over tortillas. Cover and refrigerate for 8 hours or overnight.

3. Remove from refrigerator 30 minutes before baking. Cover and bake at 350° for 25 minutes. Uncover; bake for 10 minutes. Sprinkle with remaining cheese; bake 3 minutes longer or until cheese is melted. Let stand 10 minutes before serving.

1 enchilada: 397 cal., 20g fat (10g sat. fat), 175mg chol., 846mg sod., 31g carb. (2g sugars, 2g fiber), 21g pro.

BEAR'S BREAKFAST BURRITOS

Everyone loves these hearty burritos. It's so convenient to freeze some and then bake them for a lazy Saturday breakfast.
—Larry & Sandy Kelley, Grangeville, ID

Prep: 45 min. • **Cook:** 15 min.
Makes: 12 servings

- 2 pkg. (22½ oz. each) frozen hash brown patties
- 15 large eggs, lightly beaten
- 2 Tbsp. chili powder
- 2 Tbsp. garlic salt
- 1 Tbsp. ground cumin
- ½ lb. uncooked chorizo or bulk spicy pork sausage
- 6 jalapeno peppers, seeded and minced
- 1 large green pepper, chopped
- 1 large sweet red pepper, chopped
- 1 large onion, chopped
- 1 bunch green onions, chopped
- 3 cups salsa
- 12 flour tortillas (12 in.), warmed
- 4 cups shredded Monterey Jack cheese
  Sour cream, optional

1. Cook hash browns according to package directions; crumble and keep them warm. Meanwhile, in a large bowl, whisk eggs, chili powder, garlic salt and cumin. Set aside.
2. Crumble chorizo into a large skillet; add the jalapenos, peppers and onions. Cook and stir over medium heat until chorizo is fully cooked; drain. Add egg mixture; cook and stir until eggs are set. Stir in salsa.
3. Spoon ½ cup hash browns and ½ cup egg mixture off center on each tortilla; sprinkle with ⅓ cup cheese. Fold sides and ends over filling and roll up. Wrap each burrito in waxed paper and foil. Serve warm, with sour cream if desired. Cool remaining burritos to room temperature; freeze for up to 1 month.
To use frozen burritos: Remove foil and waxed paper. Place burritos 2 in. apart on an ungreased baking sheet. Bake, uncovered, at 350° for 50-55 minutes or until burritos are heated through.
Note: Wear disposable gloves when cutting hot peppers; the oils can burn skin. Avoid touching your face.
1 burrito: 584 cal., 27g fat (12g sat. fat), 290mg chol., 2151mg sod., 58g carb. (5g sugars, 9g fiber), 27g pro.

APPLE-CINNAMON OATMEAL MIX

Oatmeal is a breakfast staple at our house. It's a warm, nutritious start to the day that keeps us going all morning. We used to buy the oatmeal mixes, but we think our homemade version is better! Feel free to substitute raisins or other dried fruit for the apples.
—Lynne Van Wagenen, Salt Lake City, UT

Takes: 5 min.
Makes: 8 cups mix (16 servings)

- 6 cups quick-cooking oats
- 1⅓ cups nonfat dry milk powder
- 1 cup dried apples, diced
- ¼ cup sugar
- ¼ cup packed brown sugar
- 1 Tbsp. ground cinnamon
- 1 tsp. salt
- ¼ tsp. ground cloves

ADDITIONAL INGREDIENT (EACH SERVING)
- ½ cup water

Combine the first 8 ingredients in a large bowl. Store in an airtight container in a cool, dry place for up to 6 months.
To prepare oatmeal: Shake mix well. In a small saucepan, bring water to a boil; slowly stir in ½ cup mix. Cook and stir over medium heat for 1 minute. Remove from heat. Cover and let stand for 1 minute or until oatmeal reaches desired consistency.
½ cup: 171 cal., 2g fat (0 sat. fat), 1mg chol., 185mg sod., 34g carb. (13g sugars, 4g fiber), 6g pro. **Diabetic exchanges:** 2 starch.

HAM & CHEESE BREAKFAST BUNDLES

My family looks forward to these rich and delicious egg bundles. They're perfect for holidays, brunches and birthdays.
—Cindy Bride, Bloomfield, IA

Prep: 35 min. • **Bake:** 15 min.
Makes: 12 servings

15   **sheets phyllo dough (14x9 in.)**
¾   **cup butter, melted**
4   **oz. cream cheese,**
     cut into 12 pieces
12   **large eggs**
½   **tsp. salt**
½   **tsp. pepper**
½   **cup cubed fully cooked ham**
½   **cup shredded provolone cheese**
2   **Tbsp. seasoned bread crumbs**
2   **Tbsp. minced fresh chives**

1. Preheat oven to 400°. Place 1 sheet of phyllo dough on a work surface; brush with butter. Layer with 4 additional phyllo sheets, brushing each layer. (Keep remaining phyllo covered with a damp towel to keep it from drying out.) Cut layered sheets crosswise in half, then lengthwise in half. Cover stacks to keep them from drying; repeat with remaining phyllo and butter.
2. Place each stack in a greased muffin cup. Fill each with a piece of cream cheese. Carefully break 1 egg into each cup. Sprinkle with salt and pepper; top with ham, cheese, bread crumbs and chives. Bring the phyllo together over filling; pinch to seal and form bundles. Bake until golden brown, 15-18 minutes. Serve warm.
1 bundle: 273 cal., 21g fat (12g sat. fat), 233mg chol., 478mg sod., 10g carb. (1g sugars, 0 fiber), 11g pro.

HALE LANI STRAWBERRY FRENCH TOAST

Our visitors love this dish and write about it in our guest books. I like to make it extra special by topping it with butter that I shape into palm tree, flower and leaf shapes.
—Ruth Johnson, Kapaa Kauai, HI

Prep: 30 min. + chilling • **Bake:** 10 min.
Makes: 10 servings

2   **cups frozen unsweetened**
     strawberries
¼   **cup sugar**
1   **loaf (1 lb.) Hawaiian sweet bread**
6   **large eggs**
1   **cup 2% milk**
3   **tsp. vanilla extract**
1½   **tsp. ground cinnamon**
½   **tsp. ground nutmeg**
¼   **cup canola oil**
     Confectioners' sugar and
     maple syrup

1. Place berries in a small bowl; sprinkle with sugar. Thaw in refrigerator overnight.
2. Slice strawberries and divide between 2 greased 13x9-in. baking dishes; set aside.
3. Cut bread into 20 slices. In a shallow bowl, whisk eggs, milk, vanilla, cinnamon and nutmeg. Dip bread in egg mixture. In a large skillet over medium heat, cook French toast in oil in batches for 2-3 minutes on each side or until golden brown. Place toast over strawberries in prepared dishes.
4. Bake at 350° for 10-15 minutes or until heated through. Sprinkle with the confectioners' sugar. Serve with syrup.
2 slices: 290 cal., 12g fat (3g sat. fat), 145mg chol., 198mg sod., 36g carb. (17g sugars, 2g fiber), 9g pro.

BRUNCH RISOTTO

This light, flavorful and inexpensive risotto makes a surprising addition to a traditional brunch menu. It's gotten lots of compliments from my friends.
—Jennifer Dines, Brighton, MA

Prep: 10 min. • **Cook:** 30 min.
Makes: 8 servings

5¼ to 5¾ cups reduced-sodium
    chicken broth
¾ lb. Italian turkey sausage links,
    casings removed
2 cups uncooked arborio rice
1 garlic clove, minced
¼ tsp. pepper
1 Tbsp. olive oil
1 medium tomato, chopped

1. In a large saucepan, heat the broth and keep warm. In a large nonstick skillet, cook sausage until no longer pink, breaking it into crumbles; drain and set aside.
2. In the same skillet, saute the rice, garlic and pepper in oil for 2-3 minutes. Return sausage to skillet. Carefully stir in 1 cup heated broth. Cook and stir until all of the liquid is absorbed.
3. Add remaining broth, ½ cup at a time, stirring constantly. Allow liquid to absorb between additions. Cook just until risotto is creamy and rice is almost tender, about 20 minutes total. Add the tomato and heat through. Serve immediately.
⅔ cup: 279 cal., 6g fat (2g sat. fat), 23mg chol., 653mg sod., 42g carb. (1g sugars, 1g fiber), 12g pro. **Diabetic exchanges:** 2½ starch, 1 lean meat, ½ fat.

MAKE AHEAD

CARAMEL APPLE STRATA

If you're planning to host a breakfast or early brunch, you'll appreciate this overnight strata. It works fabulously as your something sweet, tastes like a sticky bun and won't dry out as coffee cakes sometimes do.
—Kelly Boe, Whiteland, IN

Prep: 20 min. + chilling
Bake: 50 min. + standing
Makes: 12 servings

2 cups packed brown sugar
½ cup butter, cubed
¼ cup corn syrup
3 large apples, peeled and chopped
2 Tbsp. lemon juice
1 Tbsp. sugar
1 tsp. apple pie spice
1 loaf (1 lb.) day-old cinnamon bread
½ cup chopped pecans
10 large eggs
1 cup 2% milk
1 tsp. salt
1 tsp. vanilla extract

1. In a small saucepan, combine the brown sugar, butter and corn syrup. Bring to a boil over medium heat, stirring constantly. Cook and stir 2 minutes or until thickened. Set sauce aside.
2. In a small bowl, combine apples, lemon juice, sugar and pie spice. Arrange half the bread slices in a greased 13x9-in. baking dish. Top with apples; drizzle with half the caramel sauce. Sprinkle with pecans; top with remaining bread.
3. In a large bowl, combine the eggs, milk, salt and vanilla. Pour over top. Cover and refrigerate overnight. Cover and refrigerate remaining caramel sauce.
4. Remove the strata from refrigerator 30 minutes before baking. Bake, uncovered, at 350° for 50-55 minutes or until a knife inserted in the center comes out clean. Let stand 10 minutes before cutting.
5. In a microwave, heat reserved sauce. Drizzle warm sauce over strata.
1 piece: 462 cal., 19g fat (7g sat. fat), 198mg chol., 472mg sod., 67g carb. (49g sugars, 4g fiber), 10g pro.

Teriyaki
Shish Kabobs
page 75

Main Dishes

Be a potluck superstar when you share a standout casserole, grilled meat, crowd-sized sammie or other praiseworthy main dish. These recipes will make you proud!

ANTIPASTO SALAD PLATTER

I used to work in a pizza shop where this salad was the most popular item on the menu. The dish is perfect for nights when it's just too hot to cook.
—Webbie Carvajal, Alpine, TX

Takes: 25 min. • **Makes:** 8 servings

- 1½ cups cubed fully cooked ham
- 1 jar (10 oz.) pimiento-stuffed olives, drained and sliced
- 1 can (3.8 oz.) sliced ripe olives, drained
- 1 pkg. (3½ oz.) sliced pepperoni, quartered
- 8 cups shredded lettuce
- 10 to 12 cherry tomatoes, quartered
- 1 cup Italian salad dressing
- 1½ cups shredded part-skim mozzarella cheese

In a large bowl, combine the ham, olives and pepperoni. On a platter or individual salad plates, arrange the lettuce, olive mixture and tomatoes. Drizzle with dressing; sprinkle with cheese.

1 serving: 342 cal., 29g fat (7g sat. fat), 41mg chol., 1830mg sod., 9g carb. (3g sugars, 2g fiber), 13g pro.

ARTICHOKE SPINACH LASAGNA

Friends of ours served this homey dish when we visited them in Maryland. We just had to get the recipe and have since added a few items to make it even tastier.
—Carole Rago, Altoona, PA

Prep: 25 min.
Bake: 55 min. + standing
Makes: 12 servings

1   Tbsp. olive oil
1   small onion, chopped
½   cup sliced fresh mushrooms
4   garlic cloves, minced
1   can (14½ oz.) vegetable or chicken broth
1   can (14 oz.) water-packed artichoke hearts, drained and coarsely chopped
1   pkg. (10 oz.) frozen chopped spinach, thawed and squeezed dry
1   tsp. dried rosemary, crushed
¼   tsp. ground nutmeg
¼   tsp. pepper
1   jar (16 oz.) roasted garlic Parmesan or roasted garlic Alfredo sauce

ASSEMBLY
12   no-cook lasagna noodles

3   cups shredded part-skim mozzarella cheese
1   cup crumbled tomato and basil feta cheese or feta cheese
⅛   tsp. garlic powder
⅛   tsp. each dried oregano, parsley flakes and basil

1. Preheat oven to 350°. In large saucepan, heat oil over medium-high heat. Add onion and mushrooms; cook and stir until tender. Add garlic; cook 1 minute longer. Stir in the broth, artichokes, spinach, rosemary, nutmeg and pepper; bring just to a boil. Reduce heat; simmer 5 minutes, stirring occasionally. Stir in Alfredo sauce; remove from heat.

2. Spread 1 cup sauce into a greased 13x9-in. baking dish. Layer with 3 noodles and ⅔ cup mozzarella cheese. Repeat layers 3 times. Top with remaining sauce and mozzarella cheese. Sprinkle with feta cheese, garlic powder and herbs.

3. Bake, covered, 40 minutes. Bake, uncovered, 15 minutes longer or until noodles are tender. Let stand 10 minutes before serving.

1 piece: 269 cal., 14g fat (7g sat. fat), 49mg chol., 755mg sod., 22g carb. (3g sugars, 2g fiber), 14g pro.

BIG-BATCH JAMBALAYA

I make this dish for football-watching parties because it feeds so many people. Of course it's good any time of year!
—Kecia McCaffrey, South Dennis, MA

Prep: 25 min. • **Cook:** 55 min.
Makes: 13 servings

- 1 boneless skinless chicken breast, cubed
- 3 Tbsp. olive oil, divided
- ½ lb. cubed fully cooked ham
- ½ lb. smoked kielbasa or Polish sausage, cubed
- 2 medium green peppers, coarsely chopped
- 2 medium onions, coarsely chopped
- 6 garlic cloves, minced
- 2 cans (14½ oz. each) beef broth
- 1 can (28 oz.) crushed tomatoes
- 1½ cups water
- ¾ cup Dijon mustard
- ¼ cup minced fresh parsley
- 2 Tbsp. Worcestershire sauce
- 1½ to 2 tsp. cayenne pepper
- ½ tsp. dried thyme
- 1½ cups uncooked long grain rice
- 1 lb. uncooked medium shrimp, peeled and deveined

1. In a Dutch oven, cook chicken in 1 Tbsp. oil until no longer pink; remove and set aside. In the same pan, cook and stir the ham, kielbasa, peppers and onions in remaining oil until onions are tender. Add garlic; cook 1 minute longer.

2. Stir in broth, tomatoes, water, mustard, parsley, Worcestershire, cayenne and thyme. Bring to a boil. Reduce heat; cover and simmer for 10 minutes.

3. Add rice and return to a boil. Reduce heat; cover and simmer for 25-30 minutes or until rice is tender. Stir in shrimp and chicken; cook 2-4 minutes longer or until shrimp turn pink.

1 cup: 288 cal., 11g fat (3g sat. fat), 71mg chol., 1185mg sod., 30g carb. (2g sugars, 2g fiber), 18g pro.

HONEY CHIPOTLE RIBS

Nothing is better than having a sauce with the perfect slather consistency. Here's one that will ensure a lip-smacking feast. Go ahead and prepare the sauce up to a week in advance for an easier grilling experience.
—Caitlin Hawes, Westwood, MA

Prep: 10 min. • **Grill:** 1½ hours
Makes: 12 servings

- 6 lbs. pork baby back ribs

BARBECUE SAUCE
- 3 cups ketchup
- 2 bottles (11.2 oz. each) Guinness beer
- 2 cups barbecue sauce
- ⅔ cup honey
- 1 small onion, chopped
- ¼ cup Worcestershire sauce
- 2 Tbsp. Dijon mustard
- 2 Tbsp. chopped chipotle peppers in adobo sauce
- 4 tsp. ground chipotle pepper
- 1 tsp. salt
- 1 tsp. garlic powder
- ½ tsp. pepper

1. Wrap ribs in large pieces of heavy-duty foil; seal edges of foil. Grill, covered, over indirect medium heat for 1-1½ hours or until tender.

2. In a large saucepan, combine sauce ingredients; bring to a boil. Reduce heat; simmer, uncovered, for about 45 minutes or until thickened, stirring occasionally.

3. Carefully remove ribs from foil. Place over direct heat; baste with some of the sauce. Grill, covered, over medium heat for about 30 minutes or until browned, turning once and basting occasionally with additional sauce. Serve with the remaining sauce.

1 serving: 515 cal., 21g fat (8g sat. fat), 81mg chol., 1674mg sod., 54g carb. (49g sugars, 1g fiber), 23g pro.

CONTEST-WINNING HOLIDAY GLAZED HAM

I like to serve this juicy, mouthwatering ham with mashed potatoes and colorful vegetables. The apricot glaze is delicious, and the pineapple and cloves assure a lovely presentation.
—Diane Freeman, Falkland, BC

- -

Prep: 20 min. • **Bake:** 2 hours
Makes: 16 servings

1 boneless fully cooked ham (about 6 lbs.)
1 Tbsp. whole cloves
1 can (20 oz.) sliced pineapple
1 cup apricot preserves
1 tsp. ground mustard
½ tsp. ground allspice
  Maraschino cherries

1. Preheat oven to 325°. Place ham on a rack in a shallow roasting pan. Score the surface of ham, making diamond shapes ½ in. deep; insert a clove in each diamond. Bake, uncovered, 1½ hours.
2. Drain pineapple, reserving juice. In a small saucepan, combine pineapple juice, preserves, mustard and allspice. Bring to a boil; cook and stir for 10 minutes or until slightly thickened.
3. Spoon half the glaze over ham. Secure pineapple slices and cherries on top and sides of ham with toothpicks.
4. Bake until a thermometer reads 140°, 30-45 minutes, basting twice with the remaining glaze.
5 oz. ham: 248 cal., 6g fat (2g sat. fat), 87mg chol., 1774mg sod., 18g carb. (13g sugars, 0 fiber), 32g pro.

GOURMET BURGERS WITH SUN-DRIED TOMATO

This recipe brings together many of the flavors my family enjoys, complete with a surprise in the center of each burger. You can use almost any cheese—feta, Gorgonzola, smoked Gouda, blue or another family favorite.
—Aaron Shields, Hamburg, NY

- -

Prep: 40 min. • **Grill:** 10 min.
Makes: 8 servings

- 1   jar (7 oz.) oil-packed sun-dried tomatoes
- 3   medium onions, halved and thinly sliced
- 3   Tbsp. balsamic vinegar
- ½   cup finely chopped red onion
- 2   Tbsp. dried basil
- 2   tsp. ground cumin
- 2   tsp. ground chipotle pepper
- ½   tsp. salt
- ¼   tsp. pepper
- 3   lbs. lean ground beef (90% lean)
- 1   cup crumbled goat cheese
- 8   hamburger buns, split
     Mixed salad greens, optional

1. Drain tomatoes, reserving ⅓ cup oil; set aside. In a large skillet, saute sliced onions in 3 Tbsp. reserved oil until softened. Add vinegar. Reduce heat to medium-low; cook, stirring occasionally, until deep golden brown, 30-40 minutes.
2. Meanwhile, chop sun-dried tomatoes and transfer to large bowl. Add red onion, seasonings and remaining oil. Crumble beef over mixture and mix well. Shape into 16 thin patties. Place 2 Tbsp. goat cheese on the center of 8 patties. Top with remaining patties and press edges firmly to seal.
3. Grill burgers, covered, over medium heat until a thermometer reads 160° and juices run clear, 5-7 minutes on each side.
4. Place buns, cut side down, on grill until toasted, 1-2 minutes. Serve burgers on buns with onions and, if desired, mixed salad greens.

1 burger with 2 Tbsp. onions: 596 cal., 32g fat (10g sat. fat), 123mg chol., 588mg sod., 36g carb. (7g sugars, 5g fiber), 42g pro.

TEST KITCHEN TIP
Use a gentle hand when shaping the burgers. Overworking will make them less tender.

GRILLED ONION & SKIRT STEAK TACOS

I grew up watching my grandmother and mother in the kitchen. My grandparents came from Mexico, and this steak marinated in beer and lime juice honors their passion for cooking.
—Adan Franco, Milwaukee, WI

Prep: 15 min. + marinating
Grill: 10 min.
Makes: 8 servings

- 2 beef skirt or flank steaks (1 lb. each)
- 1 bottle (12 oz.) beer
- ¼ cup lime juice
- 3 Tbsp. olive oil, divided
- 8 spring onions or green onions
- 1¼ tsp. salt, divided
- ¾ tsp. pepper, divided
- Corn tortillas, minced fresh cilantro and lime wedges

1. Pound beef with a meat mallet to tenderize. In a large bowl, mix beer, lime juice and 2 Tbsp. oil until blended. Add beef to marinade; turn to coat. Refrigerate, covered, at least 30 minutes.

2. Meanwhile, cut partially through the onions, leaving tops intact. Drizzle with remaining oil; sprinkle with ¼ tsp. salt and ¼ tsp. pepper.

3. Drain the beef, discarding marinade; sprinkle with remaining salt and pepper. On a greased grill rack, grill steaks and onions, covered, over medium heat or broil 4 in. from heat until meat reaches desired doneness (for medium-rare, a thermometer should read 135°; medium, 140°; medium-well, 145°) and onions are crisp-tender, 2-4 minutes on each side. Cut steak diagonally across the grain into thin slices. Serve with tortillas, onions, cilantro and lime wedges.

1 serving: 288 cal., 14g fat (5g sat. fat), 67mg chol., 458mg sod., 7g carb. (3g sugars, 1g fiber), 31g pro.

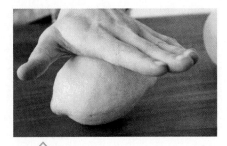

HOW TO GET THE MOST JUICE
Next time you squeeze a fresh lemon or lime, first warm the fruit in the microwave for 7-10 seconds. Then roll it back and forth under your palm on the counter, giving it firm pressure. You'll get more juice and it'll be easier to squeeze, too.

TERIYAKI SHISH KABOBS

When I was a teenager, my father worked for an airline, and my family lived on the island of Guam in the South Pacific. A friend of my mother gave her this tangy-sweet recipe, and we enjoyed it often. Now I make it for my family, and they're big fans as well.
—Suzanne Pelegrin, Ocala, FL

Prep: 20 min. + marinating • **Grill:** 15 min.
Makes: 8 servings

- 1 cup sugar
- 1 cup reduced-sodium soy sauce
- 1 cup ketchup
- 2 tsp. garlic powder
- 2 tsp. ground ginger
- 2 lbs. beef top sirloin steak, cut into 1½-in. cubes
- 2 to 3 small zucchini, cut into 1-in. slices
- ½ lb. medium fresh mushrooms
- 1 large green or sweet red pepper, cut into 1-in. pieces
- 1 small onion, cut into 1-in. pieces
- 2 cups cubed fresh pineapple

1. For marinade, mix the first 5 ingredients. In a large bowl or shallow dish, add half the marinade and the beef. Turn beef to coat. Cover and reserve the remaining marinade. Cover and refrigerate beef and marinade overnight.

2. On metal or soaked wooden skewers, thread the vegetables and, on separate skewers, thread beef with pineapple. Discard remaining marinade from beef bowl. Grill kabobs, covered, over medium heat 12-15 minutes or until the vegetables are tender and beef reaches desired doneness, turning occasionally.

3. In a small saucepan, bring reserved marinade to a boil, stirring occasionally; cook 1 minute. Remove the vegetables, pineapple and beef from skewers before serving. Serve with sauce.

1 serving: 306 cal., 5g fat (2g sat. fat), 46mg chol., 1203mg sod., 38g carb. (32g sugars, 2g fiber), 27g pro.

FAVORITE BARBECUED CHICKEN

Is there a better place than Texas to find a fantastic barbecue sauce? That's where this one is from—it's my father-in-law's own recipe. We have served it at many family reunions and think it's the best!
—Bobbie Morgan, Woodstock, GA

Prep: 15 min. • **Grill:** 35 min.
Makes: 12 servings

- 2 broiler/fryer chickens (3 to 4 lbs. each), cut into 8 pieces each
  Salt and pepper

BARBECUE SAUCE
- 2 Tbsp. canola oil
- 2 small onions, finely chopped
- 2 cups ketchup
- ¼ cup lemon juice
- 2 Tbsp. brown sugar
- 2 Tbsp. water
- 1 tsp. ground mustard
- ½ tsp. garlic powder
- ¼ tsp. pepper
- ⅛ tsp. salt
- ⅛ tsp. hot pepper sauce

1. Sprinkle chicken pieces with salt and pepper. Grill skin side down, uncovered, on a greased grill rack over medium heat for 20 minutes.

2. Meanwhile, in a small saucepan, make barbecue sauce by heating oil over medium heat. Add onion; saute until tender. Stir in remaining sauce ingredients and bring to a boil. Reduce heat; simmer, uncovered, for 10 minutes.

3. Turn chicken pieces; brush with barbecue sauce. Grill 15-25 minutes longer, brushing frequently with sauce, until a thermometer reads 165° when inserted in the breast and 170°-175° in the thigh.

1 serving: 370 cal., 19g fat (5g sat. fat), 104mg chol., 622mg sod., 15g carb. (14g sugars, 0 fiber), 33g pro.

ASIAN BARBECUED SHORT RIBS

Here in beef country, we find all sorts of different ways to serve beef. A former boss of mine, who owned a midwestern meat plant, gave me this recipe. It was an immediate hit with my family!
—Connie McDowell, Lincoln, NE

Prep: 25 min. • **Bake:** 1¾ hours
Makes: 8 servings

4	lbs. bone-in beef short ribs
1	Tbsp. canola oil
1	medium onion, sliced
¾	cup ketchup
¾	cup water, divided
¼	cup reduced-sodium soy sauce
2	Tbsp. lemon juice
1	Tbsp. brown sugar
1	tsp. ground mustard
½	tsp. ground ginger
¼	tsp. salt
⅛	tsp. pepper
1	bay leaf
2	Tbsp. all-purpose flour
	Optional: Julienned green onions and sesame seeds

1. In a Dutch oven, brown the ribs in oil on all sides in batches. Remove ribs; set aside. In the same pan, saute onion until tender, 2 minutes. Return ribs to the pan.

2. Combine the ketchup, ½ cup water, soy sauce, lemon juice, brown sugar, mustard, ginger, salt, pepper and bay leaf; pour over ribs.

3. Cover and bake at 325° until ribs are tender, 1¾-2 hours.

4. Remove ribs and keep warm. Discard bay leaf. Skim fat from pan drippings. In a small bowl, combine flour and remaining water until smooth; gradually stir into drippings. Bring to a boil; cook and stir until thickened, 2 minutes. Serve with ribs. If desired, top with green onions and sesame seeds.

1 serving: 240 cal., 13g fat (5g sat. fat), 55mg chol., 854mg sod., 11g carb. (9g sugars, 1g fiber), 20g pro.

FAVORITE DEEP-DISH PIZZA

My kids love to get pizza delivered, but it is expensive and not very healthy. I came up with a one-bowl pizza that is healthier than delivery and allows the kids to add the toppings of their choice.
—Sara LaFountain, Rockville, MD

Prep: 20 min. • **Bake:** 20 min.
Makes: 8 servings

- 1¾ cups whole wheat flour
- 1¾ cups all-purpose flour
- 2 pkg. (¼ oz. each) quick-rise yeast
- 4 tsp. sugar
- 1 tsp. salt
- 1½ cups warm water (120° to 130°)
- ¼ cup olive oil
- 1 can (8 oz.) pizza sauce
- 8 oz. fresh mozzarella cheese, sliced
- 2 cups shredded Italian cheese blend
- ½ tsp. dried oregano
- ½ tsp. Italian seasoning
  Optional: Sliced red onion, chopped green pepper, fresh oregano and crushed red pepper flakes

1. In a large bowl, combine wheat flour, 1 cup all-purpose flour, yeast, sugar and salt. Add water and oil; beat until smooth. Stir in enough remaining flour to form a soft dough. Press dough onto the bottom and up the sides of a greased 13x9-in. baking dish.
2. Top with pizza sauce. Place mozzarella slices over sauce. Sprinkle with shredded cheese, oregano and Italian seasoning. If desired, top with red onion and green pepper. Bake, uncovered, at 400° for 20-25 minutes or until golden brown. If desired, top with fresh oregano leaves and crushed red pepper flakes.

1 slice: 449 cal., 20g fat (9g sat. fat), 42mg chol., 646mg sod., 47g carb. (4g sugars, 5g fiber), 19g pro.

BRING IT
Pizza-making is an awesome team activity that kids love! Why not prep a variety of toppings and let the little chefs assist in designing their own dream pizza creations? Think veggies, meats, pineapple...

GREEK CHICKEN BAKE

As soon as the weather turns cold, I know it's time to pull out this go-to recipe. I assemble it in the morning, then put it in the oven just before dinner.
—Kelly Maxwell, Plainfield, IL

Prep: 30 min. • **Bake:** 50 min.
Makes: 8 servings

- 3 Tbsp. olive oil, divided
- 1 medium onion, chopped
- 7 garlic cloves, minced
- 2 tsp. minced fresh thyme or ¾ tsp. dried thyme
- 2 tsp. minced fresh rosemary or ¾ tsp. dried rosemary, crushed
- ¾ tsp. pepper, divided
- 2 lbs. red potatoes, cut into ½-in. cubes
- 2 cans (14½ oz. each) diced tomatoes, undrained
- 2 cups cut fresh green beans (1-in. pieces)
- 2 Tbsp. finely chopped ripe olives
- 8 bone-in chicken thighs (about 3 lbs.), skin removed
- ½ tsp. salt
- ½ cup crumbled feta cheese
  Minced fresh parsley
  Hot cooked orzo pasta, optional

1. Preheat oven to 375°. In a large skillet, heat 1 Tbsp. oil over medium heat. Add onion; cook and stir 3-4 minutes or until tender. Add garlic, thyme, rosemary and ½ tsp. pepper; cook 1 minute longer. Remove from pan.

2. In same pan, heat remaining oil over medium heat. Add potatoes; cook and stir until potatoes are lightly browned. Return onion mixture to pan; stir in the tomatoes, green beans and olives. Cook 1 minute longer.

3. Transfer to a greased 13x9-in. baking dish. Sprinkle the chicken with salt and remaining pepper; place over top of the potato mixture. Bake, covered, 40 minutes.

Bake, uncovered, 10-15 minutes longer or until a thermometer reads 170°-175°. Sprinkle with feta and parsley. If desired, serve with orzo.

To make ahead: Can be made a few hours in advance. Cover and refrigerate. Remove from the refrigerator 30 minutes before baking. Bake as directed.

1 chicken thigh with 1 cup potato mixture: 352 cal., 16g fat (4g sat. fat), 91mg chol., 312mg sod., 23g carb. (3g sugars, 3g fiber), 28g pro.

MUFFULETTA PASTA

A friend gave me this recipe when she learned that I love muffuletta sandwiches. Very rich and filling, this easy skillet supper goes together quickly on a busy weeknight. Serve with some cheesy garlic bread.
—Jan Hollingsworth, Houston, MS

Takes: 25 min.
Makes: 8 servings

- 1 pkg. (16 oz.) bow tie pasta
- 1 bunch green onions, chopped
- 2 tsp. plus ¼ cup butter, divided
- 1 Tbsp. minced garlic
- 1 pkg. (16 oz.) cubed fully cooked ham
- 1 jar (12.36 oz.) tapenade or ripe olive bruschetta topping, drained
- 1 pkg. (3½ oz.) sliced pepperoni
- 1 cup heavy whipping cream
- 2 cups shredded Italian cheese blend

1. Cook pasta according to package directions. Meanwhile, in a large skillet, saute onions in 2 tsp. butter until tender. Add garlic; cook 1 minute longer. Add the ham, tapenade and pepperoni; saute 2 minutes longer.

2. Cube remaining butter; stir butter and cream into skillet. Bring to a boil over medium heat. Reduce heat; simmer, uncovered, for 3 minutes.

3. Drain pasta; toss with ham mixture. Sprinkle with cheese.

1½ cups: 739 cal., 48g fat (21g sat. fat), 119mg chol., 1638mg sod., 48g carb. (2g sugars, 2g fiber), 27g pro.

RANCH PORK ROAST

This simple pork roast with a mild rub is perfect for new cooks. The leftover meat is tender and flavorful enough to be used in countless recipes.
—Taste of Home Test Kitchen

Prep: 10 min. • **Bake:** 50 min. + standing
Makes: 8 servings

1	boneless pork loin roast (2½ lbs.)
2	Tbsp. olive oil
1	Tbsp. ranch salad dressing mix
2	tsp. Dijon mustard
1	garlic clove, minced
½	tsp. pepper

1. Preheat oven to 350°. If desired, tie pork with kitchen string at 2-in. intervals to help roast hold its shape. Combine the next 5 ingredients; rub over roast. Place on a rack in a shallow roasting pan. Pour 1 cup water into the pan.

2. Bake, uncovered, until a thermometer reads 145°, 50-55 minutes. Let stand for 10-15 minutes before slicing.

4 oz. cooked pork: 212 cal., 10g fat (3g sat. fat), 70mg chol., 248mg sod., 2g carb. (0 sugars, 0 fiber), 27g pro.
Diabetic exchanges: 4 lean meat, ½ fat.

MAKEOVER MEATLESS LASAGNA

If you have never tried tofu before, go for it with this recipe. The tofu blends in with all the other ingredients, adding protein without the fat and calories of ground beef.
—Mary Lou Moeller, Wooster, OH

- -

Prep: 30 min. • **Bake:** 45 min. + standing
Makes: 12 servings

- 10 uncooked whole wheat lasagna noodles
- 1½ cups sliced fresh mushrooms
- ¼ cup chopped onion
- 2 garlic cloves, minced
- 1 can (14½ oz.) Italian diced tomatoes, undrained
- 1 can (12 oz.) tomato paste
- 1 pkg. (14 oz.) firm tofu, drained and cubed
- 2 large eggs, lightly beaten
- 3 cups 2% cottage cheese
- ½ cup grated Parmesan cheese
- ½ cup packed fresh parsley leaves
- ½ tsp. pepper
- 2 cups shredded part-skim mozzarella cheese, divided

1. Preheat oven to 375°. Cook noodles according to package directions for al dente. Meanwhile, in a large saucepan, cook mushrooms and onion over medium heat until tender. Add garlic; cook 1 minute. Add tomatoes and tomato paste; cook and stir until heated through.

2. Pulse the tofu in a food processor until smooth. Add the next 5 ingredients; pulse until combined. Drain noodles.

3. Place 5 noodles into a 13x9-in. baking dish coated with cooking spray, overlapping as needed. Layer with half the tofu mixture, half the sauce and half the mozzarella. Top with the remaining noodles, tofu mixture and sauce.

4. Bake, covered, 35 minutes. Sprinkle with the remaining mozzarella. Bake, uncovered, until cheese is melted, 10-15 minutes. Let stand 10 minutes before serving.

1 piece: 258 cal., 9g fat (4g sat. fat), 48mg chol., 498mg sod., 26g carb. (9g sugars, 3g fiber), 19g pro. **Diabetic exchanges:** 2 medium-fat meat, 1½ starch.

MEXICAN MANICOTTI

Serve this hearty entree with Spanish rice, homemade salsa and tortilla chips. I've also made it without ground beef, and our friends who are vegetarians requested the recipe.
—Lucy Shifton, Wichita, KS

- -

Prep: 15 min. + chilling
Bake: 65 min. + standing
Makes: 8 servings

- 1   lb. lean ground beef
- 1   can (16 oz.) refried beans
- 2½ tsp. chili powder
- 1½ tsp. dried oregano
- 1   pkg. (8 oz.) uncooked manicotti shells
- 2½ cups water
- 1   jar (16 oz.) picante sauce
- 2   cups sour cream
- 1   cup shredded Monterey Jack or Mexican cheese blend
- ¼   cup sliced green onions
      Sliced ripe olives, optional

1. In a large bowl, combine the uncooked beef, beans, chili powder and oregano. Spoon into uncooked manicotti shells; arrange in a greased 13x9-in. baking dish. Combine water and picante sauce; pour over shells. Cover and refrigerate overnight.
2. Remove from refrigerator 30 minutes before baking. Bake, covered, at 350° for 1 hour. Uncover; spoon sour cream over the top. Sprinkle with cheese, onions and olives if desired. Bake 5-10 minutes longer or until the cheese is melted.
1 serving: 431 cal., 20g fat (12g sat. fat), 90mg chol., 554mg sod., 36g carb. (6g sugars, 4g fiber), 23g pro.

HEARTY MEATBALL SUB SANDWICHES

Making the saucy meatballs in advance and reheating them saves me precious time when expecting company. These subs are excellent for casual parties.
—Deena Hubler, Jasper, IN

- -

Takes: 30 min. • **Makes:** 12 servings

- 2   large eggs, lightly beaten
- 1   cup dry bread crumbs
- 2   Tbsp. grated Parmesan cheese
- 2   Tbsp. finely chopped onion
- 1   tsp. salt
- ½   tsp. pepper
- ½   tsp. garlic powder
- ¼   tsp. Italian seasoning
- 2   lbs. ground beef
- 1   jar (28 oz.) spaghetti sauce
- 12 sandwich rolls, split
      Optional: Sliced onion and sliced green pepper

1. In a large bowl, combine the first 8 ingredients. Crumble beef over mixture; mix well. Shape into 1-in. balls. Place in a single layer in 3-qt. microwave-safe dish.
2. Cover and microwave on high for 3-4 minutes. Turn the meatballs; cook 3-4 minutes longer or until no longer pink. Drain. Add spaghetti sauce.
3. Cover and microwave on high for 2-4 minutes or until heated through. Serve on rolls. If desired, top with additional Parmesan and sliced onion and green peppers.
1 serving: 464 cal., 18g fat (7g sat. fat), 88mg chol., 1013mg sod., 49g carb. (10g sugars, 3g fiber), 26g pro.

CHICKEN PARMESAN STUFFED SHELLS

When chicken Parmesan meets stuffed shells, it's love at first bite. The texture of the chicken holds up in the deliciously creamy cheesy mixture.
—Cyndy Gerken, Naples, FL

- -

Prep: 45 min.
Bake: 40 min.
Makes: 12 servings

- 1 pkg. (12 oz.) uncooked jumbo pasta shells
- 2 Tbsp. olive oil

FILLING
- 1 lb. boneless skinless chicken breasts, cut into ½-in. cubes
- 1½ tsp. Italian seasoning
- 1 tsp. salt, divided
- ½ tsp. pepper, divided
- 1 Tbsp. olive oil
- 2 Tbsp. butter
- ⅓ cup seasoned bread crumbs
- 3 cups part-skim ricotta cheese
- 1 cup shredded part-skim mozzarella cheese
- ½ cup grated Parmesan cheese
- ½ cup 2% milk
- ¼ cup chopped fresh Italian parsley

ASSEMBLY
- 4 cups meatless pasta sauce
- ¼ cup grated Parmesan cheese
- 8 oz. fresh mozzarella cheese, thinly sliced and halved

1. Preheat oven to 375°. Cook shells according to package directions for al dente; drain. Toss with oil; spread in an even layer on a baking sheet.
2. For filling, toss chicken with Italian seasoning, ½ tsp. salt and ¼ tsp. pepper. In a large skillet, heat oil over medium-high heat; saute chicken just until lightly browned, about 2 minutes. Reduce heat to medium; stir in butter until melted. Stir in bread crumbs; cook until crumbs are slightly toasted, 2-3 minutes, stirring occasionally. Cool slightly.
3. In a large bowl, mix cheeses, milk, parsley and the remaining salt and pepper. Fold in the chicken.
4. Spread 2 cups pasta sauce into a greased 13x9-in. baking dish. Fill each shell with 2½ Tbsp. cheese mixture; place over sauce. Top with the remaining sauce and cheeses (dish will be full).
5. Cover with greased foil; bake 30 minutes. Uncover and bake until heated through, 10-15 minutes.

1 serving: 431 cal., 19g fat (10g sat. fat), 71mg chol., 752mg sod., 36g carb. (8g sugars, 2g fiber), 28g pro.

GRILLED RIBEYES WITH BLUE CHEESE BUTTER

Fire up the grill for steaks that practically melt in your mouth. They are garlic-infused, and the grilled flavor is off the charts. With this recipe on hand, any menu is sure to sizzle!

—Mona Engelbrecht, Wichita, KS

- -

Takes: 25 min. • **Makes:** 8 servings

- 8   beef ribeye steaks (10 oz. each)
- 12   garlic cloves, sliced
- ¼   cup olive oil
- 1   tsp. salt
- ¾   tsp. cayenne pepper
- ½   tsp. pepper
- ½   cup crumbled blue cheese
- ¼   cup butter, softened

1. Cut slits into each steak; insert garlic slices. Brush with oil and sprinkle with salt, cayenne and pepper.
2. Grill, covered, over medium heat or broil 4 in. from heat for 4-6 minutes on each side or until meat reaches desired doneness (for medium-rare, a thermometer should read 135°; medium, 140°; medium-well, 145°).
3. Combine blue cheese and butter. Serve with steaks.

1 steak with 1 Tbsp. butter mixture: 766 cal., 60g fat (24g sat. fat), 189mg chol., 567mg sod., 2g carb. (0 sugars, 0 fiber), 52g pro.

BRING IT
Grilled beef is a tasty, food-safe choice for get-togethers. Prep these steaks at home and tote them along with your blue cheese butter. They'll only improve from chilling in the oil, garlic and spices before they hit the hot grill!

BLT CHICKEN SALAD

Featuring all the fun fixings for a BLT chicken sandwich, this salad is so lovable. I can prep the ingredients ahead of time and just throw it together at the last minute. Barbecue sauce in the dressing gives it unexpected flavor. Even picky eaters love it.

—Cindy Moore, Mooresville, NC

- -

Takes: 20 min. • **Makes:** 8 servings

- ½   cup mayonnaise
- 3   to 4 Tbsp. barbecue sauce
- 2   Tbsp. finely chopped onion
- 1   Tbsp. lemon juice
- ¼   tsp. pepper
- 8   cups torn salad greens
- 2   large tomatoes, chopped
- 1½   lbs. boneless skinless chicken breasts, cooked and cubed
- 10   bacon strips, cooked and crumbled
- 2   hard-boiled large eggs, sliced

In a small bowl, combine the first 5 ingredients; mix well. Cover and refrigerate until serving. Place salad greens in a large bowl. Sprinkle with tomatoes, chicken and bacon; garnish with eggs. Drizzle with dressing.

1 serving: 281 cal., 19g fat (4g sat. fat), 112mg chol., 324mg sod., 5g carb. (3g sugars, 2g fiber), 23g pro.

FOIL-PACKET POTATOES & SAUSAGE

My family enjoys camping and cooking over a fire. These hearty foil-packet meals turn out beautifully over a campfire, on the grill or in the oven at home.
—Julie Koets, Elkhart, IN

Prep: 20 min. • **Cook:** 30 min.
Makes: 8 servings

- 3 lbs. red potatoes, cut into ½-in. cubes
- 2 pkg. (12 oz. each) smoked sausage links, cut into ½-in. slices
- 4 bacon strips, cooked and crumbled
- 1 medium onion, chopped
- 2 Tbsp. chopped fresh parsley
- ¼ tsp. salt
- ¼ tsp. garlic salt
- ¼ tsp. pepper
  Additional chopped fresh parsley, optional

1. Prepare campfire or grill for medium heat. In a large bowl, toss the potatoes with sausage, bacon, onion, parsley, salts and pepper.
2. Divide mixture among eight 18x12-in. pieces of heavy-duty nonstick foil, placing food on dull side of foil. Fold foil around potato mixture, sealing tightly.
3. Place packets over campfire or grill; cook 15 minutes on each side or until potatoes are tender. Open packets carefully to allow steam to escape. If desired, sprinkle with additional parsley.
1 packet: 414 cal., 25g fat (10g sat. fat), 61mg chol., 1181mg sod., 31g carb. (4g sugars, 3g fiber), 17g pro.

TEST KITCHEN TIPS

- Change up the flavor with other types of fully cooked sausage, like spinach and feta chicken sausage.
- If you don't have heavy-duty foil on hand, use a double thickness of regular foil.

BEST SPAGHETTI & MEATBALLS

One evening we had unexpected company. Since I had some of these meatballs left over in the freezer, I warmed them up as appetizers. Everyone raved! This classic recipe makes a big batch and is perfect for entertaining.
—Mary Lou Koskella, Prescott, AZ

Prep: 30 min. • **Cook:** 2 hours
Makes: 16 servings

- 2 Tbsp. olive oil
- 1½ cups chopped onions
- 3 garlic cloves, minced
- 2 cans (12 oz. each) tomato paste
- 3 cups water
- 1 can (29 oz.) tomato sauce
- ⅓ cup minced fresh parsley
- 1 Tbsp. dried basil
- 2 tsp. salt
- ½ tsp. pepper

MEATBALLS
- 4 large eggs, lightly beaten
- 2 cups soft bread cubes (cut into ¼-in. pieces)
- 1½ cups whole milk
- 1 cup grated Parmesan cheese
- 3 garlic cloves, minced
- 2 tsp. salt
- ½ tsp. pepper
- 3 lbs. ground beef
- 2 Tbsp. canola oil
- 2 lbs. spaghetti, cooked

1. In a Dutch oven, heat olive oil over medium heat. Add the onions; saute until softened. Add garlic; cook 1 minute longer. Stir in tomato paste; cook 3-5 minutes. Add the next 6 ingredients. Bring to a boil. Reduce heat; simmer, covered, 50 minutes.
2. Combine the first 7 meatball ingredients. Add beef; mix lightly but thoroughly. Shape into 1½-in. balls.
3. In a large skillet, heat canola oil over medium heat. Add meatballs; brown in batches until no longer pink. Drain. Add to the sauce; bring to a boil. Reduce heat; simmer, covered, until flavors are blended, about 1 hour, stirring occasionally. Serve with hot cooked spaghetti.
½ cup sauce with 4 meatballs and 1¼ cups spaghetti: 519 cal., 18g fat (6g sat. fat), 106mg chol., 1043mg sod., 59g carb. (8g sugars, 4g fiber), 30g pro.

1. In a large bowl, whisk together oil, vinegar and honey. Add both melons, ham and cucumber; toss to coat.
2. To serve, arrange arugula on a platter. Top with the melon mixture; sprinkle with cheese.

2 cups: 202 cal., 10g fat (3g sat. fat), 32mg chol., 646mg sod., 17g carb. (15g sugars, 2g fiber), 12g pro. **Diabetic exchanges:** 2 lean meat, 1½ fat, 1 vegetable, ½ fruit.

HAM SALAD

I first made this for a shower, and everyone raved about it. Now when I go to a potluck, I take it along with copies of the recipe.
—Patricia Reed, Pine Bluff, AR

- -

Takes: 15 min. • **Makes:** 10 servings

¾	cup mayonnaise
½	cup finely chopped celery
¼	cup sliced green onions
2	Tbsp. minced fresh chives
1	Tbsp. honey
2	tsp. spicy brown mustard
½	tsp. Worcestershire sauce
½	tsp. seasoned salt
5	cups diced fully cooked ham or turkey
⅓	cup chopped pecans and almonds, toasted
	Slider buns, split, optional

1. Mix the first 8 ingredients. Stir in ham. Refrigerate, covered, until serving.
2. Stir in pecans before serving. If desired, serve on buns.

½ cup ham salad: 254 cal., 20g fat (3g sat. fat), 43mg chol., 1023mg sod., 4g carb. (2g sugars, 1g fiber), 16g pro.

MELON ARUGULA SALAD WITH HAM

I love to think about all the healthy antioxidants in this salad that I serve to my summer dining guests. I like to save the melon rinds, cutting them into large wedges and using them as serving dishes. It makes a lovely presentation, and cleanup is a breeze!
—Shawn Jackson, Fishers, IN

- -

Takes: 20 min. • **Makes:** 8 servings

¼	cup olive oil
3	Tbsp. white wine vinegar
3	Tbsp. honey
3	cups cubed watermelon
2	cups cubed honeydew
2½	cups cubed fully cooked ham
1	small cucumber, coarsely chopped
8	cups fresh arugula
¾	cup crumbled feta cheese

CHICKEN & CHEESE NOODLE BAKE

This is the meal my daughters and I often make for new parents when they come home from the hospital. Recently I served several batches for our Wednesday night church supper and was asked for the recipe by many people.
—Fancheon Resler, Albion, IN

Prep: 20 min. • **Bake:** 25 min.
Makes: 2 casseroles (6 servings each)

- 1 pkg. (16 oz.) spaghetti, broken
- 2 medium onions, chopped
- 1 medium green pepper, chopped
- 1 medium sweet red pepper, chopped
- ½ cup butter, cubed
- 6 Tbsp. all-purpose flour
- 2 cups 2% milk
- 4 cups cubed cooked chicken
- 1 can (10¾ oz.) condensed cream of chicken and mushroom soup, undiluted
- 1 can (10¾ oz.) condensed cream of mushroom soup, undiluted
- 1 cup sour cream
- ½ tsp. celery salt
- ½ tsp. pepper
- 2 cups shredded part-skim mozzarella cheese
- 1 cup shredded cheddar cheese

1. Preheat oven to 350°. Cook spaghetti according to package directions.
2. Meanwhile, in a Dutch oven, saute onions and peppers in butter until tender. Stir in flour until blended; gradually add milk. Bring to a boil; cook and stir 2 minutes or until thickened. Stir in chicken, soups, sour cream, celery salt and pepper.
3. Drain spaghetti; add to sauce mixture and toss to coat. Transfer to 2 greased 11x7-in. baking dishes. Sprinkle with cheeses. Cover and bake 20 minutes. Uncover and bake 5-10 minutes longer or until bubbly.

1 cup: 509 cal., 24g fat (13g sat. fat), 102mg chol., 691mg sod., 42g carb. (7g sugars, 3g fiber), 29g pro.

SANDWICH FOR A CROWD

My husband and I live on a 21-acre horse ranch and love to have friends over to enjoy it with us. When entertaining, I rely on no-fuss, make-ahead entrees like this satisfying sandwich.
—Helen Hougland, Spring Hill, KS

Prep: 10 min. + chilling • **Makes:** 14 servings

- 2 loaves (1 lb. each) unsliced Italian bread (about 11 in. long)
- 1 pkg. (8 oz.) cream cheese, softened
- 1 cup shredded cheddar cheese
- ¾ cup sliced green onions
- ¼ cup mayonnaise
- 1 Tbsp. Worcestershire sauce
- 1 lb. thinly sliced fully cooked ham
- 1 lb. thinly sliced roast beef
- 14 thin slices dill pickle

1. Cut the bread loaves in half lengthwise. Hollow out both halves of each loaf, leaving a ½-in. shell (discard removed bread or save for another use).
2. Combine cheeses, onions, mayonnaise and Worcestershire sauce; spread over cut sides of bread. Layer ham and roast beef on bottom and top halves; place pickles on bottom halves. Gently press sandwich halves together.
3. Wrap and refrigerate for at least 2 hours. Cut each loaf into 7 slices.

1 slice: 297 cal., 15g fat (7g sat. fat), 53mg chol., 1141mg sod., 21g carb. (3g sugars, 1g fiber), 21g pro.

SMOKED SALMON PASTA

This pasta originally came to be from the miscellaneous ingredients in my fridge, and depending on whom I'm cooking for, it changes a little each time I make it. The recipe makes enough for a party or for leftovers, which is a bonus because it is excellent the next day whether you serve it cold or reheated.
—Jackie Hennon, Boise, ID

- -

Takes: 25 min. • **Makes:** 8 servings

- 1   lb. uncooked spiral or penne pasta
- 2   Tbsp. olive oil
- 2   large tomatoes, diced
- 2   cups water-packed artichoke hearts, drained and chopped
- 1½ cups kalamata olives, pitted and halved
- 1   cup chopped oil-packed sun-dried tomatoes
- ¾   cup chopped onion
- 8   oz. smoked salmon fillets
- 2   Tbsp. sun-dried tomato pesto
- 2   tsp. dried basil
- ¾   tsp. crushed red pepper flakes
- ¼   cup grated Parmesan cheese
- ¼   cup crumbled feta cheese

1. In a large saucepan, cook the pasta according to package directions for al dente. Meanwhile, in a Dutch oven, heat olive oil over medium-low heat. Add the next 5 ingredients. Break the salmon into bite-sized pieces; add to tomato mixture. Stir in pesto, basil and red pepper flakes. Cook, stirring occasionally, until vegetables are crisp-tender, 8-10 minutes.
2. Drain pasta. Add to salmon mixture; stir to combine. Top with cheeses.
¾ cup: 433 cal., 16g fat (3g sat. fat), 11mg chol., 924mg sod., 55g carb. (4g sugars, 4g fiber), 17g pro.

TEST KITCHEN TIP

This is a very forgiving recipe, so use more of the ingredients you like! If you love salmon, add more. If you're not fond of olives, cut back.

POTLUCK FRIED CHICKEN

This Sunday dinner staple is first fried and then baked to a crispy golden brown. Well-seasoned with oregano and sage, this classic is sure to satisfy diners at church potlucks or late-summer picnics. I love fixing it for family and friends.
—Donna Kuhaupt, Slinger, WI

- -

Prep: 40 min. • **Bake:** 25 min.
Makes: 12 servings

- 1½ cups all-purpose flour
- ½   cup cornmeal
- ¼   cup cornstarch
- 3   tsp. salt
- 2   tsp. paprika
- 1   tsp. dried oregano
- 1   tsp. rubbed sage
- 1   tsp. pepper
- 2   large eggs
- ¼   cup water
- 2   broiler/fryer chickens (3 to 4 lbs. each), cut up
    Oil for frying

1. In a large shallow dish, combine flour, cornmeal, cornstarch, salt, paprika, oregano, sage and pepper. In a shallow bowl, beat eggs and water. Dip chicken in egg mixture; place in flour mixture, a few pieces at a time, and turn to coat.
2. In an electric skillet, heat 1 in. oil to 375°. Fry chicken, a few pieces at a time, until golden and crispy, 3-5 minutes on each side.
3. Place in 2 ungreased 15x10x1-in. baking pans. Bake, uncovered, at 350° until juices run clear, 25-30 minutes.
5 oz. cooked chicken: 497 cal., 29g fat (6g sat. fat), 135mg chol., 693mg sod., 20g carb. (0 sugars, 1g fiber), 36g pro.

SOURDOUGH BREAD BOWL SANDWICH

I created this recipe for when my husband and I go to the lake. I don't like to spend a lot of time hovering over a stove or grill, especially in the hot Oklahoma summer months, and this sandwich is ready in minutes. For extra flavor, brush melted garlic and herb butter over the top prior to cooking.
—Shawna Welsh-Garrison, Owasso, OK

Prep: 15 min. • **Cook:** 25 min. + standing
Makes: 8 servings

- 1 **round loaf sourdough bread (1½ lbs.)**
- ½ **cup honey mustard salad dressing**
- 4 **slices sharp cheddar cheese**
- ⅓ **lb. thinly sliced deli ham**
- 4 **slices smoked provolone cheese**
- ⅓ **lb. thinly sliced deli smoked turkey**
- 1 **Tbsp. butter, melted**

1. Prepare campfire or grill for low heat. Cut a thin slice off top of bread loaf. Hollow out bottom of loaf, leaving a ½-in.-thick shell (save removed bread for another use). Spread dressing on inside of hollowed loaf and under the bread top. Layer inside with cheddar, ham, provolone and turkey. Replace top. Place on a piece of heavy-duty foil (about 24x18 in.). Brush the loaf with butter. Fold foil edges over top, crimping to seal.

2. Cook sandwich over campfire or grill until heated through, 25-30 minutes. Let stand 15 minutes before removing foil. Cut into wedges.

1 piece: 346 cal., 17g fat (6g sat. fat), 46mg chol., 865mg sod., 30g carb. (5g sugars, 1g fiber), 19g pro.

TEST KITCHEN TIP

This giant sandwich can be tricky to slice. Cut it with a serrated knife using a sawing motion. Consider inserting kabob skewers through each piece prior to cutting to hold layers together.

FAVORITE BAKED SPAGHETTI

This is my grandchildren's most-loved dish. It feels like such a special dinner and is so cozy for winter.
—Louise Miller, Westminster, MD

Prep: 25 min. • **Bake:** 1 hour + standing
Makes: 10 servings

- 1   pkg. (16 oz.) spaghetti
- 1   lb. ground beef
- 1   medium onion, chopped
- 1   jar (24 oz.) pasta sauce
- ½   tsp. seasoned salt
- 2   large eggs
- ⅓   cup grated Parmesan cheese
- 5   Tbsp. butter, melted
- 2   cups 4% cottage cheese
- 4   cups shredded part-skim mozzarella cheese
     Chopped fresh basil, optional

1. Preheat oven to 350°. Cook spaghetti according to package directions for al dente. Meanwhile, in a large skillet, cook beef and onion over medium heat until beef is no longer pink and onion is tender, 6-8 minutes, breaking beef into crumbles; drain. Stir in pasta sauce and seasoned salt; set aside.

2. In a large bowl, whisk the eggs, Parmesan cheese and butter. Drain spaghetti; add to egg mixture and toss to coat.

3. Place half the spaghetti mixture in a greased 13x9-in. or 3-qt. baking dish. Top with half the cottage cheese, meat sauce and mozzarella cheese. Repeat layers. Place baking dish on a rimmed baking sheet.

4. Cover and bake for 40 minutes. Uncover; bake until heated through, 20-25 minutes longer. Let stand 15 minutes before serving. If desired, sprinkle with basil.

1¼ cups: 526 cal., 24g fat (13g sat. fat), 127mg chol., 881mg sod., 45g carb. (9g sugars, 3g fiber), 31g pro.

Baked Spaghetti Puttanesca: Add 1 Tbsp. minced garlic while cooking the ground beef mixture. After draining, stir in 3 Tbsp. rinsed and drained capers, 1 cup coarsely chopped black olives, 3 finely chopped anchovy fillets and ¾ tsp. red pepper flakes. Proceed as directed, topping with additional olives and capers before serving.

HERBED SEAFOOD CASSEROLE

When I wanted a seafood dish for my annual Christmas Eve buffet, my friend gave me a wonderful recipe. This is a rich, creamy casserole loaded with shrimp, scallops and crab.
—Donna Schmuland, Wetaskiwin, AB

Prep: 40 min. • **Bake:** 50 min. + standing
Makes: 12 servings

- 1½ cups uncooked long grain rice
- 2 Tbsp. butter

- 3 celery ribs, thinly sliced
- 1 medium onion, finely chopped
- 1 medium carrot, shredded
- 3 garlic cloves, minced
- ½ tsp. salt
- ¼ tsp. pepper
- 2 Tbsp. minced fresh parsley
- 1½ tsp. snipped fresh dill or ½ tsp. dill weed

SEAFOOD
- 1 lb. uncooked shrimp (31-40 per pound), peeled and deveined
- 1 lb. bay scallops

- 1 can (16 oz.) crabmeat, drained, flaked and cartilage removed
- 5 Tbsp. butter, cubed
- ¼ cup all-purpose flour
- 1½ cups half-and-half cream
- 1 pkg. (8 oz.) cream cheese, cubed
- 1½ tsp. snipped fresh dill or ½ tsp. dill weed
- ½ tsp. salt
- ¼ tsp. pepper
- ¼ tsp. dried thyme

TOPPING
- 1½ cups soft bread crumbs
- 2 Tbsp. butter, melted

1. Preheat the oven to 325°. Cook the rice according to the package directions. Meanwhile, in a large skillet, heat butter over medium-high heat. Add celery, onion and carrot; cook and stir until crisp-tender. Add the garlic, salt and pepper; cook 1 minute longer.

2. Add to cooked rice. Stir in parsley and dill. Transfer to a greased 13x9-in. baking dish.

3. Fill a large saucepan two-thirds full with water; bring to a boil. Reduce heat to medium. Add shrimp; simmer, uncovered, 30 seconds. Add the scallops; simmer 2-3 minutes longer or just until shrimp turn pink and scallops are firm and opaque. Drain, reserving 1 cup cooking liquid. Place seafood in a large bowl; stir in crab.

4. In a small saucepan, melt butter over medium heat. Stir in flour until blended; gradually stir in the cream and reserved cooking liquid. Bring to a boil; cook and stir 2 minutes or until thickened and bubbly. Reduce heat. Stir in the cream cheese, dill and seasonings until smooth. Stir into seafood mixture.

5. Pour over rice mixture. Toss bread crumbs with melted butter; sprinkle over top. Bake, uncovered, 50-55 minutes or until golden brown. Let stand 10 minutes before serving.

1 cup: 404 cal., 20g fat (12g sat. fat), 150mg chol., 616mg sod., 29g carb. (3g sugars, 1g fiber), 26g pro.

BARBECUE SLIDERS

When guests dropped in by surprise, all I had was sausage and ground beef defrosted. We combined the two for juicy burgers on the grill.
—B.J. Larsen, Erie, CO

Takes: 25 min. • **Makes:** 8 servings

- 1 lb. ground beef
- 1 lb. bulk pork sausage
- 1 cup barbecue sauce, divided
- 16 Hawaiian sweet rolls, split
  Optional toppings: Lettuce leaves, sliced plum tomatoes and red onion

1. In a large bowl, mix beef and sausage lightly but thoroughly. Shape into sixteen ½-in.-thick patties.
2. Grill patties, covered, over medium heat or broil 4-5 in. from heat until a thermometer reads 160°, 3-4 minutes on each side. Brush with ¼ cup sauce during last 2 minutes of cooking. Serve on rolls with remaining sauce; top as desired.

Freeze option: Place patties on a waxed paper-lined baking sheet; cover and freeze until firm. Remove from pan and transfer to an airtight container; return to freezer. To use, grill frozen patties as directed, increasing time as necessary.

2 sliders: 499 cal., 24g fat (9g sat. fat), 96mg chol., 885mg sod., 47g carb. (23g sugars, 2g fiber), 24g pro.

HEALTH TIP
Make these with 90% lean ground beef and turkey breakfast sausage to save nearly 100 calories and more than half the fat per serving.

HOMEMADE SLOPPY JOES

I simmer a big batch of this hot, tangy sandwich filling and freeze the extras. Then I just thaw and reheat it for a quick dinner.
—Sandra Castillo, Janesville, WI

Prep: 10 min. • **Cook:** 30 min.
Makes: 12 servings

- 2 lbs. ground beef
- 2 medium onions, chopped
- 2 to 3 garlic cloves, minced
- 2 cups ketchup
- 1 cup barbecue sauce
- ¼ cup packed brown sugar
- ¼ cup cider vinegar
- 2 Tbsp. prepared mustard
- 1 tsp. Italian seasoning
- 1 tsp. onion powder
- ½ tsp. pepper
- 12 hamburger buns, split

In a large skillet, cook beef, onions and garlic over medium heat until meat is no longer pink, breaking meat into crumbles; drain. Stir in ketchup, barbecue sauce, brown sugar, vinegar, mustard, Italian seasoning, onion powder and pepper. Bring to a boil. Reduce heat; simmer, uncovered, 20 minutes. Serve on buns.

Freeze option: Freeze cooled meat mixture in freezer containers. To use, partially thaw in refrigerator overnight. Heat through in a saucepan, stirring occasionally; add water if necessary.

1 sandwich: 368 cal., 11g fat (4g sat. fat), 47mg chol., 1029mg sod., 49g carb. (27g sugars, 1g fiber), 18g pro.

EASY SAUERBRATEN

Here's my simplified take on traditional German fare. This beef roast's definitive pickled flavor is sure to delight fans of Bavarian cuisine.
—Patricia Rutherford, Winchester, IL

- -

Prep: 25 min. + marinating • **Bake:** 3 hours
Makes: 10 servings

- 4 cups water
- 2 cups red wine vinegar
- 12 whole cloves
- 2 bay leaves
- 3 tsp. salt
- 3 tsp. brown sugar
- 1 boneless beef chuck roast or rump roast (4 lbs.)
- ¼ cup all-purpose flour
- 2 Tbsp. canola oil
- 1 large onion, cut into wedges
- 5 medium carrots, cut into 1½-in. pieces
- 2 celery ribs, cut into 1½-in. pieces

1. In a large bowl, combine water, vinegar, cloves, bay leaves, salt and brown sugar. Remove 2 cups to a small bowl; cover and refrigerate. Add roast to large bowl with remaining marinade; turn to coat. Cover and refrigerate for 1-2 days, turning twice each day.

2. Discard marinade and spices from large bowl. Pat roast dry; dredge in flour. In a large skillet over medium-high heat, brown roast in oil on all sides. Transfer to a small roasting pan. Add onion, carrots, celery and reserved marinade.

3. Cover and bake at 325° for 3-3½ hours or until meat is tender. With a slotted spoon, remove meat and vegetables to a serving platter. Strain cooking juices; thicken if desired.

1 serving: 365 cal., 20g fat (7g sat. fat), 118mg chol., 368mg sod., 9g carb. (3g sugars, 1g fiber), 36g pro.

CHILE TAMALE PIE

This crowd-pleasing potluck dish packs a little heat, a little sweet and a big-time authentic southwestern flavor. There is no substitute for freshly ground chiles. A small food processor on high speed may be used to grind the chiles and cumin, or use a dedicated coffee grinder for fresh spices. It's a terrific $15 investment for fresh spices anytime—and your palate will thank you!
—Ralph Stamm, Dayton, OH

- -

Prep: 45 min. • **Bake:** 50 min. + standing
Makes: 12 servings

1	can (15¼ oz.) whole kernel corn
2	cups masa harina
1	can (14½ oz.) chicken broth
2	Tbsp. butter, melted
1	large egg, lightly beaten
2½	lbs. boneless pork loin roast, cut into ½-in. pieces
1	medium onion, chopped
1	can (16 oz.) refried beans
2	dried Anaheim chiles, chopped
2	dried ancho chiles, chopped
3	oz. Mexican or semisweet chocolate, grated
⅓	cup orange juice
2	Tbsp. lime juice
1	Tbsp. garlic powder
3	tsp. cumin seeds, toasted and crushed
¾	cup minced fresh cilantro, optional
1	jalapeno pepper, seeded and chopped, optional
2	cups shredded cheddar cheese

1. Drain the corn, reserving liquid; set corn aside. Place masa harina in a large bowl. In a small bowl, combine broth, butter, egg and reserved corn liquid; stir into masa harina just until moistened. Set aside.

2. In a large skillet coated with cooking spray, cook pork and onion over medium heat until pork is no longer pink. Add the beans, chiles, chocolate, orange juice, lime juice, garlic powder, cumin, reserved corn, and, if desired, cilantro and jalapeno. Bring to a boil. Reduce heat; simmer, uncovered, for 15 minutes. Meanwhile, preheat oven to 325°.

3. Transfer to a greased 13x9-in. baking dish; sprinkle with cheese. Spread masa harina mixture over cheese.

4. Bake, uncovered, until golden brown, 50-60 minutes. Let stand for 10 minutes before serving.

1 cup: 371 cal., 15g fat (8g sat. fat), 93mg chol., 496mg sod., 32g carb. (7g sugars, 6g fiber), 28g pro.

OKTOBERFEST CASSEROLE

In northeastern Ohio, we love German flavors. This delicious casserole is a trifecta mashup of my favorite dishes. It combines the flavors of classic cheesy hash brown casserole with bratwursts and sauerkraut, pretzels and beer cheese. It takes less than 10 minutes to mix and only one bowl. It's sure to please everyone any time of the year.
—Sarah Markley, Ashland, OH

Prep: 15 min. • **Bake:** 1½ hours + standing
Makes: 12 servings

- 2 cans (10½ oz. each) condensed cheddar cheese soup, undiluted
- 1 cup beer or chicken broth
- 1 cup sour cream
- 1 pkg. (32 oz.) frozen cubed hash brown potatoes, thawed
- 1 can (14 oz.) sauerkraut, rinsed and well drained
- 2 cups shredded cheddar cheese
- 1 pkg. (14 oz.) fully cooked bratwurst links, chopped
- 2 cups pretzel pieces

1. Preheat oven to 350°. In a large bowl, whisk soup, beer and sour cream until combined. Stir in potatoes, sauerkraut, cheese and chopped bratwurst. Transfer to a greased 13x9-in. baking dish. Cover and bake for 45 minutes.
2. Uncover; bake 30 minutes. Top with pretzel pieces. Bake until bubbly and heated through, 12-15 minutes longer. Let stand 10 minutes before serving.
Freeze option: Freeze cooled potato mixture in freezer containers. To use, partially thaw in refrigerator overnight. Heat through in a saucepan, stirring occasionally; add broth or water if necessary.
1 serving: 356 cal., 21g fat (10g sat. fat), 49mg chol., 884mg sod., 29g carb. (4g sugars, 3g fiber), 13g pro.

SPICY OVEN-FRIED CHICKEN

My family adores this recipe. The coating keeps the chicken nice and moist. With the taste enhanced by marinating, the result is delicious.
—Stephanie Otten, Byron Center, MI

Prep: 25 min. + marinating • **Bake:** 35 min.
Makes: 8 servings

- 2 cups buttermilk
- 2 Tbsp. Dijon mustard
- 2 tsp. salt
- 2 tsp. hot pepper sauce
- 1½ tsp. garlic powder
- 8 bone-in chicken breast halves, skin removed (8 oz. each)
- 2 cups soft bread crumbs
- 1 cup cornmeal
- 2 Tbsp. canola oil
- ½ tsp. poultry seasoning
- ½ tsp. ground mustard
- ½ tsp. paprika
- ½ tsp. cayenne pepper
- ¼ tsp. dried oregano
- ¼ tsp. dried parsley flakes

1. Preheat oven to 400°. In a large bowl or dish, combine the first 5 ingredients. Add chicken and turn to coat. Refrigerate 1 hour or overnight.
2. Drain chicken, discarding marinade. In a large bowl, combine remaining ingredients. Add chicken, 1 piece at a time, and coat with crumb mixture. Place on a parchment-lined baking sheet. Bake 35-40 minutes or until a thermometer reads 170°.
Note: To make soft bread crumbs, tear bread into pieces and place in a food processor or blender. Cover and pulse until crumbs form. A slice of bread yields ½-¾ cup crumbs.
1 chicken breast half: 296 cal., 7g fat (2g sat. fat), 103mg chol., 523mg sod., 15g carb. (2g sugars, 1g fiber), 40g pro. **Diabetic exchanges:** 6 lean meat, 1 starch, ½ fat.

Summer
Squash Salad
page 125

Sides & Salads

Round out your meal with crispy salads, creamy potatoes, flavorful veggies, flaky biscuits and more. Find wonderful sides for every season.

FLAMBOYANT FLAMENCO SUMMER SALAD

I came up with this salad simply by choosing the best-looking vegetables at a local farmers market—the colors are so beautiful! Turn it into a full vegetarian meal by adding roasted garbanzo beans or cooked white beans as protein.
—Crystal Schlueter, Northglenn, CO

- -

Takes: 25 min. • **Makes:** 8 servings

3	medium rainbow carrots
4	medium blood oranges, peeled and segmented
½	small red onion, thinly sliced
½	medium fresh beet, thinly sliced
½	medium watermelon radish, thinly sliced
2	radishes, thinly sliced
2	Tbsp. chopped pistachios, toasted
2	Tbsp. chopped oil-packed sun-dried tomatoes
1	Tbsp. capers, drained
¼	tsp. salt
¼	tsp. pepper
¼	cup white balsamic vinaigrette
4	cups torn leaf lettuce
¼	cup shaved Manchego or Parmesan cheese

Using a vegetable peeler, shave carrots lengthwise into very thin slices; place in a large bowl. Add oranges, red onion, beet, radishes, pistachios, tomatoes, capers, salt and pepper. Drizzle with vinaigrette; lightly toss to coat. Arrange lettuce on a platter; top with vegetable mixture. Top with cheese.

1 cup: 103 cal., 6g fat (1g sat. fat), 4mg chol., 203mg sod., 12g carb. (8g sugars, 3g fiber), 2g pro. **Diabetic exchanges:** 1 vegetable, 1 fat, ½ fruit.

CRANBERRY RICOTTA GNOCCHI WITH BROWN BUTTER SAUCE

To make light and airy gnocchi, work quickly and handle the dough as little as possible. You'll be pleased with the resulting pillowy dumplings.
—Sally Sibthorpe, Shelby Township, MI

- -

Prep: 30 min. + standing • **Cook:** 15 min.
Makes: 8 servings

¾	cup dried cranberries, divided
2	cups ricotta cheese
1	cup all-purpose flour
½	cup grated Parmesan cheese
1	large egg, lightly beaten
¾	tsp. salt, divided
¾	cup butter, cubed
2	Tbsp. minced fresh sage
½	cup chopped walnuts, toasted
⅛	tsp. white pepper

1. Finely chop ¼ cup cranberries. In a large bowl, combine ricotta cheese, flour, Parmesan cheese, egg, ½ tsp. salt and chopped cranberries; mix until blended. On a lightly floured surface, knead mixture 10-12 times, forming a soft dough. Cover and let rest for 10 minutes.

2. Divide dough into 4 portions. On a floured surface, roll each portion into a ¾-in.-thick rope; cut into ¾-in. pieces. Press and roll each piece with a lightly floured fork.

3. In a Dutch oven, bring 4 qt. water to a boil. Cook the gnocchi in batches 30-60 seconds or until they float. Remove with a slotted spoon; keep warm.

4. In a large heavy saucepan, cook butter over medium heat 5 minutes. Add sage; cook 3-5 minutes longer or until butter is golden brown, stirring occasionally. Stir in walnuts, white pepper and the remaining cranberries and salt. Add gnocchi; stir gently to coat.

¾ cup: 411 cal., 30g fat (16g sat. fat), 101mg chol., 503mg sod., 26g carb. (11g sugars, 1g fiber), 13g pro.

EASY PEASY BISCUITS

I love that I can make these biscuits and have enough left over to freeze for another meal. They are wonderful with homemade peach preserves.
—Amanda West, Shelbyville, TN

Prep: 25 min. • **Bake:** 10 min.
Makes: 2 dozen

- 4 cups all-purpose flour
- 4 Tbsp. baking powder
- 1 Tbsp. sugar
- 1 Tbsp. ground flaxseed
- 1 tsp. sea salt
- 1 cup solid coconut oil
- 1½ cups 2% milk

1. Preheat oven to 450°. In a large bowl, whisk flour, baking powder, sugar, flaxseed and salt. Add coconut oil and cut in with a pastry blender until mixture resembles coarse crumbs. Add milk; stir just until moistened.

2. Turn onto a lightly floured surface; knead gently 8-10 times. Pat or roll dough into a rectangle ½ in. thick; fold dough into thirds (as you would a letter). Pat or roll dough again into a rectangle ½ in. thick; cut with a pizza cutter or knife into 24 biscuits, each about 2½ in. square. Place 1½ in. apart on ungreased baking sheets. Bake until light brown, 8-10 minutes. Serve warm.

Freeze option: Freeze cut biscuit dough on waxed paper-lined baking sheets until firm. Transfer to airtight containers; return to freezer. To use, bake biscuits in a preheated 350° oven until light brown, 15-20 minutes. Or, freeze cooled baked biscuits in airtight containers. To use, heat in a preheated 350° oven until warmed, 5-10 minutes.

1 biscuit: 167 cal., 10g fat (8g sat. fat), 1mg chol., 328mg sod., 17g carb. (1g sugars, 1g fiber), 3g pro.

TABBOULEH

Tabbouleh, also known as tabouleh, is a classic Middle Eastern salad. The fresh veggies and mint leaves make it light and refreshing on a hot day.
—Michael & Mathil Chebat, Lake Ridge, VA

Takes: 30 min. • **Makes:** 8 servings

- ¼ cup bulgur
- 3 bunches fresh parsley, minced (about 2 cups)
- 3 large tomatoes, finely chopped
- 1 small onion, finely chopped
- ¼ cup lemon juice
- ¼ cup olive oil
- 5 fresh mint leaves, minced
- ½ tsp. salt
- ½ tsp. pepper
- ¼ tsp. cayenne pepper

Prepare bulgur according to package directions; cool. Transfer to a large bowl. Stir in remaining ingredients. If desired, chill before serving.

⅔ cup: 100 cal., 7g fat (1g sat. fat), 0 chol., 164mg sod., 9g carb. (3g sugars, 2g fiber), 2g pro. **Diabetic exchanges:** 1½ fat, ½ starch.

Freeze option: Cool unbaked casserole; cover and freeze. To use, partially thaw in refrigerator overnight. Remove from refrigerator 30 minutes before baking. Preheat oven to 350°. Bake casserole as directed, increasing time as necessary to heat through and for a thermometer inserted in center to read 165°.

¾ cup: 370 cal., 13g fat (9g sat. fat), 41mg chol., 456mg sod., 55g carb. (8g sugars, 6g fiber), 9g pro.

COLESLAW WALDORF SALAD

Potlucks tend to have a lot of heavy dishes, so a bright, fresh salad is a welcome addition. I came up with this recipe as a way to serve something crunchy and fruity with a touch of sweetness. Sometimes I add shredded coconut and use toasted pecans instead of walnuts.

—Trisha Kruse, Eagle, ID

Prep: 20 min. + chilling
Makes: 18 servings

- 8   cups shredded cabbage
- 1   cup vanilla yogurt
- ½   cup mayonnaise
- ¼   cup orange juice
- 2   Tbsp. cider vinegar
- 2   large red apples, chopped
- 2   cups green grapes, halved
- 2   celery ribs, thinly sliced
- ¾   cup chopped walnuts, toasted
- ½   cup golden raisins
- ½   cup chopped dried apricots

Place cabbage in a large bowl. In another bowl, whisk yogurt, mayonnaise, orange juice and vinegar until combined. Pour over cabbage; toss to coat. Stir in the remaining ingredients. Refrigerate until serving.

¾ cup: 139 cal., 8g fat (1g sat. fat), 1mg chol., 55mg sod., 17g carb. (12g sugars, 2g fiber), 2g pro. **Diabetic exchanges:** 1½ fat, 1 starch.

MAKE AHEAD
GOLDEN MASHED POTATOES

When there's no gravy with the meat, this dish is fabulous to serve in place of regular mashed potatoes. I make it often to take to picnics and church socials. My husband even made it for his family's reunion one year when I couldn't go!

—Cindy Stith, Wickliffe, KY

Prep: 40 min. • **Bake:** 30 min.
Makes: 12 servings

- 9   large potatoes (about 4 lbs.), peeled and cubed
- 1   lb. carrots, cut into ½-in. chunks
- 8   green onions, thinly sliced
- ½   cup butter
- 1   cup sour cream
- 1½ tsp. salt
- ⅛   tsp. pepper
- ¾   cup shredded cheddar cheese

1. In a soup kettle or Dutch oven, cook the potatoes and carrots in boiling salted water until tender; drain. Place in a bowl; mash and set aside.
2. In a skillet, saute onions in butter until tender. Add to the potato mixture. Add sour cream, salt and pepper; mix until blended. Transfer to a greased 13x9-in. baking dish. Sprinkle with cheese. Bake, uncovered, at 350° until heated through, 30-40 minutes.

GARLIC-ROSEMARY BRUSSELS SPROUTS

This is my go-to Thanksgiving side dish. It is healthy and easy, and it doesn't take very much time or effort to make. I usually use rosemary for my turkey, so this lets me use some of the leftover herbs.
—Elisabeth Larsen, Pleasant Grove, UT

Prep: 15 min. • **Bake:** 25 min.
Makes: 8 servings

- ¼ cup olive oil
- 4 garlic cloves, minced
- 1 tsp. salt
- ½ tsp. pepper
- 2 lbs. Brussels sprouts (about 8 cups), trimmed and halved
- 1 cup panko bread crumbs
- 1 to 2 Tbsp. minced fresh rosemary

1. Preheat oven to 425°. Place the first 4 ingredients in a small microwave-safe bowl; microwave on high 30 seconds.
2. Place Brussels sprouts in a 15x10x1-in. pan; toss with 3 Tbsp. oil mixture. Roast 10 minutes.
3. Toss bread crumbs with rosemary and remaining oil mixture; sprinkle over sprouts. Bake until crumbs are browned and sprouts are tender, 12-15 minutes. Serve immediately.
¾ cup: 134 cal., 7g fat (1g sat. fat), 0 chol., 342mg sod., 15g carb. (3g sugars, 4g fiber), 5g pro. **Diabetic exchanges:** 1½ fat, 1 vegetable, ½ starch.

TEST KITCHEN TIP

Heating the oil and garlic together infuses the oil with garlic flavor for even distribution over the sprouts. When roasting vegetables, give them breathing room. If the pan is too crowded, the vegetables will steam and not get nicely browned.

CLASSIC MACARONI SALAD

This classic recipe is a refreshingly light take on an all-time favorite. It's perfect for a fast weeknight dinner or a festive weekend barbecue.
—Dorothy Bayes, Sardis, OH

Takes: 30 min. • **Makes:** 8 servings

- 2 cups uncooked elbow macaroni
- 1 cup fat-free mayonnaise
- 2 Tbsp. sweet pickle relish
- 2 tsp. sugar
- ¾ tsp. ground mustard
- ¼ tsp. salt
- ⅛ tsp. pepper
- ½ cup chopped celery
- ⅓ cup chopped carrot
- ¼ cup chopped onion
- 1 hard-boiled large egg, chopped
  Dash paprika

1. Cook macaroni according to package directions; drain and rinse with cold water. Cool completely.
2. For dressing, in a small bowl, combine mayonnaise, pickle relish, sugar, mustard, salt and pepper. In a large bowl, combine the macaroni, celery, carrot and onion. Add dressing and toss gently to coat.
3. Refrigerate until serving. Garnish with egg and paprika.
¾ cup: 115 cal., 2g fat (0 sat. fat), 27mg chol., 362mg sod., 21g carb. (6g sugars, 2g fiber), 4g pro. **Diabetic exchanges:** 1½ starch.

BAKING POWDER DROP BISCUITS

One day I had company coming and realized I had run out of biscuit mix. I'd never made biscuits from scratch before, but I decided to give this recipe a try. Now this is the only way I make them!
—Sharon Evans, Clear Lake, IA

Takes: 20 min. • **Makes:** 1 dozen

- 2 cups all-purpose flour
- 2 Tbsp. sugar
- 4 tsp. baking powder
- ½ tsp. cream of tartar
- ½ tsp. salt
- ½ cup shortening
- ⅔ cup 2% milk
- 1 large egg

1. Preheat oven to 450°. In a large bowl, combine the first 5 ingredients. Cut in shortening until the mixture resembles coarse crumbs. In a small bowl, whisk milk and egg. Stir into crumb mixture just until moistened.

2. Drop by ¼ cupfuls 2 in. apart onto an ungreased baking sheet. Bake until golden brown, 10-12 minutes. Serve warm.

1 biscuit: 170 cal., 9g fat (2g sat. fat), 17mg chol., 271mg sod., 19g carb. (3g sugars, 1g fiber), 3g pro.

★ ★ ★ ★ ★ **READER REVIEW**

"A simple but delicious recipe easy enough for my 12-year-old daughter to make with confidence! We make this recipe when we don't have time to cut out traditional biscuits—and, honestly, these are just as good!"

MOM2LAUREN TASTEOFHOME.COM

MOM'S APPLE CORNBREAD STUFFING

My speedy recipe is the be-all and end-all stuffing in our family. Not surprisingly, we never have leftovers.
—Marie Forte, Raritan, NJ

Prep: 15 min. • **Bake:** 35 min.
Makes: 16 servings

- 6 large Granny Smith apples, peeled and chopped
- 1 pkg. (14 oz.) crushed cornbread stuffing
- ½ cup butter, melted
- 1 can (14½ oz.) chicken broth

1. Preheat oven to 350°. Combine apples, stuffing and butter. Add broth; mix well.
2. Transfer mixture to a greased 13x9-in. baking dish. Bake until golden brown, 35-40 minutes.

¾ cup: 183 cal., 7g fat (4g sat. fat), 16mg chol., 434mg sod., 28g carb. (8g sugars, 2g fiber), 3g pro. **Diabetic exchanges:** 2 starch, 1½ fat.

TROPICAL GINGER RICE

This change-of-pace side dish comes together in moments and rounds out any family meal with a burst of sweet-tart flavor. Try it with dried cherries, too!
—Charlene Chambers, Ormond Beach, FL

Takes: 25 min. • **Makes:** 8 servings

- 2 cups uncooked long grain rice
- 1 Tbsp. minced fresh gingerroot
- 4 cups chicken broth
- ⅔ cup dried tropical fruit
- ⅔ cup chopped pecans, toasted

In a large saucepan, combine rice, ginger and broth; bring to a boil. Reduce heat; simmer, covered, 18-22 minutes or until liquid is absorbed and rice is tender. Stir in dried fruit and pecans.

1 cup: 186 cal., 5g fat (0 sat. fat), 2mg chol., 408mg sod., 32g carb. (5g sugars, 1g fiber), 4g pro.

1 tsp. salt, divided
1 tsp. pepper, divided
4 Tbsp. butter, cubed
3 Tbsp. all-purpose flour
2 cups 2% milk
1 cup shredded Swiss cheese
½ cup grated Parmesan cheese
½ tsp. onion powder
½ tsp. ground mustard
½ tsp. Worcestershire sauce
⅛ tsp. cayenne pepper
 Chopped fresh thyme, optional

1. Preheat oven to 375°. Place cauliflower on a rimmed baking sheet. Drizzle with oil; sprinkle with ½ tsp. salt and ½ tsp. pepper. Toss to coat. Bake 8 minutes. Stir; bake until crisp-tender and lightly browned, 7-8 minutes longer.
2. In a large saucepan, melt butter over medium heat. Stir in flour until smooth; gradually whisk in milk. Bring to a simmer, stirring constantly; cook and stir until thickened, 2-3 minutes. Remove from heat. Stir in the next 6 ingredients and remaining ½ tsp. salt and ½ tsp. pepper until smooth.
3. Pour ¾ cup cheese sauce into a greased 2-qt. baking dish. Top with cauliflower and the remaining cheese sauce. Bake, uncovered, until bubbly and lightly browned, 30-35 minutes. If desired, top with chopped fresh thyme.
¾ cup: 196 cal., 14g fat (7g sat. fat), 34mg chol., 291mg sod., 11g carb. (5g sugars, 2g fiber), 9g pro.

FIESTA CORN

Corn with tomatoes and jalapenos is one of the first dishes I cooked for my husband. Don't like heat? Use green bell peppers instead of jalapenos.
—Cassandra Ramirez, Bardstown, KY

- -

Takes: 25 min. • **Makes:** 8 servings

¼ cup butter, cubed
1 small onion, chopped
2 to 3 jalapeno peppers, seeded and chopped
6 plum tomatoes, seeded and chopped
5 cups fresh or frozen corn
1½ tsp. salt
 Lime wedges, optional

1. In a 6-qt. stockpot, heat butter over medium heat. Add onion and jalapenos; cook and stir until onion is crisp-tender, 3-4 minutes. Stir in tomatoes; cook 3 minutes longer.
2. Add corn; cook, uncovered, until tender, stirring occasionally, 8-10 minutes. Stir in salt. If desired, serve with lime wedges.
Note: Wear disposable gloves when cutting hot peppers; the oils can burn skin. Avoid touching your face.
¾ cup: 142 cal., 7g fat (4g sat. fat), 15mg chol., 505mg sod., 20g carb. (7g sugars, 3g fiber), 4g pro.

CAULIFLOWER AU GRATIN

This is a lower-carb side dish that pairs well with pork, ham or beef. It is so creamy and delicious that even kids will ask for seconds! If you like a little crunch, sprinkle buttered bread crumbs over the top after 30 minutes of baking.
—Mary Zinchiak, Boardman, OH

- -

Prep: 25 min. • **Bake:** 45 min.
Makes: 8 servings

1 large head cauliflower, cut into florets
2 Tbsp. olive oil

TEST KITCHEN TIPS
- Freshly shredded Parmesan cheese works best in this recipe. Canned, grated Parmesan cheese will make the texture grainy.
- To make this a vegetarian dish, simply omit Worcestershire sauce.
- Add more texture by topping the dish with buttered panko bread crumbs before baking.

HEIRLOOM TOMATO PIE

My green-thumbed neighbors like to share produce with me. I return the delicious favor by baking tomato pies for all.

—Angela Benedict, Dunbar, WV

Prep: 45 min. • **Bake:** 35 min. + cooling
Makes: 8 servings

- 1¼ lbs. heirloom tomatoes (about 4 medium), cut into ¼-in. slices
- ¾ tsp. salt, divided
- 1½ cups shredded extra-sharp cheddar cheese
- ¾ cup all-purpose flour
- ¼ cup cold butter, cubed
- 1 to 2 Tbsp. half-and-half cream
- 5 bacon strips, cooked and crumbled

FILLING
- 1 pkg. (8 oz.) cream cheese, softened
- ½ cup loosely packed basil leaves, thinly sliced
- 2 Tbsp. minced fresh marjoram
- 1½ tsp. minced fresh thyme
- ½ tsp. garlic powder
- ⅛ tsp. coarsely ground pepper

1. Preheat oven to 350°. Place tomato slices in single layer on paper towels; sprinkle with ½ tsp. salt. Let stand 45 minutes. Pat dry.
2. Meanwhile, place cheese, flour and remaining salt in a food processor; pulse until blended. Add butter; pulse until butter is the size of peas. While pulsing, add just enough cream to form moist crumbs. Press dough onto bottom and up sides of an ungreased 9-in. fluted tart pan with removable bottom. Gently press bacon into dough. Bake 20-22 minutes or until light brown. Cool on a wire rack.
3. In a large bowl, beat cream cheese, herbs and garlic powder until blended. Spread over crust. Top with tomato slices; sprinkle with pepper. Bake 35-40 minutes longer or until the edges are golden brown and tomatoes are softened. Cool on a wire rack. Refrigerate leftovers.

1 slice: 320 cal., 25g fat (14g sat. fat), 74mg chol., 603mg sod., 14g carb. (3g sugars, 1g fiber), 11g pro.

SWEET CORN MUFFINS

I love to make cornbread and corn muffins, but often the results are not moist or sweet enough for my taste. I experimented until I came up with these light, pleasantly sweet muffins. They ended up winning a blue ribbon at our county fair.

—Patty Bourne, Owings, MD

Prep: 10 min. • **Bake:** 25 min.
Makes: 1 dozen

- 1½ cups all-purpose flour
- 1 cup sugar
- ¾ cup cornmeal
- 1 Tbsp. baking powder
- ½ tsp. salt
- 2 large eggs, room temperature
- ½ cup shortening
- 1 cup 2% milk, divided

In a bowl, combine the dry ingredients. Add eggs, shortening and ½ cup milk; beat for 1 minute. Add remaining milk; beat just until blended. Fill 12 paper-lined muffin cups three-fourths full. Bake at 350° until muffins test done, 25-30 minutes.

1 muffin: 254 cal., 10g fat (3g sat. fat), 33mg chol., 241mg sod., 38g carb. (18g sugars, 1g fiber), 4g pro.

BARBECUED BEAN SALAD

This tangy, hearty salad is a refreshing dish to serve at a summertime picnic. Mild spices blend nicely with the beans and garden ingredients. Be prepared to bring home an empty bowl.
—Linda Ault, Newberry, IN

Prep: 40 min. + standing
Cook: 1½ hours + chilling
Makes: 20 servings

- 1 pkg. (16 oz.) dried pinto beans, rinsed
- 1 medium onion, chopped
- 1 medium green pepper, diced
- 1 medium sweet red pepper, diced
- 1 can (15¼ oz.) whole kernel corn, drained

DRESSING
- ¼ cup ketchup
- ¼ cup cider vinegar
- ¼ cup olive oil
- 3 Tbsp. brown sugar
- 1 Tbsp. Worcestershire sauce
- 1 Tbsp. chili powder
- 5 tsp. Dijon mustard
- 1 tsp. ground cumin
- 1 tsp. salt
- ¼ tsp. pepper

1. In a large kettle, cover beans with water; bring to a boil. Boil for 2 minutes. Remove from the heat and let stand 1 hour. Drain and rinse beans; return to the kettle. Cover with water again and bring to a boil. Reduce heat; cover and simmer for 1½ hours or until beans are tender.

2. Drain and rinse beans; place in a large bowl and cool to room temperature. Add the onion, peppers and corn; toss.

3. In a saucepan, combine all dressing ingredients; simmer for 10 minutes. Pour over vegetables and mix well. Cover and chill.

¾ cup: 138 cal., 3g fat (0 sat. fat), 0 chol., 260mg sod., 22g carb. (5g sugars, 6g fiber), 5g pro.

GRILLED ELOTE FLATBREAD

Here's a fun twist on a classic Mexican dish! Keep your kitchen cooled down during the summer by grilling this fresh flatbread outdoors.
—Amanda Phillips, Portland, OR

Prep: 20 min. • **Grill:** 15 min.
Makes: 12 servings

- 2 medium ears sweet corn, husked
- 3 Tbsp. olive oil, divided
- 1 lb. fresh or frozen pizza dough, thawed
- ½ cup mayonnaise
- ⅓ cup crumbled Cotija cheese, divided
- ⅓ cup chopped fresh cilantro, divided
- 1 Tbsp. lime juice
- ½ tsp. chili powder
- ⅛ tsp. pepper

1. Brush corn with 1 Tbsp. oil. Grill corn, covered, over medium heat until lightly browned and tender, 10-12 minutes, turning occasionally. Cool slightly. Cut corn from cobs; transfer to a large bowl.

2. On a lightly floured surface, roll or press dough into a 15x10-in. oval (about ¼ in. thick); place on a greased sheet of foil. Brush top with 1 Tbsp. oil.

3. Carefully invert crust onto grill rack, removing foil. Brush top with remaining 1 Tbsp. oil. Grill, covered, over medium heat until the bottom is golden brown, 2-3 minutes on each side. Remove from grill; cool slightly.

4. Add mayonnaise, 3 Tbsp. cheese, 3 Tbsp. cilantro, lime juice, chili powder and pepper to corn; stir to combine. Spread over warm crust. Sprinkle with the remaining cheese and cilantro.

1 piece: 211 cal., 13g fat (2g sat. fat), 4mg chol., 195mg sod., 20g carb. (2g sugars, 1g fiber), 5g pro.

MARYLAND CORN POPS

Fresh-picked sweet corn is a big thing in Maryland. Here's my homespun version of Mexican street corn that brings in local bay flavors.
—Kristie Schley, Severna Park, MD

Prep: 25 min. • **Grill:** 10 min.
Makes: 2 dozen

8	medium ears sweet corn, husked
2	Tbsp. canola oil
1½	cups mayonnaise
1½	tsp. garlic powder
¼	tsp. freshly ground pepper
24	corncob holders
2	cups crumbled feta cheese
2	Tbsp. seafood seasoning
¼	cup minced fresh cilantro
	Lime wedges, optional

1. Brush all sides of corn with oil. Grill, covered, over medium heat until tender and lightly browned, 10-12 minutes, turning occasionally. Remove from grill; cool slightly.

2. Meanwhile, in a small bowl, mix the mayonnaise, garlic powder and pepper. Cut each ear of corn into thirds. Insert 1 corncob holder into each piece. Spread corn with mayonnaise mixture; sprinkle with the cheese, seafood seasoning and cilantro. If desired, serve with lime wedges.

1 corn pop: 164 cal., 14g fat (3g sat. fat), 10mg chol., 336mg sod., 7g carb. (2g sugars, 1g fiber), 3g pro.

SWEET POTATO & CARROT CASSEROLE

This zesty and sweet carrot casserole is full of flavor. We've served it at many celebrations over the years, and it's always been a big hit!
—Gloria Mezikofsky, Wakefield, MA

Prep: 55 min. • **Bake:** 25 min. + standing
Makes: 12 servings

½	cup golden raisins
3½	lbs. medium sweet potatoes (about 6 potatoes)
4	large carrots, cut into 1½-in. pieces
¼	cup butter
1½	cups packed brown sugar
⅓	cup orange juice

1. Preheat oven to 375°. In a small bowl, cover raisins with hot water; let stand 30 minutes.

2. Place sweet potatoes in a 6-qt. stockpot; add water to cover. Bring to a boil. Reduce heat; cook, uncovered, just until tender, 15-20 minutes. Remove potatoes and cool slightly. Add the carrots to same pot of boiling water; cook, uncovered, until tender, 15-20 minutes; drain.

3. Peel sweet potatoes and cut crosswise into 1½-in.-thick slices. Arrange potatoes and carrots in a greased 13x9-in. baking dish, cut sides down.

4. Drain raisins. In a small saucepan, melt butter over medium heat; stir in raisins. Add brown sugar and orange juice, stirring to dissolve sugar. Pour over vegetables.

5. Bake, uncovered, until heated through and sauce is bubbly, 25-30 minutes; if desired, baste occasionally with sauce. Let stand 10 minutes; toss before serving.

¾ cup: 307 cal., 4g fat (2g sat. fat), 10mg chol., 69mg sod., 67g carb. (45g sugars, 5g fiber), 3g pro.

NORTH WOODS WILD RICE SALAD

This is my Minnesota version of a vintage German slaw that's popular at church suppers. The wild rice has a nutty flavor that fits perfectly with tangy sauerkraut.
—Jeanne Holt, Saint Paul, MN

- -

Prep: 20 min. + chilling
Cook: 40 min. + cooling • **Makes:** 8 servings

- ⅔ cup uncooked wild rice
- 2 cans (14 oz. each) sauerkraut, rinsed and well drained
- 1 medium apple, peeled and chopped
- ¾ cup chopped celery
- ¾ cup shredded carrot
- ½ cup finely chopped red onion

DRESSING

- ½ cup sugar
- ⅓ cup cider vinegar
- 3 Tbsp. canola oil
- ¼ tsp. salt
- ¼ tsp. pepper
- 3 Tbsp. minced fresh parsley
- 1 Tbsp. minced fresh tarragon or 1 tsp. dried tarragon
- ¾ cup chopped walnuts, toasted

1. Cook wild rice according to package directions. Cool completely.
2. In a large bowl, combine sauerkraut, apple, celery, carrot, onion and cooled rice. In a small bowl, whisk the first 5 dressing ingredients until sugar is dissolved; stir in herbs. Add to the sauerkraut mixture; toss to combine.
3. Refrigerate, covered, at least 4 hours to allow flavors to blend. Stir in walnuts just before serving.

Note: To toast nuts, bake in a shallow pan in a 350° oven for 5-10 minutes or cook in a skillet over low heat until lightly browned, stirring occasionally.

¾ cup: 290 cal., 17g fat (1g sat. fat), 0 chol., 747mg sod., 33g carb. (18g sugars, 5g fiber), 5g pro.

SUPER ITALIAN CHOPPED SALAD

Antipasto ingredients are sliced and diced to make this substantial salad. I like to buy sliced meat from the deli and chop it all so we can get a bit of everything in each bite.
—Kim Molina, Duarte, CA

Takes: 25 min. • **Makes:** 10 servings

- 3 cups torn romaine
- 1 can (15 oz.) garbanzo beans or chickpeas, rinsed and drained
- 1 jar (6½ oz.) marinated artichoke hearts, drained and chopped
- 1 medium green pepper, chopped
- 2 medium tomatoes, chopped
- 1 can (2¼ oz.) sliced ripe olives, drained
- 5 slices deli ham, chopped
- 5 thin slices hard salami, chopped
- 5 slices pepperoni, chopped
- 3 slices provolone cheese, chopped
- 2 green onions, chopped
- ¼ cup olive oil
- 2 Tbsp. red wine vinegar
- ¼ tsp. salt
- ⅛ tsp. pepper
- 2 Tbsp. grated Parmesan cheese
  Pepperoncini, optional

In a large bowl, combine first 11 ingredients. For dressing, in a small bowl, whisk the oil, vinegar, salt and pepper. Pour over salad; toss to coat. Sprinkle with cheese. Top with pepperoncini, if desired.
Note: Look for pepperoncini (pickled peppers) in the pickle and olive section of your grocery store.
¾ cup: 185 cal., 13g fat (3g sat. fat), 12mg chol., 444mg sod., 11g carb. (3g sugars, 3g fiber), 7g pro.

BAKED THREE-CHEESE MACARONI

Legendary mac and cheese is a must-have for large family events. This ultimate comfort food is a divine blend of cheddar, Gruyere and Parmesan.
—Joan Sullivan, Gambrills, MD

- -

Prep: 20 min. • **Bake:** 30 min.
Makes: 12 servings

- 1 pkg. (16 oz.) elbow macaroni or fusilli pasta
- 6 Tbsp. butter, cubed
- ½ cup all-purpose flour
- 4 cups 2% milk, warmed
- 4 cups shredded Gruyere cheese
- 2 cups shredded extra-sharp cheddar cheese
- 2 tsp. salt
- ¾ tsp. freshly ground pepper
- ¼ tsp. freshly ground nutmeg
- 1½ cups panko bread crumbs
- ½ cup grated Parmesan cheese
- 2 Tbsp. butter, melted

1. Preheat oven to 350°. Cook macaroni in a 6-qt. stockpot according to package directions for al dente. Drain; return to pot.
2. In a large saucepan, melt 6 Tbsp. butter over medium heat. Stir in the flour until smooth; whisk in warmed milk. Bring to a boil, stirring constantly; cook and stir 2-3 minutes or until thickened.
3. Remove from heat; stir in Gruyere and cheddar cheeses, salt, pepper and nutmeg. Add to macaroni, tossing to coat.
4. Transfer to a greased 13x9-in. baking dish. Toss bread crumbs with Parmesan cheese and melted butter; sprinkle over casserole. Bake, uncovered, 30-40 minutes or until bubbly and top is golden brown.

¾ cup: 487 cal., 24g fat (14g sat. fat), 76mg chol., 515mg sod., 41g carb. (6g sugars, 2g fiber), 27g pro.

CAULIFLOWER WITH WHITE CHEDDAR SAUCE

My mother served this cheesy cauliflower on Thanksgiving and Christmas for as long as I can remember. I've embellished the recipe over the years, but I've kept the family tradition around for more than 47 years of marriage. When I visit my children and their families, this dish is a must for them as well! You can easily double the recipe for larger groups.
—Charlene Chambers, Ormond Beach, FL

Takes: 25 min. • **Makes:** 8 servings

- 1 large head cauliflower, cut into florets (about 6 cups)
- 5 tsp. cornstarch
- ½ tsp. salt
- ⅛ tsp. white pepper
- 1¼ cups 2% milk
- 2 Tbsp. butter
- 1 cup shredded extra sharp white cheddar cheese
  Paprika, optional

1. In a large saucepan, place steamer basket over 1 in. water. Place cauliflower in basket. Bring water to a boil. Reduce the heat to maintain a simmer; steam, covered, just until tender, 10-12 minutes.
2. Meanwhile, in a small saucepan, mix cornstarch, salt and white pepper. Stir in milk and butter until smooth. Bring to a boil, stirring constantly; cook and stir until thickened, 2-4 minutes.
3. Stir in cheese until melted. Drain cauliflower. Transfer to a serving bowl; top with the sauce. If desired, sprinkle with paprika.
¾ cup: 144 cal., 9g fat (6g sat. fat), 27mg chol., 328mg sod., 9g carb. (4g sugars, 2g fiber), 7g pro.

VEGAN GREEN GODDESS POTATO SALAD

Don't be fooled by the green color—this salad is absolutely delicious! It's perfect for potlucks and for those with dietary restrictions.
—Laura Wilhelm, West Hollywood, CA

Prep: 30 min. + chilling • **Makes:** 8 servings

- 2 lbs. baby red potatoes, halved
- 4 green onions
- 2 medium ripe avocados, peeled and pitted
- ½ cup sprigs fresh parsley, stems removed
- ½ cup vegan mayonnaise
- 3 tarragon sprigs, stems removed
- 2 tsp. capers, drained
- 1 tsp. seasoned salt
- 1 celery rib, finely chopped
  Sliced radishes

1. Place potatoes in a large saucepan; add water to cover. Bring to a boil. Reduce heat; cook, uncovered, until tender, 8-10 minutes.
2. Meanwhile, chop green onions, reserving the white portions for salad. Add green portions to a blender. Add avocados, parsley, mayonnaise, tarragon, capers and seasoned salt. Cover and process until blended, scraping down sides as needed.
3. Drain potatoes; transfer to a large bowl. Add celery, white portions of green onions and dressing; toss to coat. Refrigerate, covered, at least 1 hour. Top with radishes and additional parsley.
¾ cup: 235 cal., 15g fat (2g sat. fat), 0 chol., 295mg sod., 24g carb. (1g sugars, 4g fiber), 3g pro. **Diabetic exchanges:** 3 fat, 1½ starch.

MAKE AHEAD

PARSNIPS & TURNIPS AU GRATIN

You don't need potatoes to make a delicious au gratin dish! Sometimes I even substitute rutabaga for the turnips. I definitely cherish having this recipe in my collection.

—Priscilla Gilbert, Indian Harbour Beach, FL

- -

Prep: 20 min. • **Bake:** 15 min.
Makes: 8 servings

- 1½ lbs. parsnips, peeled and sliced
- 1¼ lbs. turnips, peeled and sliced
- 1 can (10¾ oz.) reduced-fat reduced-sodium condensed cream of celery soup, undiluted
- 1 cup fat-free milk
- ½ tsp. pepper
- 1 cup shredded sharp cheddar cheese
- ½ cup panko bread crumbs
- 1 Tbsp. butter, melted

1. Place parsnips and turnips in a large saucepan; cover with water. Bring to a boil. Reduce heat; simmer, uncovered, until crisp-tender, 5-7 minutes.
2. Meanwhile, in a small saucepan, combine the soup, milk and pepper. Bring to a boil; reduce heat to low. Stir in cheese until melted. Drain vegetables; transfer to an 11x7-in. baking dish coated with cooking spray. Pour sauce over vegetables.
3. Combine bread crumbs and butter; sprinkle over top. Bake, uncovered, at 400° until vegetables are tender and crumbs are golden brown, 15-20 minutes.
Freeze option: Cool unbaked casserole; cover and freeze. To use, partially thaw in refrigerator overnight. Remove from refrigerator 30 minutes before baking. Preheat oven to 375°. Bake casserole as directed, increasing time as necessary to heat through and for a thermometer inserted in center to read 165°.
¾ cup: 189 cal., 7g fat (4g sat. fat), 21mg chol., 309mg sod., 27g carb. (9g sugars, 4g fiber), 7g pro. **Diabetic exchanges:** 1 starch, 1 high-fat meat, 1 vegetable.

CHEDDAR & SPINACH TWICE-BAKED POTATOES

My husband is a rancher who loves a hearty potato dish, so consider these spuds with cheddar and spinach cowboy approved! My crowd never leaves any leftovers.

—Jody Augustyn, Loup City, NE

- -

Prep: 1¼ hours • **Bake:** 20 min.
Makes: 12 servings

- 6 large baking potatoes (about 12 oz. each)
- ½ cup 2% milk
- 6 Tbsp. butter, softened
- 1 pkg. (10 oz.) frozen chopped spinach, thawed and squeezed dry
- ¾ cup shredded Monterey Jack cheese
- ¾ cup shredded cheddar cheese, divided
- ¼ cup finely chopped red onion
- 1 tsp. salt
- ¼ tsp. pepper

1. Preheat oven to 375°. Scrub potatoes; pierce each several times with a fork. Place in a foil-lined 15x10x1-in. baking pan; bake 60-70 minutes or until tender.
2. When cool enough to handle, cut each potato lengthwise in half. Scoop out pulp, leaving ¼-in.-thick shells. In a large bowl, mash pulp with milk and butter, adding spinach, Monterey Jack cheese, ¼ cup cheddar cheese, onion, salt and pepper.
3. Spoon into potato shells; return to baking pan. Sprinkle with the remaining cheddar cheese. Bake 20-25 minutes or until heated through and cheese is melted.
1 stuffed potato half: 261 cal., 11g fat (7g sat. fat), 30mg chol., 363mg sod., 34g carb. (2g sugars, 5g fiber), 9g pro.

SUMMER SQUASH SALAD

Packing a perfect crunch, this salad is a tasty alternative to coleslaw. Like most gardeners, we usually have an abundance of squash and zucchini in summer, so this dish is an amazing way to use our fresh produce.
—Diane Hixon, Niceville, FL

Prep: 15 min. + chilling • **Makes:** 12 servings

- 4 cups julienned zucchini
- 4 cups julienned yellow squash
- 2 cups sliced radishes
- 1 cup canola oil
- ⅓ cup cider vinegar
- 2 Tbsp. Dijon mustard
- 2 Tbsp. snipped fresh parsley
- 1½ tsp. salt
- 1 tsp. dill weed
- ½ tsp. pepper

In a large bowl, toss zucchini, squash and radishes. In a small bowl, whisk the remaining ingredients. Pour over vegetables. Cover and refrigerate for at least 2 hours. If desired, top with additional snipped fresh parsley.

¾ cup: 188 cal., 19g fat (1g sat. fat), 0 chol., 368mg sod., 4g carb. (3g sugars, 1g fiber), 1g pro.

ROMAINE & CHERRY TOMATO SALAD

My mother made this tasty salad for me as a child, and it was my favorite. Now I serve it as a sunny appetizer or entree.
—Blythe Twiggs, Buford, GA

Takes: 20 min. • **Makes:** 8 servings

- 1 small bunch romaine, torn
- 2 cups grape tomatoes, halved
- 1 pkg. (12 oz.) frozen peas, thawed
- 1 small red onion, thinly sliced
- 1½ cups reduced-fat mayonnaise
- 1 cup shredded Parmesan cheese
- 8 bacon strips, cooked and crumbled

In a 3-qt. trifle bowl or glass bowl, layer romaine, tomatoes, peas and onion. Spread mayonnaise over onion. Sprinkle with the cheese and bacon. Refrigerate until serving.

1 cup: 284 cal., 21g fat (5g sat. fat), 31mg chol., 729mg sod., 14g carb. (6g sugars, 3g fiber), 10g pro.

KALE CAESAR SALAD

I love Caesar salads, so I created this blend of kale and romaine lettuces with a creamy Caesar dressing. It's perfect paired with chicken or steak for a light weeknight meal.
—Rashanda Cobbins, Milwaukee, WI

Takes: 15 min. • **Makes:** 8 servings

- 4 cups chopped fresh kale
- 4 cups torn romaine
- 1 cup Caesar salad croutons
- ½ cup shredded Parmesan cheese
- ½ cup mayonnaise
- 2 Tbsp. lemon juice
- 1 Tbsp. Worcestershire sauce
- 2 tsp. Dijon mustard
- 2 tsp. anchovy paste
- 1 garlic clove, minced
- ¼ tsp. salt
- ¼ tsp. pepper

In a large salad bowl, toss kale, romaine, croutons and cheese. For the dressing, combine remaining ingredients in a small bowl; pour over the salad and toss to coat. Serve immediately.

1 cup: 148 cal., 13g fat (3g sat. fat), 10mg chol., 417mg sod., 6g carb. (1g sugars, 1g fiber), 3g pro. **Diabetic exchanges:** 2½ fat, 1 vegetable.

GLORIFIED HASH BROWNS

You will be surprised at how quick and easy it is to put together this dressed-up potato casserole! When a friend made it for a church supper, I had to have the recipe. It's ideal for parties, potlucks and family reunions.
—Betty Kay Sitzman, Wray, CO

- -

Prep: 10 min. • **Bake:** 40 min.
Makes: 10 servings

- 2 cans (10¾ oz. each) condensed cream of celery soup, undiluted
- 2 cartons (8 oz. each) spreadable chive and onion cream cheese
- 1 pkg. (2 lbs.) frozen cubed hash brown potatoes
- 1 cup shredded cheddar cheese

1. In a large microwave-safe bowl, combine the soup and cream cheese. Cover; cook on high for 3-4 minutes or until cream cheese is melted, stirring occasionally. Add the potatoes and stir until coated.
2. Spoon into a greased 13x9-in. baking dish. Bake, uncovered, at 350° for 35-40 minutes or until potatoes are tender. Sprinkle with cheddar cheese. Bake 3-5 minutes longer or until cheese is melted.
Freeze option: Sprinkle cheddar cheese over unbaked casserole. Cover and freeze. To use, partially thaw in the refrigerator overnight. Remove from refrigerator 30 minutes before baking. Preheat oven to 350°. Bake the casserole as directed, increasing time as necessary to heat through and for a thermometer inserted in center to read 165°.
1 serving: 215 cal., 12g fat (8g sat. fat), 35mg chol., 400mg sod., 20g carb. (2g sugars, 1g fiber), 6g pro.

FIRE & ICE TOMATOES

You won't miss the salt in this refreshing tomato salad! It's well-seasoned with cayenne pepper, mustard seed and vinegar but not the least bit spicy. This dish is always a hit at potlucks.
—Nan Rickey, Yuma, AZ

Prep: 10 min. • **Cook:** 5 min. + chilling
Makes: 8 servings

- 5 large tomatoes, cut into wedges
- 1 medium onion, sliced
- ¾ cup white vinegar
- 6 Tbsp. sugar
- ¼ cup water
- 3 tsp. mustard seed
- ¼ tsp. cayenne pepper
- 1 large cucumber, sliced

1. Place tomatoes and onion in a large heatproof nonreactive bowl. In a small saucepan, combine vinegar, sugar, water, mustard seed and cayenne; bring to a boil. Cook 1 minute, stirring to dissolve sugar; pour carefully over the tomato mixture. Cool completely.

2. Stir in cucumber. Refrigerate, covered, overnight.

¾ cup: 72 cal., 1g fat (0 sat. fat), 0 chol., 7mg sod., 17g carb. (14g sugars, 2g fiber), 2g pro.
Diabetic exchanges: 1 vegetable, ½ starch.

SOUTHWESTERN SAVORY MUFFINS

When I was first married, I found a muffin recipe that used bacon. I modified it over the years, and now it's a favorite snack. My husband grew up in northern New Mexico and thinks most foods benefit from the addition of green chiles.
—Laura Parker, Los Alamos, NM

Prep: 20 min. • **Bake:** 15 min.
Makes: 14 muffins

- 10 bacon strips
- 2 cups all-purpose flour
- ¼ cup sugar
- 1 Tbsp. baking powder
- ¾ cup whole milk
- 1 large egg
- 1½ cups shredded cheddar cheese
- ¼ cup diced green chiles

1. In a skillet, cook the bacon until crisp; reserve ⅓ cup drippings. Crumble bacon and set aside.

2. In a large bowl, combine flour, sugar and baking powder. Whisk milk, egg and drippings; stir into dry ingredients just until moistened. Fold in cheese, chiles and bacon. Fill greased or paper-lined muffin cups three-fourths full. Bake at 400° for 15-20 minutes or until golden brown. Serve warm.

1 muffin: 226 cal., 14g fat (6g sat. fat), 41mg chol., 298mg sod., 18g carb. (4g sugars, 1g fiber), 7g pro.

BRING IT
To keep muffins warm in a slow cooker, dampen a cloth napkin with hot water, then tuck it into the bottom of the crock beneath a plate or trivet. Gently stack muffins inside, wrapped in a second (dry) napkin. Use the slow cooker's lowest setting.

MAKE AHEAD

FRESH GREEN BEAN SALAD

I had a green bean salad at a local deli and enjoyed it so much that I tried to re-create it at home. The result was yummy! It lasts for several days in the fridge, and the taste keeps getting better.
—Allison Brooks, Fort Collins, CO

Prep: 35 min.
Makes: 12 servings

- 4 cups fresh green beans, trimmed and halved
- 2 cups cherry tomatoes, halved
- 1 large English cucumber, seeded and chopped
- 1 cup fresh baby carrots, cut in half lengthwise
- 1 cup coarsely chopped fresh parsley

DRESSING
- ½ cup olive oil
- 2 Tbsp. lemon juice
- 1 Tbsp. white wine vinegar
- 1 Tbsp. grated lemon zest
- 1 tsp. Dijon mustard
- 1 garlic clove, minced
- ½ tsp. salt
- ½ tsp. ground mustard
- ¼ tsp. pepper

1. In a large saucepan, bring 4 cups water to a boil. Add beans; cook, uncovered, for 3 minutes. Drain and immediately place beans in ice water. Drain and pat dry.

2. In a large bowl, combine the beans, tomatoes, cucumber, carrots and parsley. In a small bowl, whisk dressing ingredients. Pour over salad; toss to coat. Refrigerate until serving. Serve with a slotted spoon.

¾ cup: 106 cal., 9g fat (1g sat. fat), 0 chol., 124mg sod., 6g carb. (3g sugars, 2g fiber), 1g pro. **Diabetic exchanges:** 2 fat, 1 vegetable.

GREEK HERB RATATOUILLE

When I lived in Florida, I went to a dinner at a friend's home. His wife, who is Greek, served a beautiful side dish that she called an eggplant fan, and she shared the recipe with me. While I've made her version many times with success, I was inspired by the movie Ratatouille *and created this version.*
—Joe Sherwood, Tryon, NE

Prep: 30 min. + chilling • **Bake:** 45 min.
Makes: 13 servings

- 1 small eggplant
- 2 small zucchini
- 2 small yellow summer squash
- 4 plum tomatoes
- 1 large sweet onion
- ½ cup butter, melted
- ½ cup minced fresh parsley
- 3 garlic cloves, minced
- ½ tsp. salt
- ½ tsp. each dried thyme, oregano, tarragon and basil
- ½ tsp. dried rosemary, crushed
- ½ tsp. pepper
- 1 cup shredded part-skim mozzarella cheese

1. Cut vegetables into ¼-in.-thick slices.
2. In a greased 13x9-in. baking dish, layer the eggplant, zucchini, squash, tomatoes and onion. In a small bowl, combine the butter, parsley, garlic and seasonings; pour over vegetables. Cover and refrigerate overnight.
3. Remove from refrigerator 30 minutes before baking. Bake, uncovered, at 375° for 35 minutes. Sprinkle with cheese. Bake 10-15 minutes longer or until the cheese is melted. Serve with a slotted spoon.
¾ cup: 120 cal., 9g fat (5g sat. fat), 24mg chol., 190mg sod., 8g carb. (5g sugars, 3g fiber), 4g pro.

SPRING GREEK PASTA SALAD

For a light meal, we toss rotini pasta with cucumber, zucchini and sweet peppers. Make it into a main dish by adding grilled chicken.
—Christine Schenher, Exeter, CA

Takes: 30 min.
Makes: 16 servings

- 4 cups veggie rotini or other spiral pasta (about 12 oz.)

VINAIGRETTE
- ¼ cup olive oil
- 3 Tbsp. lemon juice
- 2 Tbsp. balsamic vinegar
- 1 Tbsp. water
- 3 garlic cloves, minced
- 1 tsp. salt
- ¼ tsp. pepper
- 3 Tbsp. minced fresh oregano or 1 Tbsp. dried oregano

SALAD
- 3 large tomatoes, seeded and chopped
- 1 medium sweet red pepper, chopped
- 1 small cucumber, seeded and chopped
- 1 small zucchini, chopped
- 1 small red onion, halved and thinly sliced
- ⅓ cup sliced pitted Greek olives, optional
- 1 cup (4 oz.) crumbled feta cheese

1. Cook pasta according to the package directions. Drain; rinse with cold water and drain well.
2. In a small bowl, whisk oil, lemon juice, vinegar, water, garlic, salt and pepper until blended. Stir in oregano.
3. In a large bowl, combine the pasta, vegetables and, if desired, olives. Add vinaigrette and cheese; toss to combine. Refrigerate, covered, until serving.
¾ cup: 142 cal., 5g fat (1g sat. fat), 4mg chol., 219mg sod., 20g carb. (3g sugars, 2g fiber), 5g pro. **Diabetic exchanges:** 1 starch, 1 fat.

Watermelon Basket
page 153

Big Batch Dishes

Turn here to find fantastic crowd-sized dishes for your biggest bashes. The recipes here all serve 20 or more people.

MAKE AHEAD

BEST EVER CRESCENT ROLLS

My daughter and I have cranked out dozens of these homemade crescent rolls. It is a real team effort. I cut the dough into pie-shaped wedges; she rolls them up.
—Irene Yeh, Mequon, WI

Prep: 40 min. + chilling • **Bake:** 10 min./batch
Makes: 32 rolls

      3¾ to 4¼ cups all-purpose flour
      2 pkg. (¼ oz. each) active dry yeast
      1 tsp. salt
      1 cup 2% milk
      ½ cup butter, cubed
      ¼ cup honey
      3 large egg yolks. room temperature
      2 Tbsp. butter, melted

1. Combine 1½ cups flour, yeast and salt. In a small saucepan, heat milk, cubed butter and honey to 120°-130°. Add to dry ingredients; beat on medium speed 2 minutes. Add egg yolks; beat on high 2 minutes. Stir in enough remaining flour to form a soft dough (dough will be sticky).
2. Turn the dough onto a floured surface; knead until smooth and elastic, 6-8 minutes. Place in a greased bowl, turning once to grease top. Cover and let rise in a warm place until doubled, about 45 minutes.
3. Punch down the dough. Cover and refrigerate overnight.
4. Turn chilled dough onto a lightly floured surface; divide in half. Roll each portion into a 14-in. circle; cut each circle into 16 wedges. Lightly brush wedges with melted butter. Roll up from wide ends, pinching pointed ends to seal. Place 2 in. apart on parchment-lined baking sheets, point side down. Cover; let rise in a warm place until doubled, about 45 minutes.
5. Preheat oven to 375°. Bake until golden brown, 9-11 minutes. Remove from pans to wire racks; serve warm.
Freeze option: Immediately after shaping, freeze rolls on parchment-lined baking sheets until firm. Transfer to a freezer container; return to freezer. Freeze up to 4 weeks. To use, let rise, increasing rise time to 2½-3 hours, and bake as directed.
1 roll: 104 cal., 4g fat (3g sat. fat), 28mg chol., 107mg sod., 14g carb. (3g sugars, 1g fiber), 2g pro.

BLACK-AND-BLUE PIZZAS
Here, blue cheese, shiitake mushrooms and blackened seasoning lend a tasty change to traditional pizza.
—Michelle Huelskamp, Marion, NC

Prep: 40 min. • **Bake:** 15 min.
Makes: 2 pizzas (12 pieces each)

      2 loaves (1 lb. each) frozen bread dough, thawed
      8 bacon strips, chopped
      1 lb. boneless skinless chicken breasts, cut into strips
      5 tsp. blackened seasoning
      3 shallots, finely chopped
      2 garlic cloves, minced
      1 jar (15 oz.) Alfredo sauce
      2½ cups sliced fresh shiitake mushrooms
      1 can (3.8 oz.) sliced ripe olives, drained
      ½ cup finely chopped sun-dried tomatoes (not packed in oil)
      1¼ cups (5 oz.) crumbled blue cheese
      3 Tbsp. minced fresh basil or 3 tsp. dried basil
      2 Tbsp. minced fresh thyme or 2 tsp. dried thyme
     12 slices provolone cheese
      3 oz. Parmesan cheese, shaved into strips, or ¾ cup grated Parmesan cheese

1. Roll dough into two 16x10-in. rectangles; transfer to ungreased baking sheets and build up edges slightly.
2. In a large skillet, cook bacon over medium heat until crisp. Remove to paper towels with a slotted spoon; drain, reserving 2 Tbsp. drippings. Sprinkle chicken with blackened seasoning; cook chicken in the drippings until no longer pink. Add shallots and garlic; cook 1 minute longer. Set aside.
3. Spread sauce over crusts; top with the chicken mixture, bacon, mushrooms, olives and tomatoes. Sprinkle with blue cheese, basil and thyme; top with cheeses.
4. Bake at 450° for 14-18 minutes or until bubbly and cheese is melted.
1 piece: 263 cal., 12g fat (6g sat. fat), 35mg chol., 657mg sod., 22g carb. (2g sugars, 2g fiber), 15g pro.

BACON-WRAPPED WATER CHESTNUTS

Whenever I attend a potluck, folks always ask me to bring these treats—they've become my trademark. I especially like to prepare them for holiday gatherings.
—Debi Jellison, Jacksonville, FL

- -

Prep: 20 min. • **Bake:** 35 min.
Makes: about 5 dozen

- 1 lb. sliced bacon
- 2 cans (8 oz. each) whole water chestnuts, rinsed and drained
- 1 cup ketchup
- ¾ cup packed brown sugar

1. Cut bacon strips into thirds; wrap a strip around each water chestnut and secure with a wooden toothpick. Place in an ungreased 15x10x1-in. baking pan. Bake at 375° until bacon is crisp, 25 minutes.
2. Meanwhile, in a small saucepan, combine ketchup and brown sugar; cook and stir over medium heat until sugar has dissolved. Remove chestnuts to paper towels; drain. Dip in ketchup mixture; place in a lightly greased 13x9-in. baking dish. Spoon the remaining sauce over chestnuts. Return to oven for 10 minutes.

1 piece: 33 cal., 1g fat (0 sat. fat), 2mg chol., 92mg sod., 5g carb. (4g sugars, 0 fiber), 1g pro.

★ ★ ★ ★ ★ **READER REVIEW**

"I have been making these for many years. They are requested at all carry-ins!"

PALEMMER TASTEOFHOME.COM

APPLESAUCE MUFFINS

These are such a popular item at the restaurant I own that I had the recipe printed on a card to share with guests.
—Linda Williams, LaFayette, AL

- -

Prep: 10 min. • **Bake:** 20 min.
Makes: about 2 dozen

- 1 cup butter, softened
- 2 cups sugar
- 2 large eggs, room temperature
- 1 tsp. vanilla extract
- 2 cups applesauce
- 4 cups all-purpose flour
- 1 tsp. baking soda
- 1 tsp. ground cinnamon
- 1 tsp. ground allspice
- ¼ tsp. ground cloves
- 1 cup chopped walnuts, optional
  Cinnamon sugar, optional

1. Preheat oven to 350°. In a bowl, cream the butter and sugar until light and fluffy, 5-7 minutes. Beat in eggs and vanilla. Stir in applesauce. Combine flour, baking soda and spices; stir into creamed mixture. If desired, fold in nuts.
2. Fill greased or paper-lined muffin cups three-fourths full. Bake until a toothpick comes out clean, 20-25 minutes. Cool for 5 minutes before removing from pans to wire racks. If desired, sprinkle with cinnamon sugar.

1 muffin: 224 cal., 8g fat (5g sat. fat), 36mg chol., 120mg sod., 35g carb. (19g sugars, 1g fiber), 3g pro. **Diabetic exchanges:** 2 starch, 1½ fat.

DUO TATER BAKE

Cut down on holiday prep time with this creamy potato dish that combines sweet potatoes with regular spuds. I served this for Thanksgiving, and it was a winner.
—Joan McCulloch, Abbotsford, BC

- -

Prep: 40 min. • **Bake:** 20 min.
Makes: 2 casseroles (10 servings each)

4 lbs. russet or Yukon Gold potatoes, peeled and cubed
3 lbs. sweet potatoes, peeled and cubed
2 cartons (8 oz. each) spreadable chive and onion cream cheese
1 cup sour cream
¼ cup shredded Colby-Monterey Jack cheese
⅓ cup 2% milk
¼ cup shredded Parmesan cheese
½ tsp. salt
½ tsp. pepper
TOPPING
1 cup shredded Colby-Monterey Jack cheese
½ cup chopped green onions
¼ cup shredded Parmesan cheese

1. Place russet potatoes in a Dutch oven and cover with water. Bring to a boil. Reduce heat; cover and cook until tender, 10-15 minutes.
2. Meanwhile, place sweet potatoes in a large saucepan; cover with water. Bring to a boil. Reduce heat; cover and cook until tender, 10-15 minutes. Drain; mash with half the cream cheese and sour cream and the ¼ cup shredded cheese.
3. Drain russet potatoes; mash with the remaining cream cheese and sour cream. Stir in the milk, Parmesan cheese, salt and pepper.
4. Spread 2⅔ cups russet potato mixture into each of 2 greased 11x7-in. baking dishes. Layer with 4 cups sweet potato mixture. Repeat layers. Spread with remaining russet potato mixture.
5. Bake, uncovered, at 350° until heated through, about 15 minutes. Combine topping ingredients; sprinkle over the casseroles. Bake until cheese is melted, 2-3 minutes longer.
¾ cup: 236 cal., 12g fat (8g sat. fat), 38mg chol., 246mg sod., 25g carb. (7g sugars, 2g fiber), 5g pro.

PHILLY CHEESESTEAK WONTON CUPS

I love the versatility of wonton wrappers. You can fill them with any mix of flavors or ingredients to suit your tastes. The first batch of these cups I tried with a Mexican-inspired filling, which was delicious. But this fun version is a spinoff of Philly cheesesteak, one of my favorite sandwiches.
—Cyndy Gerken, Naples, FL

- -

Prep: 40 min. • **Bake:** 10 min./batch
Makes: 3 dozen

36 wonton wrappers
2 tsp. canola oil
1 large onion, chopped
1 medium green pepper, chopped
1 lb. sliced deli roast beef, cut into ¾-in. pieces
¼ cup Worcestershire sauce
3 tsp. Montreal steak seasoning
¼ tsp. pepper
2 cups shredded provolone cheese
Optional: Chopped sliced pepperoncini and steak sauce

1. Preheat oven to 375°. Press wonton wrappers in greased muffin cups. Bake until golden brown, 4-5 minutes.
2. Meanwhile, in a skillet, heat oil over medium-high heat. Saute onion and green pepper until tender, 3-5 minutes. Remove from pan.
3. Toss beef with Worcestershire sauce, steak seasoning and pepper. In same pan, cook and stir beef mixture over medium heat until heated through, about 5 minutes. Place about 2 Tbsp. beef mixture in each cup; sprinkle each with scant 1 Tbsp. cheese.
4. Bake cups until heated through, 8-10 minutes. Serve immediately. If desired, top with pepperoncini and serve with steak sauce.
1 wonton cup: 66 cal., 2g fat (1g sat. fat), 12mg chol., 360mg sod., 6g carb. (0 sugars, 0 fiber), 5g pro.

BACON-CHEDDAR POTATO CROQUETTES

Once you discover croquettes, you'll want to make extra mashed potatoes every time. The little baked balls are yummy with ranch dressing, barbecue sauce or Dijon mayonnaise for dipping.
—Pamela Shank, Parkersburg, WV

- -

Prep: 20 min. + chilling • **Bake:** 20 min.
Makes: about 5 dozen

- 4 cups cold mashed potatoes (with added milk and butter)
- 6 bacon strips, cooked and crumbled
- ½ cup shredded cheddar cheese
- 2 large eggs, lightly beaten
- ¼ cup sour cream
- 1 Tbsp. minced chives
- ½ tsp. salt
- ¼ tsp. pepper
- 40 Ritz crackers, crushed
- ¼ cup butter, melted
- 1 tsp. paprika
  Barbecue sauce, Dijon-mayonnaise blend or ranch salad dressing

1. In a large bowl, combine the first 8 ingredients. Shape by tablespoonfuls into balls. Roll in cracker crumbs. Place on parchment-lined baking sheets. Refrigerate 2 hours or overnight.

2. Combine butter and paprika; drizzle over croquettes. Bake at 375° until golden brown, 18-20 minutes. Serve with dipping sauce of your choice.

Freeze option: Prepare croquettes as directed, omitting chilling step. Transfer to waxed paper-lined baking sheets. Prepare butter mixture; drizzle over croquettes. Freeze until firm. Transfer to resealable containers; return to freezer. To use, bake croquettes as directed, increasing time to 20-25 minutes. Serve with sauce.

1 appetizer: 46 cal., 3g fat (1g sat. fat), 12mg chol., 112mg sod., 4g carb. (0 sugars, 0 fiber), 1g pro.

SMOKED MOZZARELLA MUSHROOM PIZZA

Top a refrigerated crust with portobello mushrooms, smoked mozzarella and prosciutto for a hearty starter. Made in a 15x10x1-in. pan, the pizza could even be cut into larger pieces and served as an entree.
—Edwina Gadsby, Hayden, ID

- -

Prep: 25 min. • **Bake:** 15 min.
Makes: 24 servings

- 2   Tbsp. butter, divided
- 2   Tbsp. olive oil, divided
- ⅔   cup sliced red onion
- ½   lb. sliced baby portobello mushrooms
- 1   garlic clove, minced
- 2   tsp. minced fresh rosemary or ½ tsp. dried rosemary, crushed
- 1   tube (13.8 oz.) refrigerated pizza crust
- 1½ cups shredded smoked mozzarella cheese
- 2   oz. sliced prosciutto or deli ham, finely chopped

1. Preheat oven to 400°. In a large skillet, heat 1 Tbsp. butter and 1 Tbsp. oil over medium-high heat. Add onion; cook and stir 2-3 minutes or until softened. Reduce heat to medium-low; cook 8-10 minutes or until golden brown, stirring occasionally. Remove from pan.

2. In same skillet, heat remaining butter and oil over medium-high heat. Add mushrooms; cook and stir 2-3 minutes or until tender. Add garlic and rosemary; cook 1-2 minutes longer or until liquid is evaporated.

3. Unroll and press dough onto bottom of a greased 15x10x1-in. baking pan. Using fingertips, press several dimples into dough. Sprinkle with ½ cup cheese; top with onion, mushroom mixture and prosciutto. Sprinkle with remaining cheese. Bake 15-18 minutes or until golden brown and cheese is melted.

1 piece: 90 cal., 5g fat (2g sat. fat), 11mg chol., 178mg sod., 9g carb. (1g sugars, 0 fiber), 4g pro.

CHEESECAKE POPS

The possibilities are endless with these cute cheesecake bites. Customize them for any special occasion by using different toppings.
—Evelyn Moore, Elk Grove, CA

Prep: 2 hours + freezing
Makes: 45 cheesecake pops

- 3 pkg. (8 oz. each) cream cheese, softened
- 1 cup sugar
- 1 cup sour cream
- 1 tsp. vanilla extract
- 3 large eggs, lightly beaten
- 1 cup graham cracker crumbs
- 45 lollipop sticks (4 in. long)
- 3 pkg. (10 to 12 oz. each) white baking chips
- 3 Tbsp. shortening
  Toppings: Grated coconut, grated chocolate and assorted sprinkles

1. Line the bottom of a 9-in. springform pan with parchment; coat paper and sides of pan with cooking spray.
2. In a large bowl, beat cream cheese and sugar until smooth. Beat in sour cream and vanilla until blended. Add eggs; beat on low speed just until combined. Pour into prepared pan.
3. Place pan on a baking sheet. Bake at 350° for 45-50 minutes or until center is almost set. Cool on a wire rack for 10 minutes. Carefully run a knife around edge of pan to loosen; cool 1 hour longer. Cover and freeze overnight.
4. Remove from the freezer and let stand for 30 minutes. Place cracker crumbs in a shallow bowl. Working quickly, scoop out 1-in. balls of cheesecake; roll each in cracker crumbs and insert a lollipop stick. Place on waxed paper-lined baking sheets. Freeze for 1 hour or until firm.
5. In a microwave, melt white baking chips and shortening at 70% power; stir until smooth. Place toppings in shallow bowls. Dip cheesecake pops in white chip mixture; allow excess to drip off. Roll in toppings.

Place on waxed paper; let stand until set. Store in the refrigerator.
1 cake pop: 203 cal., 14g fat (8g sat. fat), 37mg chol., 80mg sod., 18g carb. (16g sugars, 0 fiber), 3g pro.

WILD PLUM JELLY

I've had this wild plum jelly recipe for ages. Each year when the plums are ripe, I'll fill my pail and make this jelly. It's so good served with toast, pancakes or waffles!
—Ludell Heuser, Mount Horeb, WI

Prep: 55 min. • **Process:** 5 min.
Makes: about 8 half-pints

- 5 lbs. wild plums, halved and pitted
- 4 cups water
- 1 pkg. (1¾ oz.) powdered fruit pectin
- 7½ cups sugar

1. In a stockpot, simmer plums and water until tender, about 30 minutes. Line a strainer with 4 layers of cheesecloth and place over a bowl. Place plum mixture in strainer; cover with edges of cheesecloth. Let stand until liquid measures 5½ cups, about 30 minutes.
2. Return liquid to the pan. Add pectin; stir and bring to a boil. Add sugar; bring to a full rolling boil. Boil for 1 minute, stirring constantly.
3. Remove from the heat; skim off any foam. Carefully ladle hot mixture into hot sterilized half-pint jars, leaving ¼-in. headspace. Remove air bubbles; wipe rims and adjust lids. Process for 5 minutes in a boiling-water canner.
Note: The processing time listed is for altitudes of 1,000 feet or less. Add 1 minute to the processing time for each 1,000 feet of additional altitude.
2 Tbsp.: 108 cal., 0 fat (0 sat. fat), 0 chol., 0 sod., 28g carb. (27g sugars, 1g fiber), 0 pro.

CINNAMON-CANDY COOKIES

I was trying to make a unique Christmas cookie inspired by my brother's love of Red Hots. I used the candies for cinnamon flavor in these lovely lacelike cookies.
—Wendy Rusch, Cameron, WI

- -

Prep: 20 min. + chilling
Bake: 10 min./batch + cooling
Makes: about 5 dozen

⅔ cup Red Hots
2⅓ cups all-purpose flour
1 cup butter, softened
1 cup sugar
1 tsp. vanilla extract
FROSTING
2 cups confectioners' sugar
½ cup butter, softened
½ tsp. vanilla or cinnamon extract
⅛ tsp. salt
4 to 6 Tbsp. 2% milk

1. Place Red Hots in a food processor; process until fine and powdery. Add flour; pulse to combine.
2. In a large bowl, cream butter and sugar until light and fluffy, 5-7 minutes. Beat in vanilla. Gradually beat in flour mixture. Shape into two 8-in. rolls; wrap each roll in waxed paper. Refrigerate until firm, about 1 hour.
3. Preheat oven to 350°. Unwrap and cut into ¼-in. slices. Place 2 in. apart on ungreased baking sheets. Bake until edges are just lightly browned, 7-9 minutes. Cool on pans 2 minutes before removing to wire racks to cool completely.
4. For frosting, in a small bowl, beat confectioners' sugar, butter, extract, salt and enough milk to reach desired consistency. Decorate cookies as desired.
Freeze option: Place wrapped logs in a freezer container; freeze. To use, unwrap frozen logs and cut into slices. If necessary, let dough stand a few minutes at room temperature before cutting. Bake and decorate cookies as directed.
1 cookie: 98 cal., 5g fat (3g sat. fat), 12mg chol., 42mg sod., 14g carb. (9g sugars, 0 fiber), 1g pro.

★ ★ ★ ★ ★ **READER REVIEW**

"Delicious! A light, crispy alternative to the usual holiday treats. Destined to become a holiday tradition in our family! I used almond extract in this recipe, and it was amazing!"
MRSK6770 TASTEOFHOME.COM

CONEY DOGS

My mom and I always make these top dogs for get-togethers. Leftovers are no problem—there never are any!
—Donna Sternthal, Sharpsville, PA

- -

Prep: 15 min. • **Cook:** 45 min.
Makes: 24 servings

- 2 lbs. ground beef
- 3 small onions, chopped
- 3 cups water
- 1 can (12 oz.) tomato paste
- 5 tsp. chili powder
- 2 tsp. rubbed sage
- 2 tsp. salt
- 1 tsp. pepper
- ½ tsp. garlic salt
- ½ tsp. dried oregano
- ¼ tsp. cayenne pepper
- 24 hot dogs, cooked
- 24 hot dog buns
  Shredded cheddar cheese, optional

1. In a Dutch oven, cook beef and onions over medium heat until meat is no longer pink, breaking it into crumbles; drain. Stir in the water, tomato paste and seasonings.
2. Cover and simmer for 30 minutes, stirring occasionally. Serve on hot dogs on buns; sprinkle with cheese if desired.
1 hot dog: 358 cal., 20g fat (8g sat. fat), 49mg chol., 962mg sod., 27g carb. (6g sugars, 2g fiber), 17g pro.

BRING IT
For easy self-service, line up the cooked hot dogs in a chafing dish and top with the hot Coney sauce. Then place the buns and toppings, such as cheese, pickles and onion, to the side.

GREEN TOMATO CHOWCHOW

My grandmom's long-cherished chowchow has Pennsylvania Dutch roots. The pickled relish of cabbage, onions and peppers is tart and sweet with a smidge of spice.
—Sharon Tipton, Casselberry, FL

- -

Prep: 20 min. • **Cook:** 1¼ hours + cooling
Makes: 10 cups

- 3 lbs. green tomatoes (about 5 medium)
- 2 Tbsp. salt
- 1 medium head cabbage
- 1 lb. onions (about 3 medium)
- 1 lb. green and sweet red peppers (about 3 medium), seeded
- 1 jalapeno pepper, seeded and chopped, optional
- 4 cups cider vinegar
- 2¾ cups sugar
- 4 tsp. mixed pickling spices

1. Chop tomatoes. Transfer to a strainer and sprinkle with salt; let stand 10 minutes. Meanwhile, chop cabbage, onions and green and red peppers. Place in a Dutch oven. Add drained tomatoes to pan and, if desired, jalapeno.
2. Stir in vinegar and sugar. Place pickling spices on a double thickness of cheesecloth. Gather the corners to enclose spices; tie securely with string. Add to pan. Bring to a boil. Reduce heat; simmer, uncovered, until thickened, stirring occasionally, 1-1½ hours. Discard spice bag. Cool to room temperature; refrigerate leftovers.
Note: Wear disposable gloves when cutting hot peppers; the oils can burn skin. Avoid touching your face.
¼ cup: 80 cal., 0 fat (0 sat. fat), 0 chol., 276mg sod., 19g carb. (17g sugars, 1g fiber), 1g pro.

APPETIZER PINWHEELS

These sophisticated appetizers made of Gruyere, prosciutto and fresh sage never fail to receive compliments. They freeze well, so make a batch to have on hand for when guests drop in.
—Shannon Koene, Blacksburg, VA

- -

Prep: 15 min. + chilling • **Bake:** 15 min.
Makes: about 5 dozen

- 2 cups shredded Gruyere or Swiss cheese
- 3 Tbsp. minced fresh sage
- 1 pkg. (17.3 oz.) frozen puff pastry, thawed
- 4 oz. thinly sliced prosciutto or deli ham

1. In a small bowl, mix cheese and sage. Unfold puff pastry; cut each pastry in half crosswise. Top each half with prosciutto and cheese mixture to within ½ in. of edges; roll up jelly-roll style, starting with a long side. Wrap tightly in waxed paper; refrigerate at least 3 hours or overnight.
2. Preheat oven to 400°. Unwrap and cut each roll crosswise into sixteen ½-in. slices. Place cut side down on greased baking sheets. Bake 14-16 minutes or until golden brown.
To make ahead: Rolls can be made 2 days in advance. Wrap rolls in waxed paper and place in a container; close tightly and store in the refrigerator.
Freeze option: Freeze wrapped rolls in a resealable freezer container. To use, unwrap frozen rolls and cut into slices. Bake as directed.
1 piece: 56 cal., 3g fat (1g sat. fat), 5mg chol., 85mg sod., 4g carb. (0 sugars, 1g fiber), 2g pro.

BACON-COLBY LASAGNA

My grandmother added bacon to her cheesy lasagna, something she borrowed from carbonara-style pasta. I learned so much by her side.
—Cathy McCartney, Davenport, IA

- -

Prep: 30 min. • **Bake:** 45 min. + standing
Makes: 2 lasagnas (12 servings each)

- 24 uncooked lasagna noodles
- 2 lbs. lean ground beef (90% lean)
- 2 medium onions, chopped
- 1½ lbs. bacon strips, cooked and crumbled
- 2 cans (15 oz. each) tomato sauce
- 2 cans (14½ oz. each) diced tomatoes, undrained
- 2 Tbsp. sugar
- 1 tsp. salt
- 8 cups shredded Colby-Monterey Jack cheese

1. Preheat oven to 350°. Cook noodles according to package directions for al dente; drain. In a 6-qt. stockpot, cook beef and onions over medium-high heat until beef is no longer pink, breaking beef into crumbles, 10-12 minutes; drain. Stir in bacon, tomato sauce, tomatoes, sugar and salt; heat through.
2. Spread 1 cup sauce into each of 2 greased 13x9-in. baking dishes. Layer each with 4 noodles, overlapping as needed, 1⅔ cups sauce and 1⅓ cups cheese. Repeat layers twice.
3. Bake, covered, 40 minutes. Uncover; bake until bubbly, 5-10 minutes longer. Let stand 15 minutes before serving.
Freeze option: Cool unbaked lasagnas; cover and freeze. To use, partially thaw in refrigerator overnight. Remove from refrigerator 30 minutes before baking. Preheat oven to 350°. Bake the lasagna as directed, increasing time as necessary to heat through and for a thermometer inserted in center to read 165°.
1 piece: 357 cal., 18g fat (11g sat. fat), 67mg chol., 744mg sod., 25g carb. (4g sugars, 2g fiber), 23g pro.

APPETIZER PINWHEELS

These sophisticated appetizers made of Gruyere, prosciutto and fresh sage never fail to receive compliments.
They freeze well, so make a batch to have on hand for when guests drop in.
—Shannon Koene, Blacksburg, VA

- -

Prep: 15 min. + chilling • **Bake:** 15 min.
Makes: about 5 dozen

  2 **cups shredded Gruyere or Swiss cheese**
  3 **Tbsp. minced fresh sage**
  1 **pkg. (17.3 oz.) frozen puff pastry, thawed**
  4 **oz. thinly sliced prosciutto or deli ham**

1. In a small bowl, mix cheese and sage. Unfold puff pastry; cut each pastry in half crosswise. Top each half with prosciutto and cheese mixture to within ½ in. of edges; roll up jelly-roll style, starting with a long side. Wrap tightly in waxed paper; refrigerate at least 3 hours or overnight.
2. Preheat oven to 400°. Unwrap and cut each roll crosswise into sixteen ½-in. slices. Place cut side down on greased baking sheets. Bake 14-16 minutes or until golden brown.
To make ahead: Rolls can be made 2 days in advance. Wrap rolls in waxed paper and place in a container; close tightly and store in the refrigerator.
Freeze option: Freeze wrapped rolls in a resealable freezer container. To use, unwrap frozen rolls and cut into slices. Bake as directed.
1 piece: 56 cal., 3g fat (1g sat. fat), 5mg chol., 85mg sod., 4g carb. (0 sugars, 1g fiber), 2g pro.

BACON-COLBY LASAGNA

My grandmother added bacon to her cheesy lasagna, something she borrowed from carbonara-style pasta. I learned so much by her side.
—Cathy McCartney, Davenport, IA

- -

Prep: 30 min. • **Bake:** 45 min. + standing
Makes: 2 lasagnas (12 servings each)

 24 **uncooked lasagna noodles**
  2 **lbs. lean ground beef (90% lean)**
  2 **medium onions, chopped**
1½ **lbs. bacon strips, cooked and crumbled**
  2 **cans (15 oz. each) tomato sauce**
  2 **cans (14½ oz. each) diced tomatoes, undrained**
  2 **Tbsp. sugar**
  1 **tsp. salt**
  8 **cups shredded Colby-Monterey Jack cheese**

1. Preheat oven to 350°. Cook noodles according to package directions for al dente; drain. In a 6-qt. stockpot, cook beef and onions over medium-high heat until beef is no longer pink, breaking beef into crumbles, 10-12 minutes; drain. Stir in bacon, tomato sauce, tomatoes, sugar and salt; heat through.
2. Spread 1 cup sauce into each of 2 greased 13x9-in. baking dishes. Layer each with 4 noodles, overlapping as needed, 1⅔ cups sauce and 1⅓ cups cheese. Repeat layers twice.
3. Bake, covered, 40 minutes. Uncover; bake until bubbly, 5-10 minutes longer. Let stand 15 minutes before serving.
Freeze option: Cool unbaked lasagnas; cover and freeze. To use, partially thaw in refrigerator overnight. Remove from refrigerator 30 minutes before baking. Preheat oven to 350°. Bake the lasagna as directed, increasing time as necessary to heat through and for a thermometer inserted in center to read 165°.
1 piece: 357 cal., 18g fat (11g sat. fat), 67mg chol., 744mg sod., 25g carb. (4g sugars, 2g fiber), 23g pro.

CRANBERRY-ORANGE VODKA SLUSH

Years ago, my mother made a rosy and refreshing party drink I've never forgotten. The sparkle comes from fruit juices, vodka and lemon lime soda.
—Melinda Strable, Ankeny, IA

- -

Prep: 15 min. + freezing • **Makes:** 24 servings

- 9 **cups water**
- 2 **cups sugar**
- 1 **can (12 oz.) frozen cranberry juice concentrate, partially thawed**
- 1 **can (12 oz.) frozen orange juice concentrate, partially thawed**
- ¾ **cup thawed lemonade concentrate**
- 2 **cups vodka**
- 8 **cups lemon-lime soda, chilled**

1. In a 5-qt. bowl, mix water and sugar until sugar is dissolved. Stir in the juice concentrates and vodka until blended. Transfer to freezer containers, allowing headspace for expansion; freeze overnight.
2. To serve, place ⅔ cup slush in each glass. Add ⅓ cup soda.
1 cup: 210 cal., 0 fat (0 sat. fat), 0 chol., 10mg sod., 43g carb. (39g sugars, 0 fiber), 0 pro.

★ ★ ★ ★ ★ **READER REVIEW**

"Didn't make any changes, and this is one of my favorite drink recipes! Perfect for groups, and to keep handy in the freezer and enjoy over time. Fabulous!"

NHATALSKY TASTEOFHOME.COM

DRIED CHERRY & SAUSAGE DRESSING

Apples and dried cherries add a sweet-tart flavor to my homemade stuffing. It makes a holiday dinner memorable.
—Connie Boll, Chilton, WI

- -

Prep: 40 min. • **Bake:** 45 min.
Makes: 20 servings

- 1 **loaf (1 lb.) unsliced Italian bread**
- ¼ **cup cherry juice blend or unsweetened apple juice**
- 1 **cup dried cherries**
- 1 **lb. bulk Italian sausage**
- 2 **celery ribs, chopped**
- 1 **medium onion, chopped**
- 2 **medium Granny Smith apples, chopped**
- ½ **cup chopped fresh parsley**
- ½ **cup butter, melted**
- 1 **tsp. Italian seasoning**
- 1 **tsp. fennel seed**
- 1 **tsp. rubbed sage**
- ½ **tsp. salt**
- ¼ **tsp. pepper**
- 2 **large eggs**
- 2 **cups chicken stock**

1. Preheat oven to 375°. Cut bread into 1-in. cubes; transfer to two 15x10x1-in. baking pans. Bake 10-15 minutes or until toasted. Cool slightly. In a small saucepan, bring juice to a boil. Stir in cherries. Remove from heat; let stand 10 minutes. Drain.
2. Meanwhile, in a large skillet, cook the sausage, celery and onion over medium heat 8-10 minutes or until sausage is no longer pink and vegetables are tender, breaking sausage into crumbles; drain. Transfer to a large bowl; stir in apples, parsley, butter, seasonings, bread cubes and drained cherries. In a small bowl, whisk eggs and stock; pour over bread mixture and toss to coat.
3. Transfer to a greased 13x9-in. baking dish (dish will be full). Bake, covered, 30 minutes. Bake, uncovered, until golden brown, 15-20 minutes longer.
¾ cup: 204 cal., 11g fat (5g sat. fat), 43mg chol., 422mg sod., 21g carb. (8g sugars, 1g fiber), 6g pro.

RED VELVET CAKE BITES

Everyone loves red velvet, but any cake mix can work with this recipe. I've even rolled chopped macadamia nuts into pineapple cake and dipped them in white chocolate. Whatever you do, have fun!
—Anne Powers, Munford, AL

- -

Prep: 45 min. + chilling
Bake: 25 min. + cooling
Makes: 5 dozen

1   pkg. red velvet cake mix
    (regular size)
1   can (16 oz.) cream cheese frosting
1   lb. each white, milk chocolate and
    dark chocolate candy coating

1. Prepare and bake cake mix according to package directions using a 13x9-in. baking pan. Cool completely.
2. Crumble cake into a large bowl. Add frosting; beat well. Refrigerate until easy to handle, 1 hour. Shape into 1½-in. balls; transfer to waxed paper-lined baking sheets. Refrigerate at least 1 hour.
3. In a microwave, melt the white candy coating; stir until smooth. Dip 20 cake balls in coating; allow excess to drip off. Return to baking sheets; let stand until set. Repeat with milk chocolate and dark chocolate coatings and remaining cake balls. If desired, drizzle with additional candy coating. Store in airtight containers.
Freeze option: Freeze uncoated cake balls in freezer containers, layered between waxed paper. To use, thaw in covered containers. Dip in coatings as directed.

1 cake ball: 206 cal., 11g fat (7g sat. fat), 11mg chol., 79mg sod., 28g carb. (24g sugars, 0 fiber), 1g pro.

BAKED HAM WITH PINEAPPLE

I first learned the technique for cooking ham with pineapple for a themed dinner that my husband and I hosted. Since it was widely known as the symbol of hospitality, pineapple was the star ingredient on our menu and on this lovely baked ham.
—JoAnn Fox, Johnson City, TN

- -

Prep: 15 min. • **Bake:** 2 hours
Makes: 20 servings

1   fully cooked bone-in ham (6 to 8 lbs.)
     Whole cloves
1   can (20 oz.) sliced pineapple
½   cup packed brown sugar
12   maraschino cherries

1. Place ham in roasting pan. Score the surface with shallow diagonal cuts, making diamond shapes; insert cloves into diamonds.
2. Cover and bake at 325° for 1½ hours. Drain pineapple, reserving ¼ cup juice. Combine the brown sugar and reserved pineapple juice; pour over ham. Arrange pineapple slices and cherries on ham. Bake, uncovered, 30-45 minutes longer or until a thermometer reads 140° and the ham is heated through.
3 oz. cooked ham: 219 cal., 13g fat (5g sat. fat), 48mg chol., 924mg sod., 8g carb. (8g sugars, 0 fiber), 17g pro.

CREAMY GRAPE SALAD

Everyone raves when I bring this refreshing, creamy salad to potlucks. For a special finishing touch, sprinkle it with brown sugar and pecans.
—Marge Elling, Jenison, MI

Takes: 20 min. • **Makes:** 24 servings

- 1 pkg. (8 oz.) cream cheese, softened
- 1 cup sour cream
- ⅓ cup sugar
- 2 tsp. vanilla extract
- 2 lbs. seedless red grapes
- 2 lbs. seedless green grapes
- 3 Tbsp. brown sugar
- 3 Tbsp. chopped pecans

1. In a large bowl, beat cream cheese, sour cream, sugar and vanilla until blended. Add grapes and toss to coat.
2. Transfer to a serving bowl. Cover and refrigerate until serving. Sprinkle with brown sugar and pecans just before serving.

¾ cup: 131 cal., 6g fat (3g sat. fat), 17mg chol., 35mg sod., 19g carb. (18g sugars, 1g fiber), 2g pro.

RICH CLAM CHOWDER

I came across a chowder recipe I liked several years ago. I've made just enough changes to give it a unique flavor, and now it can feed a pretty large crowd. People always go back for seconds; then they ask for the recipe.
—Teresa Dastrup, Meridian, ID

- -

Prep: 45 min. • **Cook:** 25 min.
Makes: 22 servings

6	cups diced peeled red potatoes
3	large onions, finely chopped
6	celery ribs, finely chopped
3	cups water
6	cans (6½ oz. each) minced clams
1½	cups butter, cubed
1½	cups all-purpose flour
8	cups half-and-half cream
¼	cup red wine vinegar
2	Tbsp. minced fresh parsley
3	tsp. salt
¼	tsp. pepper

1. In a stockpot, combine the potatoes, onions, celery and water. Drain clams, reserving juice; set clams aside. Add juice to potato mixture. Bring to a boil. Reduce the heat; cover and simmer for 10 minutes or until potatoes are tender.
2. Meanwhile, in a large saucepan, melt butter over medium heat. Whisk in flour. Cook and stir for 5 minutes or until lightly browned. Gradually stir in cream. Bring to a boil; cook and stir for 2 minutes or until thickened. Gradually stir into the potato mixture.
3. Add the vinegar, parsley, salt, pepper and clams. Cook 5-10 minutes longer or until heated through.
1 cup: 318 cal., 21g fat (14g sat. fat), 85mg chol., 675mg sod., 20g carb. (5g sugars, 1g fiber), 8g pro.

WATERMELON BASKET

I cut a watermelon into a basket shape and then fill it with melon balls to serve with a creamy dip.
—Christine Johnson, Ricetown, KY

Prep: 30 min. + chilling
Makes: 32 servings (about 1⅓ cups dip)

- 1 large watermelon (10 lbs.)
- 1 medium honeydew, cut into balls
- 3 cups white cranberry juice
- 1 cup light corn syrup
- 2 Tbsp. lime juice

FRUIT DIP

- 1 pkg. (8 oz.) cream cheese, softened
- ¼ cup 2% milk
- 3 Tbsp. sugar
- 3 Tbsp. lemon juice
- ¾ tsp. ground cardamom

1. With a sharp knife, cut a thin slice from the bottom of the watermelon so it sits flat. Mark a horizontal cutting line 2 in. above center and around the melon.
2. For handle, score a 1½-in.-wide strip across top of melon, connecting both sides to horizontal line. With a long sharp knife, cut all the way through the rind above the cutting line in a zigzag pattern.
3. Carefully lift off the side pieces. Remove fruit from both sections and cut into balls. Refrigerate the basket.
4. In a large bowl, combine watermelon and honeydew balls. In another bowl, whisk cranberry juice, corn syrup and lime juice until blended; pour over melon balls. Cover and chill for 3 hours.
5. Drain; spoon melon into watermelon basket. In a small bowl, beat the cream cheese and milk until smooth. Beat in the sugar, lemon juice and cardamom; serve with melon.
1 serving: 127 cal., 3g fat (2g sat. fat), 8mg chol., 41mg sod., 25g carb. (22g sugars, 1g fiber), 2g pro.

MAKE AHEAD

DULCE DE LECHE HOT CHOCOLATE PODS

Give your friends a little heaven in a cup with these divine hot chocolate pods. Just add hot milk and stir.
—*Taste of Home* Test Kitchen

Prep: 20 min. + chilling • **Cook:** 5 min.
Makes: 14 pods (2 servings per pod)

- 24 oz. 53% cacao dark baking chocolate or semisweet chocolate, chopped
- 1 can (13.4 oz.) dulce de leche
- ½ cup heavy whipping cream
  Optional: Gold colored sugar and gold pearl dust

ADDITIONAL INGREDIENT (FOR EACH POD)

- 1½ cups whole milk

1. Place chocolate in a large bowl. In a small saucepan, bring dulce de leche and cream just to a boil, stirring constantly. Pour over chocolate; whisk until smooth.
2. Spoon ¼ cup chocolate mixture into each of 14 paper-lined muffin cups; if desired, sprinkle with the gold sugar. Refrigerate until firm, about 8 hours. If desired, brush with gold dust. Store in an airtight container in refrigerator for up to 3 weeks.
3. To prepare hot chocolate: Bring 1½ cups milk just to a boil; add 1 pod. Whisk until dissolved.
¾ cup: 289 cal., 17g fat (10g sat. fat), 28mg chol., 100mg sod., 30g carb. (26g sugars, 2g fiber), 8g pro.

SOUR CREAM POUND CAKE

Because I'm our town's postmaster, I can bake only in my spare time. I especially enjoy making desserts like this one. It tastes amazing as is, or tuck it under ice cream and chocolate syrup like a hot fudge sundae!
—Karen Conrad, East Troy, WI

- -

Prep: 15 min. • **Bake:** 1¼ hours + cooling
Makes: 20 servings

1 cup butter, softened
3 cups sugar
6 large eggs, room temperature
3 cups all-purpose flour
¼ tsp. baking soda
¼ tsp. salt
1 cup sour cream
2 tsp. vanilla extract
    Confectioners' sugar, optional

1. In a bowl, cream butter and sugar until light and fluffy, 5-7 minutes. Add eggs, 1 at a time, beating well after each addition. Combine flour, baking soda and salt; add to creamed mixture alternately with sour cream and vanilla. Beat on low just until blended. Pour into a greased and floured 10-in. fluted tube pan.

2. Bake at 325° for 1¼-1½ hours or until a toothpick comes out clean. Cool in pan 15 minutes before removing to a wire rack to cool completely. Sprinkle with confectioners' sugar if desired.

1 piece: 311 cal., 13g fat (7g sat. fat), 96mg chol., 163mg sod., 45g carb. (30g sugars, 1g fiber), 4g pro.

★ ★ ★ ★ ★ **READER REVIEW**

"So scrumptious! Turned out perfectly. I made a confectioners' sugar glaze, and it was delicious. Will be my go-to pound cake!"

EMILYHERRERA TASTEOFHOME.COM

FESTIVE MEAT LOAF PINWHEEL

Dress up meat loaf for a dinner during the holiday week when company's in town! This crowd-sized pinwheel features ham, Swiss cheese and a homemade tomato sauce.
—Vera Sullivan, Amity, OR

- -

Prep: 20 min. • **Bake:** 1¼ hours
Makes: 20 servings

 3 large eggs
 1 cup dry bread crumbs
 ½ cup finely chopped onion
 ½ cup finely chopped green pepper
 ¼ cup ketchup
 2 tsp. minced fresh parsley
 1 tsp. dried basil
 1 tsp. dried oregano
 1 garlic clove, minced
 2 tsp. salt
 ½ tsp. pepper
 5 lbs. lean ground beef
    (90% lean)
 ¾ lb. thinly sliced deli ham
 ¾ lb. thinly sliced Swiss cheese

TOMATO PEPPER SAUCE
 ½ cup finely chopped onion
 2 celery ribs, chopped
 ½ cup chopped green pepper
 1 garlic clove, minced
 1 to 2 tsp. olive oil
 2 cups chopped fresh tomatoes
 1 cup beef broth
 1 bay leaf
 1 tsp. sugar
 ¼ tsp. salt
 ¼ tsp. dried thyme
 1 Tbsp. cornstarch
 2 Tbsp. cold water

1. Preheat oven to 350°. In a large bowl, combine the first 11 ingredients. Crumble the beef over mixture and mix lightly but thoroughly. On a piece of heavy-duty foil, pat beef mixture into a 17x15-in. rectangle. Cover with ham and cheese slices to within ½ in. of edges.

2. Roll up tightly jelly-roll style, starting with a short side. Place seam side down in a roasting pan. Bake, uncovered, until a thermometer reads 160°, 1¼-1½ hours.

3. In a large saucepan, saute the onion, celery, green pepper and garlic in oil until tender, 3-5 minutes. Add tomatoes, broth, bay leaf, sugar, salt and thyme. Simmer, uncovered, 30 minutes. Discard bay leaf.

4. Combine cornstarch and water until smooth; stir into sauce. Bring to a boil; cook and stir until thickened, about 2 minutes. Drain meat loaf. Serve with sauce.

1 slice: 319 cal., 17g fat (7g sat. fat), 124mg chol., 732mg sod., 8g carb. (2g sugars, 1g fiber), 32g pro.

PEANUT BUTTER GRANOLA MINI BARS

Kids will flip over this deliciously oaty, sweet snack! I mean, what's not to love about peanut butter-honey-oatmeal bars? And at fewer than 100 calories, you can afford to have seconds.
—Vivian Levine, Summerfield, FL

- -

Prep: 20 min. • **Bake:** 15 min. + cooling
Makes: 3 dozen

½ cup reduced-fat
   creamy peanut butter
⅓ cup honey
1 large egg
2 Tbsp. canola oil
1 tsp. vanilla extract
3½ cups old-fashioned oats
½ cup packed brown sugar
¾ tsp. salt
⅓ cup peanut butter chips
⅓ cup miniature semisweet
   chocolate chips

1. Preheat oven to 350°. In a large bowl, beat the peanut butter, honey, egg, oil and vanilla until blended. Combine oats, brown sugar and salt; add to the peanut butter mixture and mix well. Stir in chips. (Batter will be sticky.)
2. Press into a greased 13x9-in. baking pan. Bake until mixture is set and edges are lightly browned, 12-15 minutes. Cool on a wire rack. Cut into bars.
1 piece: 96 cal., 4g fat (1g sat. fat), 5mg chol., 78mg sod., 14g carb. (8g sugars, 1g fiber), 3g pro. **Diabetic exchanges:** 1 starch, 1 fat.

BAKED BEANS WITH PINEAPPLE

This marvelous recipe is a staple at our neighborhood's annual barbecue.
—J. Hindson, Victoria, BC

- -

Prep: 25 min. • **Bake:** 45 min.
Makes: 30 servings

1 lb. bacon strips, diced
1 large onion, chopped
3 cans (two 55 oz., one 28 oz.)
   baked beans
2 cans (one 20 oz., one 8 oz.) crushed
   pineapple, drained
½ cup packed brown sugar
½ cup ketchup

1. In a large skillet, cook the bacon over medium heat until crisp. Remove with a slotted spoon to paper towels. Drain, reserving 2 Tbsp. drippings. Saute onion in drippings until tender.
2. In a very large bowl, combine beans, pineapple, bacon and onion. Combine brown sugar and ketchup; stir into the bean mixture.
3. Transfer to 2 greased 3-qt. or 13x9-in. baking dishes. Cover and bake at 350° for 20 minutes. Uncover; bake 25-35 minutes longer or until bubbly and beans reach desired thickness.
½ cup: 266 cal., 10g fat (3g sat. fat), 22mg chol., 830mg sod., 37g carb. (18g sugars, 8g fiber), 12g pro.

> **TEST KITCHEN TIP**
> These smoky, slightly sweet beans will be popular with everyone—including the kiddos.

EASY MACARONI SALAD

This hearty pasta salad is sure to please appetites of all ages—and it serves a lot of folks!
—LaVerna Mjones, Moorhead, MN

Prep: 15 min. + chilling
Makes: 34 servings

- 2 lbs. uncooked elbow macaroni
- 12 hard-boiled large eggs, chopped
- 2½ lbs. fully cooked ham, cubed
- 1 pkg. (16 oz.) frozen peas, thawed
- 3 cups sliced celery
- 1 large green pepper, chopped
- ½ cup chopped onion
- 1 jar (4 oz.) diced pimientos, drained
- 4 cups mayonnaise

1. Cook macaroni according to package directions. Rinse in cold water; drain and cool completely.

2. Place in a large bowl; stir in remaining ingredients. Cover and refrigerate for at least 3 hours.

1 cup: 380 cal., 26g fat (4g sat. fat), 102mg chol., 615mg sod., 23g carb. (2g sugars, 2g fiber), 13g pro.

★ ★ ★ ★ ★ **READER REVIEW**

"It was very good! I cut the recipe in half and it could still feed a small army. I added horseradish sauce, deli mustard, ground pepper and relish for some extra kick. It is a keeper."

JEFFODAVIS TASTEOFHOME.COM

MAKE-AHEAD MEATBALLS

My husband and I have visitors often. Keeping a supply of these frozen meatballs on hand means I can easily prepare a quick, satisfying meal. I start with a versatile meatball mix that makes about 12 dozen meatballs, then freeze them in batches for future use.
—Ruth Andrewson, Leavenworth, WA

Prep: 30 min. • **Bake:** 10 min.
Makes: 5 batches
(about 30 meatballs per batch)

- 4 **large eggs, lightly beaten**
- 2 **cups dry bread crumbs**
- ½ **cup finely chopped onion**
- 1 **Tbsp. salt**
- 2 **tsp. Worcestershire sauce**
- ½ **tsp. white pepper**
- 4 **lbs. lean ground beef (90% lean)**

1. Preheat oven to 400°. In a large bowl, combine the first 6 ingredients. Crumble the beef over mixture and mix well. Shape into 1-in. balls, about 12 dozen.
2. Place meatballs on greased racks in shallow baking pans. Bake 10-15 minutes or until no longer pink, turning often; drain. Cool.
Freeze option: Freeze cooled meatballs in freezer containers. To use, partially thaw in refrigerator overnight. Reheat on a greased 15x10x1-in. baking pan in a preheated 350° oven until heated through.
5 meatballs: 134 cal., 6g fat (2g sat. fat), 62mg chol., 334mg sod., 6g carb. (1g sugars, 0 fiber), 14g protein. **Diabetic exchanges:** 2 lean meat, ½ starch.

BIG-BATCH MARINARA SAUCE

I typically freeze part of this marinara sauce to have on hand for guests or when I'm craving a comforting pasta dish. It adds a fresh, herby layer of flavor.
—Cyndy Gerken, Naples, FL

Prep: 25 min. • **Cook:** 2¼ hours
Makes: 6 qt.

- 4 **large onions, chopped**
- 2 **Tbsp. olive oil**
- 10 **garlic cloves, minced**
- 4 **cans (28 oz. each) crushed tomatoes**
- 7 **cans (15 oz. each) tomato sauce**
- 2 **cans (6 oz. each) tomato paste**
- 1 **cup grated Parmesan cheese**
- 1 **cup minced fresh parsley**
- ¾ **cup minced fresh basil or**
     ¼ cup dried basil
- 2 **Tbsp. minced fresh oregano or**
     2 tsp. dried oregano
- 2 **Tbsp. herbes de Provence or**
     Italian seasoning
     Hot cooked spaghetti

1. In a stockpot, saute onions in oil until tender. Add garlic; cook 2 minutes longer. Add the crushed tomatoes, tomato sauce, tomato paste, cheese and herbs. Bring to a boil. Reduce heat; simmer, uncovered, for 2-3 hours or until desired consistency, stirring occasionally.
2. Serve desired amount over spaghetti.
Freeze option: Cool remaining sauce; transfer to freezer containers. Freeze for up to 3 months. Thaw in refrigerator overnight. Place in a saucepan and heat through.
Note: Look for herbes de Provence in the spice aisle.
¾ cup: 94 cal., 2g fat (1g sat. fat), 2mg chol., 605mg sod., 16g carb. (3g sugars, 4g fiber), 5g pro. **Diabetic exchanges:** 2 vegetable, ½ starch.

CALIFORNIA ROLLS

This tastes as good as any restaurant or store-bought California roll. Plus, it's one of the easiest sushi recipes to make! For the best results, use sushi rice to ensure the right sticky consistency.
—*Taste of Home* Test Kitchen

Prep: 1 hour + standing • **Makes:** 64 pieces

- 2 **cups sushi rice, rinsed and drained**
- 2 **cups water**
- ¼ **cup rice vinegar**
- 2 **Tbsp. sugar**
- ½ **tsp. salt**
- 2 **Tbsp. sesame seeds, toasted**
- 2 **Tbsp. black sesame seeds**
   Bamboo sushi mat
- 8 **nori sheets**
- 1 **small cucumber, seeded and julienned**
- 3 **oz. imitation crabmeat sticks, julienned**
- 1 **medium ripe avocado, peeled and julienned**
   Optional: Reduced-sodium soy sauce, prepared wasabi and pickled ginger slices

1. In a large saucepan, combine rice and water; let stand for 30 minutes. Bring to a boil. Reduce heat to low; cover and simmer for 15-20 minutes or until water is absorbed and rice is tender. Remove from the heat. Let stand, covered, for 10 minutes.

2. Meanwhile, in small bowl, combine the vinegar, sugar and salt, stirring until sugar is dissolved.

3. Transfer rice to a large shallow bowl; drizzle with vinegar mixture. With a wooden paddle or spoon, stir the rice with a slicing motion to cool slightly. Cover with a damp cloth to keep moist. (Rice mixture may be made up to 2 hours ahead and stored at room temperature, covered with a damp towel. Do not refrigerate.)

4. Sprinkle toasted and black sesame seeds onto a plate; set aside. Place sushi mat on a work surface so mat rolls away from you; line with plastic wrap. Place ¾ cup rice on plastic. With moistened fingers, press rice into an 8-in. square. Top with 1 nori sheet.

5. Arrange a small amount of cucumber, crab and avocado about 1½ in. from bottom edge of nori sheet. Roll up rice mixture over filling, using bamboo mat to lift and compress mixture while rolling; remove plastic wrap as you roll.

6. Remove mat; roll sushi rolls in sesame seeds. Cover with plastic wrap. Repeat with remaining ingredients to make 8 rolls. Cut each into 8 pieces. Serve with soy sauce, wasabi and ginger slices if desired.

1 piece: 35 cal., 1g fat (0 sat. fat), 0 chol., 30mg sod., 6g carb. (1g sugars, 1g fiber), 1g pro. **Diabetic exchanges:** ½ starch.

TEST KITCHEN TIP
Wasabi, a Japanese version of horseradish, is bright green in color and has a sharp, pungent and fiery-hot flavor. It is traditionally used as a condiment with sushi and sashimi. Today, many western sauces, mustards and other condiments are seasoned with wasabi. Wasabi powder and paste are available in the Asian food section of the grocery store.

SICILIAN POTATO SALAD

Fresh basil is the star of this mayo-free, Italian-inspired take on potato salad. It's sure to be popular.

—Sue Falk, Sterling Heights, MI

Prep: 20 min. • **Cook:** 20 min.
Makes: 26 servings

- 10 small russet potatoes, unpeeled
- 1½ tsp. salt, divided
- ½ lb. fresh green beans, cut into 1½-in. pieces
- ¼ tsp. pepper
- 2 medium cucumbers, halved lengthwise and cut into ¼-in. slices
- ½ lb. cherry tomatoes, halved
- 1 large red onion, halved and thinly sliced
- 1 cup thinly sliced fresh basil leaves, divided
- ½ cup olive oil
- 4 Tbsp. cider vinegar
- 3 garlic cloves, minced

1. Place potatoes and ½ tsp. salt in a Dutch oven; add water to cover. Bring to a boil. Reduce heat; cook, uncovered, until tender, 12-15 minutes. Drain; rinse with cold water. Pat dry.
2. Meanwhile, in a small saucepan, bring 1 cup water to a boil. Add the beans; cook, uncovered, just until crisp-tender, 3-4 minutes. Drain; immediately drop into ice water. Drain and pat dry.
3. Peel and cube potatoes; sprinkle with remaining salt and the pepper. Transfer to a serving bowl. Add beans, cucumbers, tomatoes, onion and ¾ cup basil leaves. Whisk together oil, vinegar and garlic. Drizzle over vegetables; toss to coat. Sprinkle with remaining basil.

¾ cup: 96 cal., 4g fat (1g sat. fat), 0 chol., 143mg sod., 13g carb. (2g sugars, 2g fiber), 2g pro. **Diabetic exchanges:** 1 starch, 1 fat.

CREAMY BUFFALO CHICKEN DIP

This slightly spicy dip cleverly captures the flavor of Buffalo chicken wings. Using canned chicken eases preparation.

—Allyson DiLascio, Saltsburg, PA

Takes: 30 min. • **Makes:** 5 cups

- 1 pkg. (8 oz.) cream cheese, softened
- 1 cup Louisiana-style hot sauce
- 1 cup ranch salad dressing
- 3 cans (4½ oz. each) chunk white chicken, drained and shredded
- 1 cup shredded cheddar cheese
  Thinly sliced green onions, optional
  Corn or tortilla chips
  Celery sticks

1. In a small bowl, combine the cream cheese, hot sauce and salad dressing. Stir in chicken.
2. Spread into an ungreased 11x7-in. baking dish. Sprinkle with cheddar cheese. Bake, uncovered, at 350° for 20-22 minutes or until heated through. If desired, sprinkle with green onions. Serve with chips and celery sticks.

2 Tbsp.: 69 cal., 6g fat (2g sat. fat), 15mg chol., 156mg sod., 1g carb. (0 sugars, 0 fiber), 3g pro.

So-Easy Sticky
Chicken Wings
page 188

Slow Cooker

Have slow cooker, will travel! Dig in to dozens of irresistible dishes, perfect for sharing, in this chapter. Nothing beats a slow-cooked recipe for potlucks.

MOROCCAN LAMB LETTUCE WRAPS

I am a huge fan of both lamb and lettuce wraps. This combination—with the creamy dressing and crunchy cucumber— makes a tasty slow-cooked dish. The wine and chili powder add extra flavor elements, too.

—Arlene Erlbach, Morton Grove, IL

- -

Prep: 25 min. • **Cook:** 5 hours
Makes: 8 servings

- 2 lbs. lamb stew meat
- 1 cup chunky salsa
- ⅓ cup apricot preserves
- 6 Tbsp. dry red wine, divided
- 1 to 2 Tbsp. Moroccan seasoning (ras el hanout)
- 2 tsp. chili powder
- ½ tsp. garlic powder
- 1 English cucumber, very thinly sliced
- 2 Tbsp. prepared ranch salad dressing
- 16 Bibb or Boston lettuce leaves

1. Combine lamb, salsa, preserves, 4 Tbsp. wine, Moroccan seasoning, chili powder and garlic powder. Transfer to a 3-qt. slow cooker. Cook, covered, on low 5-6 hours, until lamb is tender. Remove lamb; shred with 2 forks. Strain cooking juices and skim fat. Return lamb and cooking juices to slow cooker; heat through. Stir in remaining 2 Tbsp. wine; heat through.
2. Combine cucumber and ranch dressing; toss to coat. Serve lamb mixture in lettuce leaves; top with cucumber mixture.

2 filled lettuce wraps: 221 cal., 8g fat (2g sat. fat), 74mg chol., 257mg sod., 13g carb. (8g sugars, 1g fiber), 24g pro.
Diabetic exchanges: 3 lean meat, 1 starch.

VEGETARIAN BUFFALO DIP

A friend made Buffalo chicken dip and that got me thinking about creating a vegetarian dip with the same flavors. This addictive dip is so amazing, no one will miss the meat.

—Amanda Silvers, Oldfort, TN

Prep: 10 min. • **Cook:** 1½ hours
Makes: 6 cups

- 1 cup sour cream
- 8 oz. cream cheese, softened
- 1 envelope ranch salad dressing mix
- 2 cups shredded sharp cheddar cheese
- 1 can (15 oz.) black beans, rinsed and drained
- 8 oz. fresh mushrooms, chopped
- 1 cup Buffalo wing sauce
  Optional: Sliced green onions and tortilla chips

Combine sour cream, cream cheese and ranch dressing mix in a bowl until smooth. Stir in the next 4 ingredients. Transfer to a 3- or 4-qt. slow cooker. Cook, covered, on high 1½ hours. If desired, sprinkle with green onions and serve with tortilla chips.
¼ cup: 113 cal., 8g fat (5g sat. fat), 21mg chol., 526mg sod., 5g carb. (1g sugars, 1g fiber), 4g pro.

4. Remove roast; shred with 2 forks. Strain cooking juices. Reserve vegetables and 1 cup juices; discard remaining juices. Skim fat from reserved juices. Return pork and reserved vegetables and cooking juices to slow cooker; heat through. Serve on buns with avocado and mayonnaise mixture.

Freeze option: Place shredded pork and vegetables in freezer containers; top with cooking juices. Cool and freeze. To use, partially thaw in the refrigerator overnight. Heat through in a covered saucepan, stirring gently. Add a little broth if necessary.

1 sandwich: 484 cal., 29g fat (7g sat. fat), 71mg chol., 400mg sod., 36g carb. (15g sugars, 3g fiber), 18g pro.

GREEN OLIVE DIP

Olive fans will love this dip. It's cheesy and full of beef and beans. It could even be used as a filling for taco shells.
—Beth Dunahay, Lima, OH

Prep: 30 min. • **Cook:** 3 hours
Makes: 8 cups

- 1 lb. ground beef
- 1 medium sweet red pepper, chopped
- 1 small onion, chopped
- 1 can (16 oz.) refried beans
- 1 jar (16 oz.) mild salsa
- 2 cups shredded part-skim mozzarella cheese
- 2 cups shredded cheddar cheese
- 1 jar (5¾ oz.) sliced green olives with pimientos, drained
  Tortilla chips

1. In a large skillet, cook beef, pepper and onion over medium heat until meat is no longer pink, breaking it into crumbles; drain.
2. Transfer to a greased 3-qt. slow cooker. Add the beans, salsa, cheeses and olives. Cover and cook on low 3-4 hours or until cheese is melted, stirring occasionally. Serve with chips.

¼ cup: 96 cal., 6g fat (3g sat. fat), 21mg chol., 262mg sod., 4g carb. (1g sugars, 1g fiber), 7g pro.

MAKE AHEAD

MIDNIGHT CARIBBEAN PORK SANDWICHES

These sandwiches are so tasty! They have depth of flavor—savory, sweet, piquant, subtle and sublime. They're also super easy to make and worth the (slow-cooker) wait.
—Elizabeth Bennett, Mill Creek, WA

Prep: 25 min. • **Cook:** 6 hours
Makes: 12 servings

- 1 Tbsp. canola oil
- 3 medium onions, cut into ½-in. slices
- 1 bottle (12 oz.) amber beer or 1½ cups chicken broth
- ¼ cup packed brown sugar
- 10 garlic cloves, minced and divided
- 2 Tbsp. ground cumin
- 7 tsp. minced chipotle peppers in adobo sauce, divided
- ½ tsp. salt
- ½ tsp. pepper
- 1 boneless pork shoulder butt roast (2 to 3 lbs.)
- 1 cup mayonnaise
- ½ cup minced fresh cilantro
- 12 Hawaiian sweet hamburger buns
- 2 medium ripe avocados, peeled and sliced

1. In a large skillet, heat canola oil over medium-high heat. Add onions; cook and stir until tender, 6-8 minutes. Add beer, brown sugar, 8 garlic cloves, cumin, 5 tsp. chipotle peppers, salt and pepper; cook and stir until combined.
2. Place pork roast in a 5- or 6-qt. slow cooker. Pour onion mixture over meat. Cook, covered, on low 6-8 hours, until pork is tender.
3. Meanwhile, combine mayonnaise, cilantro, remaining 2 garlic cloves and chipotle peppers. Cover and refrigerate until serving.

CILANTRO & LIME CHICKEN WITH SCOOPS

I came up with this recipe when I was preparing for a large party and I wanted a healthy Tex-Mex chicken to serve in tortilla cups. You can make this party dish ahead of time to free yourself for time-sensitive dishes. Serve it in tortilla chip cups or any other savory crispy cup you like. Enjoy leftovers over salad greens or wrapped up in tender tortillas for burritos.
—Lori C. Terry, Chicago, IL

- -

Prep: 15 min. • **Cook:** 3½ hours
Makes: 16 servings (4 cups)

1 lb. boneless skinless chicken breasts
2 tsp. chili powder
2 Tbsp. lime juice
1½ cups frozen petite corn (about 5 oz.), thawed
1½ cups chunky salsa
1½ cups (6 oz.) finely shredded cheddar cheese
1 medium sweet red pepper, finely chopped
4 green onions, thinly sliced
Minced fresh cilantro
Baked tortilla chip scoops

1. Place chicken in a 1½-qt. slow cooker; sprinkle with chili powder and lime juice.

Cook, covered, on low 3-4 hours or until chicken is tender.

Remove chicken; discard cooking juices. Shred chicken with 2 forks; return to slow cooker. Add corn and salsa; cook, covered, on low about 30 minutes or until heated through, stirring occasionally.

Transfer to a large bowl, if desired. Stir in cheese, pepper and green onions. Sprinkle with cilantro; serve with tortilla scoops.

¼ cup chicken mixture: 97 cal., 4g fat (2g sat. fat), 26mg chol., 183mg sod., 5g carb. (2g sugars, 1g fiber), 9g pro. **Diabetic exchanges:** 1 medium-fat meat.

BLACK-EYED PEAS & HAM

Every New Year's Day we have these slow-cooked black-eyed peas to bring good luck for the coming year.
—Dawn Legler, Fort Morgan, CO

Prep: 20 min. + soaking • **Cook:** 5 hours
Makes: 12 servings

- 1 pkg. (16 oz.) dried black-eyed peas, rinsed and sorted
- ½ lb. fully cooked boneless ham, finely chopped
- 1 medium onion, finely chopped
- 1 medium sweet red pepper, finely chopped
- 5 bacon strips, cooked and crumbled
- 1 large jalapeno pepper, seeded and finely chopped
- 2 garlic cloves, minced
- 1½ tsp. ground cumin
- 1 tsp. reduced-sodium chicken bouillon granules
- ½ tsp. salt
- ½ tsp. cayenne pepper
- ¼ tsp. pepper
- 6 cups water
   Minced fresh cilantro, optional
   Hot cooked rice

1. Soak black-eyed peas according to package directions.

2. Transfer peas to a 6-qt. slow cooker; add the next 12 ingredients. Cover and cook on low 5-7 hours, until peas are tender. Sprinkle with cilantro if desired. Serve with rice.

Note: Wear disposable gloves when cutting hot peppers; the oils can burn skin. Avoid touching your face.

¾ cup: 170 cal., 3g fat (1g sat. fat), 13mg chol., 386mg sod., 24g carb. (5g sugars, 7g fiber), 13g pro. **Diabetic exchanges:** 1½ starch, 1 lean meat.

SLOW-COOKED PORK ROAST

Here's a tasty meal that's wonderful for summer because the oven never needs to heat up. It is so flavorful and is sure to become a favorite.
—Marion Lowery, Medford, OR

- -

Prep: 20 min. • **Cook:** 6 hours + standing
Makes: 12 servings

- 2 cans (8 oz. each) unsweetened crushed pineapple, undrained
- 1 cup barbecue sauce
- 2 Tbsp. unsweetened apple juice
- 1 Tbsp. minced fresh rosemary or 1 tsp. dried rosemary, crushed
- 1 tsp. minced garlic
- 2 tsp. grated lemon zest
- 1 tsp. liquid smoke, optional
- ½ tsp. salt
- ¼ tsp. pepper
- 2 Tbsp. olive oil
- 1 boneless pork loin roast (3 to 4 lbs.)

1. In a large saucepan, combine the first 9 ingredients. Bring to a boil. Reduce heat; simmer, uncovered, for 3 minutes.
2. Meanwhile, cut roast in half. In a nonstick skillet, heat oil over medium heat; add pork roast and brown on all sides.
3. Place pork roast in a 5-qt. slow cooker; pour barbecue sauce over pork and turn to coat. Cover and cook on low for 6-7 hours, until meat is tender. Let stand 10 minutes before slicing.

3 oz. cooked pork: 205 cal., 5g fat (2g sat. fat), 57mg chol., 364mg sod., 16g carb. (13g sugars, 1g fiber), 22g pro.

SUN-DRIED TOMATO SPINACH-ARTICHOKE DIP

Fresh veggies and crackers will disappear quickly when they're next to this cheesy slow-cooked dip. With smoked Gouda, it has an extra level of flavor that keeps everyone guessing.
—Katie Stanczak, Hoover, AL

Prep: 10 min. • **Cook:** 2 hours
Makes: 3 cups

1   pkg. (10 oz.) frozen chopped spinach, thawed and squeezed dry
1   pkg. (8 oz.) cream cheese, softened
1   cup shredded smoked Gouda cheese
½   cup shredded fontina cheese
½   cup chopped water-packed artichoke hearts
¼   to ½ cup soft sun-dried tomato halves (not packed in oil), chopped
⅓   cup finely chopped onion
1   garlic clove, minced
    Assorted fresh vegetables and crackers

In a 1½-qt. slow cooker, mix the spinach, cheeses, artichoke hearts, sun-dried tomatoes, onion and garlic. Cook, covered, on low for 2-3 hours or until the until cheese is melted. Stir before serving. Serve dip with vegetables and crackers.
¼ cup: 134 cal., 11g fat (6g sat. fat), 35mg chol., 215mg sod., 4g carb. (2g sugars, 1g fiber), 6g pro.

MAKE AHEAD
DELUXE WALKING NACHOS

This slow-cooked potluck chili makes an awesome filling for a little bag of walk-around nachos. Cut the bag lengthwise to make it easier to load up your fork.
—Mallory Lynch, Madison, WI

Prep: 20 min. • **Cook:** 6 hours
Makes: 18 servings

1   lb. lean ground beef (90% lean)
1   large sweet onion, chopped

3   garlic cloves, minced
2   cans (14½ oz. each) diced tomatoes with mild green chiles, divided
2   cans (15 oz. each) pinto beans, rinsed and drained
2   cans (15 oz. each) black beans, rinsed and drained
2   to 3 Tbsp. chili powder
2   tsp. ground cumin
½   tsp. salt
18 pkg. (1 oz. each) nacho-flavored tortilla chips
    Optional toppings: Shredded cheddar cheese, sour cream, chopped tomatoes and pickled jalapeno slices

1. In a large skillet, cook beef, onion and garlic over medium heat until beef is no longer pink, breaking beef into crumbles, 6-8 minutes; drain.

2. Transfer beef mixture to a 5-qt. slow cooker. Drain 1 can tomatoes, discarding liquid; add to slow cooker. Stir in beans, chili powder, cumin, salt and remaining can of tomatoes, undrained. Cook, covered, on low 6-8 hours to allow flavors to blend. Mash beans to desired consistency.

3. Just before serving, cut open tortilla chip bags. Divide chili among bags; add toppings as desired.

Freeze option: Freeze cooled chili in a freezer container. To use, partially thaw in refrigerator overnight. Heat through in a saucepan, stirring occasionally; adding water if necessary.

1 serving: 282 cal., 10g fat (2g sat. fat), 16mg chol., 482mg sod., 36g carb. (5g sugars, 6g fiber), 12g pro.

MAKE AHEAD

PIZZA SOUP WITH GARLIC TOAST CROUTONS

This comforting soup satisfies our pizza cravings. I sometimes substitute Italian sausage for the chicken or add a little Parmesan cheese. Go nuts and add all your favorite pizza toppings!
—Joan Hallford, North Richland Hills, TX

Prep: 10 min. • **Cook:** 6 hours
Makes: 10 servings (about 4 qt.)

1 can (28 oz.) diced tomatoes, drained
1 can (15 oz.) pizza sauce
1 lb. boneless skinless chicken breasts, cut into 1-in. pieces
1 pkg. (3 oz.) sliced pepperoni, cut in half
1 cup sliced fresh mushrooms
1 small onion, chopped
½ cup chopped green pepper
¼ tsp. pepper
2 cans (14½ oz. each) chicken broth
1 pkg. (11¼ oz.) frozen garlic Texas toast
1 pkg. (10 oz.) frozen chopped spinach, thawed and squeezed dry
1 cup shredded part-skim mozzarella cheese

1. In a 6-qt. slow cooker, combine the first 9 ingredients. Cook, covered, on low for 6-8 hours, until chicken is tender.
2. For croutons, cut Texas toast into cubes; bake according to package directions. Add spinach to soup; heat through, stirring occasionally. Top servings with cheese and warm croutons.

Freeze option: Freeze cooled soup in freezer containers. To use, partially thaw in the refrigerator overnight. Heat through in a saucepan, stirring occasionally. Prepare croutons as directed. Top soup with cheese and croutons.

1½ cups: 292 cal., 13g fat (5g sat. fat), 46mg chol., 1081mg sod., 24g carb. (7g sugars, 4g fiber), 20g pro.

TEST KITCHEN TIP
The cheesy garlic croutons put this soup over the top, but it's still amazing without them, and a lot leaner, too—just 150 calories and 6 grams of fat per serving.

VEGETABLE SOUP WITH HAMBURGER

I work full time but my family sits down to a home-cooked meal just about every night, thanks in part to simple recipes like this. I love that I can make it in the slow cooker.
—Theresa Jackson, Cicero, NY

Prep: 15 min. • **Cook:** 8 hours
Makes: 10 servings (2½ qt.)

- 1 lb. lean ground beef (90% lean)
- 1 medium onion, chopped
- 2 garlic cloves, minced
- 4 cups V8 juice
- 1 can (14½ oz.) stewed tomatoes
- 2 cups coleslaw mix
- 2 cups frozen green beans
- 2 cups frozen corn
- 2 Tbsp. Worcestershire sauce
- 1 tsp. dried basil
- ½ tsp. salt
- ¼ tsp. pepper

In a large saucepan, cook beef and onion over medium heat until meat is no longer pink. Add garlic; cook 1 minute longer. Drain. In a 5-qt. slow cooker, combine the remaining ingredients. Stir in beef mixture. Cover and cook on low for 8-10 hours or until the vegetables are tender.
1 cup: 145 cal., 4g fat (2g sat. fat), 28mg chol., 507mg sod., 17g carb. (7g sugars, 3g fiber), 11g pro. **Diabetic exchanges:** 1 lean meat, 1 vegetable, ½ starch.

MAKE AHEAD

SLOW-COOKED BARBECUED BEEF SANDWICHES

Chuck roast makes delicious shredded beef sandwiches after simmering in a rich homemade sauce all day. The meat really is tender and juicy, and it only takes a few minutes to prepare.
—Tatina Smith, San Angelo, TX

Prep: 20 min. • **Cook:** 8¼ hours
Makes: 12 servings

- 1 boneless beef chuck roast (3 lbs.)
- 1½ cups ketchup
- ¼ cup packed brown sugar
- ¼ cup barbecue sauce
- 2 Tbsp. Worcestershire sauce
- 2 Tbsp. Dijon mustard
- 1 tsp. liquid smoke, optional
- ½ tsp. salt
- ¼ tsp. garlic powder
- ¼ tsp. pepper
- 12 sandwich buns, split
  Optional: Sliced onions, dill pickles and pickled jalapenos

1. Cut roast in half and place in a 3- or 4-qt. slow cooker. In a small bowl, combine the ketchup, brown sugar, barbecue sauce, Worcestershire sauce, mustard, liquid smoke if desired, and seasonings. Pour over beef.
2. Cover and cook on low for 8-10 hours or until meat is tender. Remove meat; cool slightly. Skim fat from the cooking liquid. Shred beef with 2 forks; return to the slow cooker. Cover and cook for 15 minutes or until heated through. Using a slotted spoon, place ½ cup on each bun. Serve with onions, pickles and jalapenos if desired.
Freeze option: Place individual portions of cooled meat mixture in freezer containers. To use, partially thaw in the refrigerator overnight. Microwave, covered, on high in a microwave-safe dish until heated through, gently stirring and adding a little broth or water if necessary.
1 sandwich: 458 cal., 15g fat (5g sat. fat), 74mg chol., 1052mg sod., 49g carb. (18g sugars, 1g fiber), 30g pro.

BRING IT
Encourage sandwich artistry by placing garnish choices in a large lidded condiment bar (available at restaurant supply stores). Traditionally used to hold cocktail garnishes, it can also double as a DIY sundae bar.

ROSEMARY BEEF ROAST OVER CHEESY POLENTA

I love beef roast made in the slow cooker, and it's fun to pair it with something that's a little different than potatoes! This is true comfort food.
—Elisabeth Larsen, Pleasant Grove, UT

Prep: 20 min. • **Cook:** 7 hours
Makes: 8 servings

- ¼ cup minced fresh rosemary
- 3 garlic cloves, minced
- 3 tsp. salt, divided
- 1 tsp. pepper
- 1 boneless beef chuck roast (3 lbs.)
- 1 Tbsp. canola oil
- 1 cup beef broth
- 2 cups water
- 2 cups 2% milk
- 1 cup cornmeal
- ½ cup shredded Parmesan cheese
- 3 Tbsp. butter, cubed

1. Mix rosemary, garlic, 2 tsp. salt and pepper; rub over meat. In a large skillet, heat oil over medium-high heat; brown meat. Transfer meat a 5- or 6-qt. slow cooker. Add broth to skillet; cook 1 minute, stirring to loosen browned bits from pan. Pour over meat. Cook, covered, on low for 7-9 hours, until meat is tender.

2. For polenta, in a large heavy saucepan, bring water, milk and remaining 1 tsp. salt to a boil. Reduce heat to a gentle boil; slowly whisk in cornmeal. Cook and stir with a wooden spoon until polenta is thickened and pulls away cleanly from sides of pan, 15-20 minutes. (Mixture will be very thick.) Remove from heat; stir in Parmesan cheese and butter. Serve with roast. If desired, serve with additional fresh rosemary and Parmesan cheese.

1 serving: 471 cal., 25g fat (11g sat. fat), 130mg chol., 1216mg sod., 19g carb. (3g sugars, 1g fiber), 39g pro.

GARDEN GREEN BEANS & POTATOES

Fresh green beans paired with red potatoes make an easy and satisfying side dish. To make it even better, add crumbled bacon!
—Kelly Zinn, Cicero, IN

- -

Prep: 10 min. • **Cook:** 6 hours
Makes: 16 servings

- 2 lbs. fresh green beans, trimmed
- 1½ lbs. red potatoes, quartered
- 1 medium onion, chopped
- ½ cup beef broth
- 1½ tsp. salt
- 1 tsp. dried thyme
- ½ tsp. pepper
- ¼ cup butter, softened
- 1 Tbsp. lemon juice

In a 6-qt. slow cooker, combine the first 7 ingredients. Cook, covered, on low for 6-8 hours, until beans are tender. Stir in butter and lemon juice. Remove veggies with a slotted spoon.

¾ cup: 77 cal., 3g fat (2g sat. fat), 8mg chol., 278mg sod., 12g carb. (2g sugars, 3g fiber), 2g pro. **Diabetic exchanges:** 1 vegetable, ½ starch, ½ fat.

CREAMY CHEESE POTATOES

This easy potato dish is a comfort-food classic. It's popular at gatherings.
—Greg Christiansen, Parker, KS

- -

Prep: 10 min. • **Cook:** 3¼ hours
Makes: 10 servings

- 1 can (10¾ oz.) condensed cream of chicken soup, undiluted
- 1 can (10¾ oz.) condensed cream of mushroom soup, undiluted
- 3 Tbsp. butter, melted
- 1 pkg. (30 oz.) frozen shredded hash brown potatoes, thawed
- 2 cups shredded cheddar cheese
- 1 cup sour cream
    Minced fresh parsley, optional

1. In a 3-qt. slow cooker coated with cooking spray, combine the soups and butter. Stir in potatoes.
2. Cover and cook on low for 3-4 hours or until potatoes are tender. Stir in cheese and sour cream. Cover and cook 15-30 minutes longer or until heated through. If desired, sprinkle with parsley.

¾ cup: 278 cal., 17g fat (10g sat. fat), 52mg chol., 614mg sod., 21g carb. (2g sugars, 2g fiber), 9g pro.

LOADED BROCCOLI-CHEESE POTATO CHOWDER

For anyone who loves baked potatoes or broccoli cheese soup, this is the best of both worlds. If you have bacon lovers, offer crumbled cooked bacon as a topping. Then everyone is happy, carnivore or not!
—Vivi Taylor, Middleburg, FL

- -

Prep: 15 min. • **Cook:** 6 hours 10 min.
Makes: 8 servings (about 2 qt.)

- 1 pkg. (20 oz.) refrigerated O'Brien hash brown potatoes
- 1 garlic clove, minced
- 2 cups reduced-fat sour cream
- ¼ cup all-purpose flour
- ½ tsp. pepper
- ⅛ tsp. ground nutmeg
- 3 cups vegetable stock
- 1 pkg. (12 oz.) frozen broccoli florets, thawed
- 4 cups shredded cheddar cheese, divided
- ½ cup finely chopped green onions

1. Combine the hash browns and garlic in a 5- or 6-qt. slow cooker. In a large bowl, whisk the sour cream, flour, pepper and nutmeg until smooth; stir in stock. Pour into slow cooker; stir to combine. Cook, covered, on low 6-8 hours or until hash browns are tender.

2. Add the broccoli and 3 cups cheese; cover and cook until cheese is melted, about 10 minutes longer. Serve with green onions and remaining cheese.

1 cup: 386 cal., 23g fat (13g sat. fat), 62mg chol., 921mg sod., 26g carb. (6g sugars, 2g fiber), 20g pro.

STEAK STROGANOFF

Here's a slow-cooker recipe that makes a traditional dinner so easy. Serve tender sirloin steak with a flavorful gravy over noodles for a homestyle meal that your whole family will request time and again.
—Lisa VanEgmond, Annapolis, IL

Prep: 25 min. • **Cook:** 7 hours
Makes: 12 servings

- 3 to 4 lbs. beef top sirloin steak, cubed
- 2 cans (14½ oz. each) chicken broth
- 1 lb. sliced fresh mushrooms
- 1 can (12 oz.) regular cola
- ½ cup chopped onion
- 1 envelope onion soup mix
- 1 to 2 tsp. garlic powder
- 2 tsp. dried parsley flakes
- ½ tsp. pepper
- 2 envelopes country gravy mix
- 2 cups sour cream
  Hot cooked noodles
  Minced fresh parsley, optional

1. In a 5-qt. slow cooker, combine the first 9 ingredients. Cover and cook on low for 7-8 hours or until beef is tender.
2. With a slotted spoon, remove beef and mushrooms. Place gravy mix in a large saucepan; gradually whisk in cooking liquid. Bring to a boil; cook and stir until thickened, about 2 minutes. Remove from heat; stir in sour cream. Add beef and mushrooms to the gravy. Serve with noodles. If desired, sprinkle with parsley.

1 cup: 345 cal., 20g fat (11g sat. fat), 65mg chol., 840mg sod., 11g carb. (7g sugars, 1g fiber), 29g pro.

SLOW-COOKED CARNITAS

Simmer succulent pork the slow-cooker way. Sometimes I put the seasoned meat on top of shredded lettuce for a tasty salad, instead of using tortillas.
—Lisa Glogow, Aliso Viejo, CA

Prep: 20 min. • **Cook:** 6 hours
Makes: 12 servings

- 1 boneless pork shoulder butt roast (3 to 4 lbs.)
- 3 garlic cloves, thinly sliced
- 2 tsp. olive oil
- ½ tsp. salt
- ½ tsp. pepper
- 1 bunch green onions, chopped
- 1½ cups minced fresh cilantro
- 1 cup salsa
- ½ cup chicken broth
- ½ cup tequila or additional chicken broth
- 2 cans (4 oz. each) chopped green chiles
- 12 flour tortillas (8 in.) or corn tortillas (6 in.), warmed
  Optional: Fresh cilantro leaves, sliced red onion and chopped tomatoes

1. Cut roast in half; place in a 5-qt. slow cooker. Sprinkle with the garlic, olive oil, salt and pepper. Add the onions, cilantro, salsa, broth, tequila and chiles. Cover and cook on low for 6-8 hours or until meat is tender.
2. Remove meat; cool slightly. Shred with 2 forks and return to the slow cooker; heat through. Spoon about ⅔ cup meat mixture onto each tortilla; serve with toppings of your choice.
1 serving: 363 cal., 15g fat (5g sat. fat), 67mg chol., 615mg sod., 28g carb. (1g sugars, 1g fiber), 24g pro.

ITALIAN SAUSAGES WITH PROVOLONE

Here's an easy recipe everyone will rave about. These tangy sausages with their pepper and onion topping will go quickly.
—Shelly Bevington, Hermiston, OR

Prep: 15 min. • **Cook:** 4 hours
Makes: 10 servings

- 10 Italian sausage links (4 oz. each)
- 1 Tbsp. canola oil
- 1 each small sweet red, yellow and orange peppers, cut into strips
- 2 medium onions, halved and sliced
- 2 cups Italian salad dressing
- 10 slices provolone cheese
- 10 brat buns, split

1. In a large skillet, brown sausages in batches in oil. Drain. Transfer to a 5-qt. slow cooker. Add the peppers, onions and salad dressing. Cover and cook on low for 4-5 hours or until a thermometer reads 160° and vegetables are tender.
2. Place sausages and cheese in buns; using a slotted spoon, top with pepper mixture.
1 serving: 543 cal., 31g fat (10g sat. fat), 60mg chol., 1267mg sod., 41g carb. (9g sugars, 2g fiber), 25g pro.

CRISPY SNACK MIX

This recipe proves that you can make just about anything in the slow cooker, even a delightfully crispy snack mix.
—Jane Pair Sims, De Leon, TX

Prep: 10 min. • **Cook:** 2½ hours
Makes: about 2½ qt.

- 4½ cups crispy chow mein noodles
- 4 cups Rice Chex
- 1 can (9¾ oz.) salted cashews
- 1 cup sweetened shredded coconut, toasted
- ½ cup butter, melted
- 2 Tbsp. reduced-sodium soy sauce
- 2¼ tsp. curry powder
- ¾ tsp. ground ginger

1. In a 5-qt. slow cooker, combine the chow mein noodles, cereal, cashews and coconut. In a small bowl, whisk the butter, soy sauce, curry powder and ginger; drizzle over cereal mixture and mix well.
2. Cover and cook on low for 2½ hours, stirring every 30 minutes. Serve warm or at room temperature.
¾ cup: 298 cal., 22g fat (8g sat. fat), 16mg chol., 420mg sod., 21g carb. (4g sugars, 2g fiber), 5g pro.

MULLED GRAPE CIDER

I came up with this recipe when I tried to make grape jelly and ended up with 30 jars of delicious grape syrup instead. I simmered the syrup with spices to make this pretty autumn drink.
—Sharon Harmon, Orange, MA

- -

Prep: 20 min. • **Cook:** 3 hours
Makes: 12 servings (3 qt.)

5	lbs. Concord grapes
8	cups water, divided
1½	cups sugar
8	whole cloves
4	cinnamon sticks (4 in.)
	Dash ground nutmeg

1. In a large saucepan, combine the grapes and 2 cups water; bring to a boil, stirring constantly. Press through a strainer; reserve juice and discard skins and seeds.
2. Pour juice through a double layer of cheesecloth into a 5-qt. slow cooker. Add the sugar, cloves, cinnamon sticks, nutmeg and the remaining water. Cover and cook on low for 3 hours. Discard cloves and cinnamon sticks.

1 cup: 231 cal., 1g fat (0 sat. fat), 0 chol., 4mg sod., 59g carb. (56g sugars, 0 fiber), 1g pro.

PINEAPPLE UPSIDE-DOWN DUMP CAKE

No matter the season, this dump cake recipe is absolutely wonderful! Bonus: It works just as well with gluten-free and sugar-free cake mixes, too.
—Karin Gatewood, Dallas, TX

- -

Prep: 10 min.
Cook: 2 hours + standing
Makes: 10 servings

¾	cup butter, divided
⅔	cup packed brown sugar
1	jar (6 oz.) maraschino cherries, drained
½	cup chopped pecans, toasted

1	can (20 oz.) unsweetened pineapple tidbits or crushed pineapple, undrained
1	pkg. yellow cake mix (regular size) Vanilla ice cream, optional

1. In a microwave oven, melt ½ cup butter; stir in brown sugar. Spread evenly onto bottom of a greased 5-qt. slow cooker. Sprinkle with maraschino cherries and chopped pecans; top with pineapple. Sprinkle evenly with dry cake mix. Melt the remaining butter; drizzle over top.
2. Cook, covered, on high for 2 hours, or until the fruit mixture is bubbly. (To avoid scorching, rotate slow-cooker insert a half turn midway through cooking time, lifting carefully with oven mitts.)
3. Turn off the slow cooker; let stand, uncovered, for 30 minutes before serving. If desired, serve with ice cream.

Note: To toast nuts, bake in a shallow pan in a 350° oven for 5-10 minutes or cook in a skillet over low heat until lightly browned, stirring occasionally.

½ cup: 455 cal., 22g fat (10g sat. fat), 37mg chol., 418mg sod., 66g carb. (47g sugars, 1g fiber), 3g pro.

TEST KITCHEN TIPS

- Letting the cake stand, uncovered, after cooking allows the steam to escape. As it cools, the cake and the saucy pineapple mixture set up a bit.
- Sprinkle the cake mix in an even layer over the pineapple. If it's piled high in the center, the middle of the cake may be undercooked.
- A large slow cooker is used to keep the ingredient layers thin and promote even cooking.

THAI CHICKEN LETTUCE CUPS

Lettuce wraps make light and lively appetizers. These are easy to make because the slow cooker does most of the work. Just load it up and then let things get cooking. When the chicken is cooked, just shred and serve.
—Robin Haas, Hyde Park, MA

Prep: 10 min. • **Cook:** 2½ hours
Makes: 12 servings

1	lb. boneless skinless chicken breasts
½	cup reduced-sodium chicken broth
4	garlic cloves, minced
1	Tbsp. sugar
1	Tbsp. reduced-sodium soy sauce
2	tsp. oyster sauce
½	tsp. crushed red pepper flakes
2	cups torn basil leaves, divided
2	Tbsp. hoisin sauce
12	Bibb or Boston lettuce leaves
2	cups cooked long grain rice
4	green onions, chopped
	Shredded carrots and thinly sliced radishes

1. In a 1½-qt. slow cooker, combine the first 7 ingredients. Cook, covered, on low for about 2½ hours, or until a thermometer inserted in chicken reads 165°. Remove chicken; shred with 2 forks. Return to slow cooker. Stir in 1½ cups basil and hoisin sauce; heat through.

2. Serve chicken mixture in lettuce leaves with rice, green onions, carrots, radishes and remaining basil.

Freeze option: Freeze cooled chicken mixture and juices in freezer containers. To use, partially thaw in the refrigerator overnight. Heat through in a saucepan, stirring occasionally and adding a little broth if necessary.

1 lettuce cup: 93 cal., 1g fat (0 sat. fat), 21mg chol., 162mg sod., 11g carb. (2g sugars, 1g fiber), 9g pro.

WARM ROCKY ROAD CAKE

When served warm, this reminds me of super moist lava cake. And until I made this, I didn't think a slow-cooker cake could be so attractive. It's a real winner.
—Scarlett Elrod, Newnan, GA

- -

Prep: 20 min. • **Cook:** 3 hours
Makes: 16 servings

  1   **pkg. German chocolate cake mix (regular size)**
  1   **pkg. (3.9 oz.) instant chocolate pudding mix**
  1   **cup sour cream**
  ⅓   **cup butter, melted**
  3   **large eggs, room temperature**
  1   **tsp. vanilla extract**
  3¼ **cups 2% milk, divided**
  1   **pkg. (3.4 oz.) cook-and-serve chocolate pudding mix**
  1½ **cups miniature marshmallows**
  1   **cup semisweet chocolate chips**
  ½   **cup chopped pecans, toasted**
      Vanilla ice cream, optional

1. In a large bowl, combine the first 6 ingredients; add 1¼ cups milk. Beat on low speed 30 seconds. Beat on medium 2 minutes. Transfer to a greased 4- or 5-qt. slow cooker. Sprinkle the cook-and-serve pudding mix over batter.
2. In a small saucepan, heat remaining milk until bubbles form around sides of pan; gradually pour over contents of slow cooker.

3. Cook, covered, on high 3-4 hours, or until a toothpick inserted in cake portion comes out with moist crumbs.
4. Turn off slow cooker. Sprinkle the marshmallows, chocolate chips and pecans over cake; let stand, covered, until marshmallows begin to melt, about 5 minutes. Serve warm. If desired, serve with ice cream.
Note: To toast nuts, bake in a shallow pan in a 350° oven for 5-10 minutes or cook in a skillet over low heat until lightly browned, stirring occasionally.
¾ cup: 386 cal., 17g fat (8g sat. fat), 59mg chol., 431mg sod., 55g carb. (34g sugars, 2g fiber), 6g pro.

HOW TO TRAVEL WITH ICE CREAM
To keep ice cream firm and scoopable for hours, wrap the containers in plastic bubble wrap, a powerful insulator. If you have an ice cream maker (and room in your cooler), pack wrapped ice cream into the frozen ice cream cylinder.

MAKE AHEAD

BUTTERNUT SQUASH & BARLEY SOUP

I love to use my garden produce in this vegetable-packed soup. Serve it with oatmeal dinner rolls and you have a delicious, healthy dinner.
—Julie Sloan, Osceola, IN

Prep: 25 min. • **Cook:** 5¼ hours
Makes: 12 servings (3 qt.)

- 1   small butternut squash (2½ to 3 lbs.), peeled and cut into 1-in. cubes (about 6 cups)
- 4   cups water
- 1   carton (32 oz.) reduced-sodium chicken broth
- ¾   cup medium pearl barley
- 2   medium carrots, chopped
- 2   celery ribs, chopped
- 1   small onion, chopped
- 2   Tbsp. minced fresh parsley or 2 tsp. dried parsley flakes
- 2   garlic cloves, minced
- 1   tsp. rubbed sage
- 1¼ tsp. salt
- ½   tsp. curry powder
- ¼   tsp. pepper
- 1   cup cubed cooked turkey

1. Place all ingredients except turkey in a 5- or 6-qt. slow cooker. Cook, covered, on low for 5-7 hours or until squash and barley are tender.
2. Stir in turkey; cook, covered, for about 15 minutes or until heated through.

Freeze option: Transfer soup to freezer containers; cool. Cover and freeze up to 3 months. Thaw in the refrigerator. Place in a saucepan and heat through.

1 cup: 120 cal., 1g fat (0 sat. fat), 12mg chol., 493mg sod., 23g carb. (4g sugars, 6g fiber), 7g pro. **Diabetic exchanges:** 1½ starch.

TEST KITCHEN TIP

Leftover cubed or shredded turkey works well in this soup.

SO-EASY STICKY CHICKEN WINGS

My neighbor once shared these tangy wings with me at a potluck, and they have been a family favorite ever since.
—Jo Vanderwolf, Lillooet, BC

Prep: 20 min. • **Cook:** 3 hours
Makes: about 40 pieces

- 4   lbs. chicken wings
- 1   cup barbecue sauce
- 1   cup soy sauce
- 6   green onions, chopped, divided
- 1   Tbsp. sesame seeds

Using a sharp knife, cut through the 2 wing joints; discard wing tips. Place remaining wing pieces in a 4- or 5-qt. slow cooker. Stir in barbecue sauce, soy sauce and ¼ cup chopped green onions. Cook, covered, on high 3-4 hours or until tender. Sprinkle with sesame seeds and remaining green onions.

1 piece: 68 cal., 4g fat (1g sat. fat), 14mg chol., 452mg sod., 3g carb. (2g sugars, 0 fiber), 6g pro.

SEAFOOD CHEESE DIP

This cheesy recipe has a nice combination of seafood flavors and clings beautifully to slices of bread.
—Michelle Domm, Atlanta, NY

Prep: 15 min. • **Cook:** 1½ hours
Makes: 5 cups

- 1   pkg. (32 oz.) Velveeta, cubed
- 2   cans (6 oz. each) lump crabmeat, drained
- 1   can (10 oz.) diced tomatoes and green chiles, undrained
- 1   cup frozen cooked salad shrimp, thawed
      French bread baguette, sliced and toasted, and assorted fresh vegetables

In a greased 3-qt. slow cooker, combine the cheese, crab, tomatoes and shrimp. Cover and cook on low 1½-2 hours or until cheese is melted, stirring occasionally. Serve with baguette slices and vegetables.

¼ cup: 172 cal., 12g fat (7g sat. fat), 77mg chol., 791mg sod., 4g carb. (3g sugars, 0 fiber), 12g pro.

2 Tbsp. ground ancho chili pepper
1 Tbsp. chili powder
1½ tsp. salt
1½ tsp. ground cumin
1½ tsp. paprika
2 cans (14½ oz. each) fire-roasted diced tomatoes, undrained
1 medium sweet yellow pepper, chopped
1 medium sweet red pepper, chopped
1 can (4 oz.) chopped green chiles
1 garlic clove, minced
1 cup brewed coffee
¾ cup dry red wine or chicken broth
1 can (16 oz.) kidney beans, rinsed and drained
1 can (15 oz.) cannellini beans, rinsed and drained
  Sliced avocado and chopped green onions

1. In a large skillet, heat oil over medium heat. Add turkey and onion; cook until meat is no longer pink, breaking up turkey into crumbles, 8-10 minutes.

2. Transfer to a 5-qt. slow cooker; stir in seasonings. Add tomatoes, sweet peppers, chiles and garlic; stir in coffee and wine.

3. Cook, covered, on low 7-9 hours. Stir in cannellini beans; cook 15-20 minutes longer, until heated through. Top servings with avocado and green onions.

Freeze option: Freeze cooled chili in freezer containers. To use, partially thaw in the refrigerator overnight. Heat through in a saucepan, stirring occasionally and adding broth or water if necessary.

1⅓ cups: 360 cal., 17g fat (4g sat. fat), 58mg chol., 1033mg sod., 29g carb. (6g sugars, 7g fiber), 21g pro.

SLOW-COOKER TROPICAL ORANGE CAKE

Inspired by the fruity tropical flavors of my all-time favorite yogurt, this makes for a fresh, fun and comforting treat. Try it for a beautiful dessert that is amazingly easy to prepare!
—Lisa Renshaw, Kansas City, MO

- -

Prep: 15 min.
Cook: 4 hours + standing
Makes: 8 servings

3 cups cold 2% milk
1 pkg. (3.4 oz.) instant coconut cream pudding mix
1 pkg. orange cake mix (regular size)
¾ cup unsweetened pineapple tidbits
2 cups toasted coconut marshmallows, quartered

1. In a large bowl, whisk milk and pudding mix 2 minutes. Transfer to a greased 5-qt. slow cooker. Prepare the cake mix batter according to package directions, folding pineapple into batter. Pour the batter into slow cooker.

2. Cook, covered, on low for about 4 hours, until edges of cake are golden brown.

3. Remove the slow-cooker insert; sprinkle cake with marshmallows. Let cake stand, uncovered, 10 minutes before serving.

1 serving: 518 cal., 20g fat (6g sat. fat), 77mg chol., 596mg sod., 73g carb. (50g sugars, 1g fiber), 9g pro.

MAKE AHEAD

SLOW-COOKER TURKEY CHILI

I love this recipe because I can prepare it in the morning and have a wholesome dinner ready when I get home. And you can make a big batch to freeze!
—Terri Crandall, Gardnerville, NV

- -

Prep: 30 min. • **Cook:** 7¼ hours
Makes: 8 servings (2¾ qt.)

2 Tbsp. olive oil
1½ lbs. ground turkey
1 medium onion, chopped

MOM'S ITALIAN BEEF SANDWICHES

My mom made the best Italian beef. I've added to her recipe over the years, but it's still hers. She made these sandwiches for family reunions, and there were never any leftovers.
—Mary McVey, Colfax, NC

- -

Prep: 20 min. • **Cook:** 8 hours
Makes: 16 servings

- 1 boneless beef rump roast or bottom round roast (2 lbs.), halved
- 1 boneless beef chuck roast (2 lbs.), halved
- 1 beef sirloin tip roast (1 lb.)
- 2 Tbsp. canola oil
- 2 cups water
- 1 medium onion, chopped
- 4 garlic cloves, minced
- 2 envelopes Italian salad dressing mix
- 1 envelope zesty Italian salad dressing mix
- 1 envelope (0.87 oz.) brown gravy mix
- 1 to 2 Tbsp. crushed red pepper flakes
- 1 Tbsp. Italian seasoning
- 2 tsp. Worcestershire sauce
- 16 hoagie buns, split
  Sliced provolone cheese, optional
  Giardiniera, optional

1. In a large skillet, brown each roast in oil on all sides. Drain. Transfer meat to a 7-qt. slow cooker. Combine the water, onion, garlic, salad dressing and gravy mixes, red pepper flakes, Italian seasoning and Worcestershire sauce; pour over beef. Cover and cook on low for 8-10 hours or until meat is tender.

2. Remove beef; cool slightly. Skim fat from cooking juices. Pour juices into a large bowl. Shred beef with 2 forks; add to bowl. Using a slotted spoon, place ½ cup on each bun. Top with cheese and giardiniera if desired.

Freeze option: Cool the meat and juices; transfer to freezer containers. Freeze for up to 3 months. To use, thaw in refrigerator overnight. Place in a Dutch oven and heat through. Using a slotted spoon, place ½ cup on each bun. Top with cheese and giardiniera if desired.

1 sandwich: 450 cal., 16g fat (5g sat. fat), 89mg chol., 969mg sod., 39g carb. (8g sugars, 1g fiber), 37g pro.

★ ★ ★ ★ ★ **READER REVIEW**

"This was excellent! My husband said it was as good as Al's in Chicago! We will definitely make this again, though I used half the red pepper flakes suggested because we have a small child. Still very tasty!"
AMBERCOOKIN TASTEOFHOME.COM

SPICY COWBOY CHILI

Toasting the peppers for this chili releases their earthy flavors, but wear gloves when handling peppers and seeds.

—Rachel Sprinkel, Hilo, HI

Prep: 45 min. • **Cook:** 7 hours
Makes: 14 servings (3½ qt.)

1 whole garlic bulb
2 to 3 Tbsp. olive oil, divided
2 dried ancho chiles
2 dried chipotle chiles
1 bottle (12 oz.) dark beer
3 lbs. beef stew meat, cut into ¾-in. pieces
2 large onions, chopped
3 cans (16 oz. each) kidney beans, rinsed and drained
3 cans (14½ oz. each) diced tomatoes, undrained
2 cans (8 oz. each) tomato sauce
2 Tbsp. Worcestershire sauce
1 Tbsp. chili powder
1 tsp. pepper
½ tsp. salt
Optional: Shredded cheddar cheese and sliced jalapeno pepper, seeded

1. Preheat oven to 425°. Remove papery outer skin from garlic bulb, but do not peel or separate the cloves. Cut off top of garlic bulb, exposing individual cloves. Brush cut cloves with 1 tsp. oil. Wrap in foil. Bake until the cloves are soft, 30-35 minutes. Unwrap and cool slightly. Squeeze garlic from skins; mash with a fork.

2. Meanwhile, in a large dry skillet over medium-high heat, toast chiles on both sides until puffy, 3-6 minutes. (Do not blacken.) Cool. Remove stems and seeds; coarsely chop chiles. Place in a small bowl; cover with beer. Let stand until softened, about 30 minutes.

3. In the same skillet, heat 1 Tbsp. oil over medium-high heat. Brown beef in batches, adding additional oil if needed; transfer to a 6-qt. slow cooker. In the skillet, heat 2 tsp. oil over medium heat. Add onions; cook and stir until tender. Add to beef.

4. Stir in the remaining ingredients, mashed garlic and dried chiles mixture. Cover and cook on low for 7-9 hours or until the meat is tender. If desired, serve with shredded cheddar cheese and jalapenos.

Note: One-half teaspoon ground chipotle pepper may be substituted for the dried chipotle chiles; add ground chipotle when adding the mashed garlic and beer mixture to slow cooker.

1 cup: 301 cal., 9g fat (3g sat. fat), 60mg chol., 588mg sod., 27g carb. (7g sugars, 8g fiber), 27g pro. **Diabetic exchanges:** 4 lean meat, 1½ starch, 1 vegetable.

ONION-GARLIC HASH BROWNS

Quick to assemble, these slow-cooked hash browns are one of my go-to sides. Stir in hot sauce if you like a bit of heat. I top my finished dish with a sprinkling of shredded cheddar cheese.
—Cindi Boger, Ardmore, AL

- -

Prep: 20 min. • **Cook:** 3 hours
Makes: 12 servings

- ¼ cup butter, cubed
- 1 Tbsp. olive oil
- 1 large red onion, chopped
- 1 small sweet red pepper, chopped
- 1 small green pepper, chopped
- 4 garlic cloves, minced
- 1 pkg. (30 oz.) frozen shredded hash brown potatoes
- ½ tsp. salt
- ½ tsp. pepper
- 3 drops hot pepper sauce, optional
- 2 tsp. minced fresh parsley

1. In a large skillet, heat butter and oil over medium heat. Add red onion and peppers. Cook and stir until crisp-tender. Add garlic; cook 1 minute longer. Stir in hash browns, salt, pepper and, if desired, pepper sauce.

2. Transfer to a 5-qt. slow cooker coated with cooking spray. Cook, covered, for 3-4 hours or until heated through. Sprinkle with parsley just before serving.

½ cup: 110 cal., 5g fat (3g sat. fat), 10mg chol., 136mg sod., 15g carb. (1g sugars, 1g fiber), 2g pro.
Diabetic Exchanges: 1 starch, 1 fat.

SWEET & SPICY MEATBALLS

You'll usually find a batch of these meatballs in my freezer. The slightly sweet sauce nicely complements the spicy pork sausage.
—Genie Brown, Roanoke, VA

- -

Prep: 30 min. • **Cook:** 2 hours
Makes: about 4 dozen

- 2 lbs. bulk spicy pork sausage
- 1 large egg, lightly beaten
- 1 cup packed brown sugar
- 1 cup red wine vinegar
- 1 cup ketchup
- 1 Tbsp. soy sauce
- 1 tsp. ground ginger

1. In a large bowl, combine sausage and egg. Shape into 1-in. balls. Place on a greased rack in a shallow baking pan. Bake at 400° for 15-20 minutes or until a thermometer reads 160°; drain.

2. Meanwhile, in a 4- or 5-qt. slow cooker, combine remaining ingredients. Carefully add the meatballs; stir gently to coat. Cover and cook on low heat for 2-3 hours or until meatballs are heated through and the sugar is dissolved.

1 meatball: 70 cal., 4g fat (1g sat. fat), 14mg chol., 200mg sod., 6g carb. (6g sugars, 0 fiber), 2g pro.

BUTTER & HERB TURKEY

My kids love turkey for dinner, and this easy recipe lets me make it whenever I want. No special occasion required! The meat is so tender it comes right off the bone.
—Rochelle Popovic, South Bend, IN

Prep: 10 min. • **Cook:** 5 hours
Makes: 12 servings (3 cups gravy)

- 1 bone-in turkey breast (6 to 7 lbs.)
- 2 Tbsp. butter, softened
- ½ tsp. dried rosemary, crushed
- ½ tsp. dried thyme
- ¼ tsp. garlic powder
- ¼ tsp. pepper
- 1 can (14½ oz.) chicken broth
- 3 Tbsp. cornstarch
- 2 Tbsp. cold water

1. Rub turkey with butter. Combine the rosemary, thyme, garlic powder and pepper; sprinkle over turkey. Place in a 6-qt. slow cooker. Pour broth over top. Cover and cook on low 5-6 hours or until tender.

2. Remove turkey to a serving platter; keep warm. Skim fat from the cooking juices; transfer to a small saucepan. Bring to a boil. Combine the cornstarch and water until smooth. Gradually stir into the pan. Bring to a boil; cook and stir until thickened, about 2 minutes. Serve with turkey.

5 oz. cooked turkey with ¼ cup gravy: 339 cal., 14g fat (5g sat. fat), 128mg chol., 266mg sod., 2g carb. (0 sugars, 0 fiber), 48g pro.

HOISIN PORK WRAPS

For a casual get-together, set a buffet with pork, tortillas and red cabbage slaw and have your guests make their own wraps.
—Linda Woo, Derby, KS

Prep: 25 min. • **Cook:** 7 hours
Makes: 15 servings

- 1 boneless pork loin roast (3 lbs.)
- 1 cup hoisin sauce, divided
- 1 Tbsp. minced fresh gingerroot
- 6 cups shredded red cabbage
- 1½ cups shredded carrots
- ¼ cup thinly sliced green onions
- 3 Tbsp. rice vinegar
- 4½ tsp. sugar
- 15 flour tortillas (8 in.), warmed

1. Cut roast in half. Combine ⅓ cup hoisin sauce and ginger; rub over pork. Transfer to a 4 or 5-qt. slow cooker. Cover and cook on low for 7-8 hours or until pork is tender.
2. Meanwhile, in a large bowl, combine the cabbage, carrots, onions, vinegar and sugar. Chill until serving.
3. Shred meat with 2 forks and return to the slow cooker; heat through. Place 2 tsp. remaining hoisin sauce down the center of each tortilla; top with ⅓ cup shredded pork and ⅓ cup coleslaw. Roll up.
1 serving: 314 cal., 8g fat (2g sat. fat), 46mg chol., 564mg sod., 37g carb. (7g sugars, 1g fiber), 23g pro. **Diabetic exchanges:** 2½ starch, 2 lean meat.

Strawberry Jam
Cake
page 212

The Sweetest Treats

Get ready for oohs and aahs when you prepare one of the desserts in this chapter. From summer fruit cobblers to keto cookies and luscious Christmas sweets, you'll find every meal's happy ending here.

CHERRY PLUM SLAB PIE

I love to make desserts with fruit all summer! If you use store-bought crust, I recommend stacking your two pie crusts on top of each other and then rolling them to the correct size.
—Elisabeth Larsen, Pleasant Grove, UT

Prep: 25 min. • **Bake:** 50 min. + cooling
Makes: 20 servings

- 1 lb. fresh sweet cherries, pitted
- 4 medium red plums, thinly sliced
- ½ cup sugar
- ¼ cup cornstarch
- 2 Tbsp. lemon juice
  Dough for double-crust pie

TOPPING
- ½ cup old-fashioned oats
- ½ cup chopped walnuts
- ⅓ cup all-purpose flour
- ¼ cup sugar
- ¼ cup packed brown sugar
- 1 tsp. ground cinnamon
- ¼ tsp. salt
- ½ cup cold unsalted butter

1. Preheat oven to 375°. In a large bowl, combine cherries, plums, sugar, cornstarch and lemon juice; toss to coat.

2. On a lightly floured surface, roll dough into a 16x12-in. rectangle; transfer to an ungreased 13x9-in. baking dish. Trim even with rim of dish. Add filling. For topping, in a small bowl, mix oats, walnuts, flour, sugar, brown sugar, cinnamon and salt; cut in butter until crumbly. Sprinkle over filling.

3. Bake until filling is bubbly and crust is golden brown, 50-55 minutes. Cool on a wire rack.

1 piece: 279 cal., 16g fat (9g sat. fat), 36mg chol., 155mg sod., 32g carb. (15g sugars, 2g fiber), 3g pro.

Dough for double-crust pie: Combine 2½ cups all-purpose flour and ½ tsp. salt; cut in 1 cup cold butter until crumbly. Gradually add ⅓-⅔ cup ice water, tossing with a fork until dough holds together when pressed. Divide dough in half. Shape each into a disk; wrap and refrigerate 1 hour.

CRANBERRY NUT COOKIES

In fall, I stock up on fresh cranberries and freeze them so I can make these cookies throughout the year. Tangy cranberries are a nice addition to a buttery cookie.
—Machelle Wall, Rosamond, CA

- -

Prep: 15 min. • **Bake:** 20 min./batch
Makes: 5 dozen

⅔ cup butter, softened
1 cup sugar
1 cup packed brown sugar
1 large egg, room temperature
¼ cup 2% milk
2 Tbsp. lemon juice
3 cups all-purpose flour
¼ cup ground walnuts
1 tsp. baking powder
½ tsp. salt
¼ tsp. baking soda
2½ cups halved fresh or
   frozen cranberries
1 cup chopped walnuts

1. In a large bowl, cream butter and s[u] until light and fluffy, 5-7 minutes. Beat in egg, milk and lemon juice. Combine the flour, ground walnuts, baking powder, salt and baking soda; gradually add to the creamed mixture and mix well. Stir in the cranberries and chopped walnuts.
2. Drop by heaping tablespoonfuls 2 in. apart onto lightly greased baking sheets. Bake at 350° for 16-18 minutes or until golden brown. Remove to wire racks to cool.
1 cookie: 87 cal., 4g fat (1g sat. fat), 9mg chol., 52mg sod., 13g carb. (7g sugars, 0 fiber), 1g pro.

TEST KITCHEN TIP

Dark brown sugar has more molasses than light or golden brown sugar. They're generally interchangeable in recipes. If you like a bolder flavor, choose dark brown sugar.

KETO CHOCOLATE CHIP COOKIES

Keto eaters, rejoice! This ultra soft cookie recipe is a perfectly tasty guilt-free treat.
—*Taste of Home* Test Kitchen

Prep: 10 min. • **Bake:** 10 min./batch + cooling
Makes: 28 cookies

- ½ cup butter, softened
  Granulated erythritol equivalent to ⅓ cup granulated sugar
- 1 large egg, room temperature
- 1 tsp. vanilla extract
- 1¾ cups almond flour
- ¼ tsp. baking soda
- ¼ tsp. salt
- ¾ cup sugar-free dark chocolate baking chips

1. In a large bowl, cream butter and erythritol until light and fluffy, 5-7 minutes. Beat in egg and vanilla. In another bowl, whisk almond flour, baking soda and salt; gradually beat into creamed mixture. Stir in chocolate chips.

2. Preheat oven to 325°. Drop dough by tablespoonfuls 2 in. apart onto ungreased baking sheets. Using a wet finger, press down on cookies to flatten. Bake until edges are lightly browned, 7-10 minutes. Cool completely on pans on wire racks.

1 cookie: 102 cal., 9g fat (4g sat. fat), 15mg chol., 63mg sod., 7g carb. (0 sugars, 1g fiber), 2g pro.

HOLIDAY PRETZEL SALAD

I gave a classic summer salad a holiday twist by making green, white and red layers. The combination of salty, sweet, creamy and fruity is always a hit!
—Renee Conneally, Northville, MI

Prep: 35 min. + chilling • **Bake:** 10 min.
Makes: 15 servings

- ¾ cup butter, melted
- 3 Tbsp. sugar
- 2 cups crushed pretzels

LIME LAYER
- 1 cup boiling water
- 1 pkg. (3 oz.) lime gelatin
- 1 pkg. (8 oz.) cream cheese, softened
- 1 carton (8 oz.) frozen whipped topping, thawed
- 3 to 5 drops green food coloring, optional

CREAM CHEESE LAYER
- 1 pkg. (8 oz.) cream cheese, softened
- ½ cup sugar
- 1 carton (8 oz.) frozen whipped topping, thawed

STRAWBERRY LAYER
- 2 cups boiling water
- 2 pkg. (3 oz. each) strawberry gelatin
- 4 cups sliced fresh strawberries
  Optional: Additional whipped topping and miniature pretzels

1. Preheat oven to 350°. Mix melted butter and sugar; stir in the pretzels. Press onto bottom of an ungreased 13x9-in. baking dish. Bake 10 minutes. Cool completely on a wire rack.

2. Meanwhile, for lime layer, in a large bowl, add boiling water to lime gelatin; stir 2 minutes to completely dissolve. Refrigerate until partially set, about 1 hour. In a bowl, beat cream cheese until smooth. Add cooled lime gelatin mixture; beat until smooth. Fold in whipped topping; if desired, add green food coloring. Spread over crust. Refrigerate until set but not firm, 25-30 minutes.

3. For cream cheese layer, in a bowl, beat cream cheese and sugar until smooth. Fold in whipped topping. Spread over lime layer. Refrigerate until set.

4. For strawberry layer, in a large bowl, add boiling water to strawberry gelatin; stir 2 minutes to completely dissolve. Refrigerate until partially set, about 1 hour. Stir in strawberries. Gently spoon over cream cheese layer. Refrigerate, covered, until firm, 2-4 hours. To serve, cut into squares. If desired, top with additional whipped topping and miniature pretzels.

1 serving: 407 cal., 25g fat (17g sat. fat), 55mg chol., 368mg sod., 40g carb. (29g sugars, 1g fiber), 5g pro.

CHOCOLATE-STRAWBERRY CELEBRATION CAKE

I have some terrific from-scratch recipes, but this uses a boxed mix with plenty of doctoring. As a groom's cake, it's often more popular than the wedding cake.
—Nora Fitzgerald, Sevierville, TN

- -

Prep: 30 min. • **Bake:** 30 min. + cooling
Makes: 16 servings

- 1 pkg. chocolate cake mix (regular size)
- 1 pkg. (3.9 oz.) instant chocolate pudding mix
- 4 large eggs, room temperature
- 1 cup sour cream
- ¾ cup water
- ¼ cup canola oil
- 4 oz. semisweet chocolate, melted

FROSTING
- 2 cups butter, softened
- 4 cups confectioners' sugar
- ¾ cup baking cocoa
- ½ cup 2% milk

GARNISHES
- 4 oz. semisweet chocolate, chopped
- ½ cup heavy whipping cream
- 1 lb. fresh strawberries, hulled
  Seedless strawberry jam, warmed, optional

1. Preheat oven to 350°. Combine the first 7 ingredients; beat on low speed for 30 seconds. Beat on medium for 2 minutes. Transfer to 2 greased and floured 9-in. round baking pans.

2. Bake until a toothpick inserted in the center comes out clean, 28-32 minutes. Cool 10 minutes before removing from pans to wire racks to cool completely.

3. In a large bowl, cream the butter, confectioners' sugar and cocoa until light and fluffy. Beat in milk until smooth. Spread frosting between layers and over top and sides of cake.

4. For ganache, place chocolate in a small bowl. Heat cream just to a boil; pour over chocolate and whisk until smooth. Drizzle over top of cake, allowing the ganache to drape down the sides. Arrange strawberries on top of cake. If desired, brush jam onto the strawberries.

1 slice: 666 cal., 40g fat (23g sat. fat), 120mg chol., 485mg sod., 69g carb. (50g sugars, 2g fiber), 6g pro.

★ ★ ★ ★ ★ **READER REVIEW**

"I made this cake for an auction. The cake itself is rich and decadent. The frosting seemed more like a mousse to me—not too sweet, but airy. The auctioneer saved this to be the last thing auctioned off because it looked so good. It sold for $150. Wow!"

ROBRRD TASTEOFHOME.COM

MOM'S CHOCOLATE CHIP COOKIES

My mom always brightened my lunch with these yummy cookies.
—Tammy Orr, Wharton, NJ

- -

Prep: 20 min. • **Bake:** 10 min./batch
Makes: 4 dozen

1	cup butter, softened
¾	cup packed brown sugar
¼	cup sugar
1	pkg. (3.4 oz.) instant vanilla pudding mix
2	large eggs, room temperature, lightly beaten
1	tsp. vanilla extract
2¼	cups all-purpose flour
1	tsp. baking soda
2	cups semisweet chocolate chips

Preheat oven to 375°. Cream butter and sugars until light and fluffy, 5-7 minutes. Add pudding mix, eggs and vanilla. Combine flour and baking soda. Add to mixture; mix well. Fold in chips. Drop by teaspoonfuls onto ungreased baking sheets. Bake until lightly browned, 10-12 minutes.
1 cookie: 117 cal., 5g fat (3g sat. fat), 8mg chol., 45mg sod., 20g carb. (14g sugars, 1g fiber), 1g pro.

> **TEST KITCHEN TIP**
> Unless otherwise specified, *Taste of Home* recipes are tested with lightly salted butter. Unsalted, or sweet, butter is sometimes used to achieve a buttery flavor, such as in shortbread cookies or buttercream frosting. In these recipes, added salt would detract from the buttery taste desired.

HEALTHY BLACKBERRY COBBLER

This lovely treat has helped my family stay healthy, lose weight and still be able to enjoy dessert! Other kinds of berries or even fresh peaches are just as delicious in this cobbler.
—Leslie Browning, Lebanon, KY

- -

Prep: 15 min. + standing • **Bake:** 45 min.
Makes: 10 servings

½	cup sugar
4½	tsp. quick-cooking tapioca
¼	tsp. ground allspice
5	cups fresh or frozen blackberries, thawed
2	Tbsp. orange juice

DOUGH

1	cup all-purpose flour
⅓	cup plus 1 Tbsp. sugar, divided
¼	tsp. baking soda
¼	tsp. salt
⅓	cup vanilla yogurt
⅓	cup fat-free milk
3	Tbsp. butter, melted

1. Preheat oven to 350°. In a large bowl, combine sugar, tapioca and allspice. Add blackberries and orange juice; toss to coat. Let stand for 15 minutes. Spoon into a greased 2-qt. baking dish.
2. In a large bowl, combine flour, ⅓ cup sugar, baking soda and salt. Combine yogurt, milk and butter; stir into dry ingredients until smooth. Spread over berry mixture.
3. Bake for 20 minutes; sprinkle with remaining sugar. Bake until golden brown, 25-30 minutes. Serve warm.
1 serving: 194 cal., 4g fat (2g sat. fat), 10mg chol., 128mg sod., 38g carb. (23g sugars, 4g fiber), 3g pro.

DUTCH OVEN CHERRY CHOCOLATE DUMP CAKE

Looking for a super quick dessert that will make people think you spent all day in the kitchen? This easy dessert will wow your guests. Feel free to use your favorite pie filling in place of cherry.
—Rashanda Cobbins, Milwaukee, WI

Prep: 5 min. • **Bake:** 35 min.
Makes: 8 servings

- 1 can (21 oz.) cherry pie filling
- 1 can (12 oz.) evaporated milk
- 1 pkg. chocolate cake mix (regular size)
- ⅓ cup sliced almonds
- ¾ cup butter, melted
  Vanilla ice cream, optional

1. Preheat the oven to 350°. Line a 4-qt. Dutch oven with parchment; lightly spray with cooking spray. Combine pie filling and evaporated milk; spread filling mixture into bottom of Dutch oven. Sprinkle with cake mix (unprepared) and almonds; drizzle with butter.
2. Bake, covered, until cake springs back when touched, 35-40 minutes. If desired, serve with ice cream.
1 cup: 515 cal., 24g fat (15g sat. fat), 61mg chol., 605mg sod., 68g carb. (44g sugars, 3g fiber), 7g pro.

BANANA CREAM CHEESECAKE

Here is a delightful no-bake dessert. Add a dash of cinnamon to the graham cracker crust if you'd like.
—Margie Snodgrass, Wilmore, KY

Prep: 25 min. + chilling • **Makes:** 10 servings

- 1¾ cups graham cracker crumbs
- ¼ cup sugar
- ½ cup butter, melted

FILLING
- 1 pkg. (8 oz.) cream cheese, softened
- ½ cup sugar
- 1 carton (8 oz.) frozen whipped topping, thawed, divided
- 3 to 4 medium firm bananas, sliced
- 1¾ cups cold 2% milk
- 1 pkg. (3.4 oz.) instant banana cream pudding mix

1. In a small bowl, combine cracker crumbs and sugar; stir in butter. Set aside ½ cup for topping. Press remaining crumb mixture onto bottom and up the sides of a greased 9-in. springform pan or 9-in. square baking pan. Bake at 350° for 5-7 minutes. Cool on wire rack.

2. In a large bowl, beat cream cheese and sugar until smooth. Fold in 2 cups whipped topping. Arrange half the banana slices in crust; top with half the cream cheese mixture. Repeat layers.
3. In a small bowl, whisk milk and pudding mix for 2 minutes. Let stand for 2 minutes or until soft-set; fold in remaining whipped topping. Pour over the cream cheese layer. Sprinkle with reserved crumb mixture. Refrigerate for 1-2 hours or until set.
1 slice: 436 cal., 24g fat (16g sat. fat), 55mg chol., 405mg sod., 51g carb. (36g sugars, 1g fiber), 5g pro.

SOUTHERN PEACH UPSIDE-DOWN CAKE

A dear friend from the South gave me the idea for this peachy cake. I add bourbon and top each slice with vanilla or cinnamon ice cream.
—Trista Jefferson, Batavia, OH

Prep: 25 min. • **Bake:** 40 min.
Makes: 10 servings

    2   cups sliced peeled fresh or
        frozen peaches, thawed
    2   Tbsp. bourbon, optional
    ¼   cup butter
    ½   cup packed brown sugar
BATTER
    ½   cup butter, softened
    ¾   cup sugar
    1   large egg, room temperature
    1   tsp. vanilla extract
    1¼ cups all-purpose flour
    1¼ tsp. baking powder
    ¼   tsp. salt
    ½   cup 2% milk

1. Preheat oven to 350°. If desired, combine peaches and bourbon; let stand 10 minutes.
2. Meanwhile, place ¼ cup butter in a 10-in. cast-iron or other ovenproof skillet; heat in oven until butter is melted, 5-7 minutes. Sprinkle brown sugar evenly over butter. Arrange peach slices over brown sugar.
3. For batter, in a large bowl, cream butter and sugar until light and fluffy, 5-7 minutes. Beat in egg and vanilla. In another bowl, whisk flour, baking powder and salt; add to the creamed mixture alternately with milk, beating after each addition just until combined. Spread batter evenly over peaches.
4. Bake until a toothpick inserted in center comes out clean, 40-45 minutes. Cool for 5 minutes before inverting onto a serving plate. Serve warm.
1 slice: 306 cal., 15g fat (9g sat. fat), 56mg chol., 235mg sod., 41g carb. (29g sugars, 1g fiber), 3g pro.

LEMON LIME DESSERT

This make-ahead treat offers a wonderfully refreshing blend of citrus flavors. Topped with a smooth lemon sauce, it's the perfect ending to any meal. Using an electric mixer makes it easy to combine the lime sherbet and vanilla ice cream.
—Marsha Schindler, Fort Wayne, IN

Prep: 20 min. • **Cook:** 10 min. + freezing
Makes: 15 servings

    1½ cups graham cracker crumbs
    14 Tbsp. butter, melted, divided
    1¼ cups sugar, divided
    ½   gallon vanilla ice cream, softened
    1   qt. lime sherbet, softened
    2   large eggs, lightly beaten
    ¼   cup lemon juice

1. In a large bowl, combine the cracker crumbs, 7 Tbsp. butter and ¼ cup sugar. Press into an ungreased 13x9-in. dish; freeze until firm. In a large bowl, combine ice cream and sherbet; pour over crust. Freeze until firm.
2. In a heavy saucepan, combine the eggs and remaining sugar. Stir in the lemon juice and remaining butter. Cook and stir until mixture reaches 160° and coats the back of a spoon. Transfer to a bowl; refrigerate until cooled.
3. Spread over ice cream mixture. Cover and freeze for 3 hours or overnight. May be frozen for up to 2 months.
4. Just before serving, remove from the freezer and cut into squares.
1 piece: 401 cal., 21g fat (12g sat. fat), 90mg chol., 242mg sod., 52g carb. (40g sugars, 0 fiber), 4g pro.

DOUBLE BUTTERSCOTCH COCONUT CAKE

I got this recipe from a co-worker years ago, and then I changed it a bit by adding a family favorite: butterscotch. It is super easy to throw together and is a perfect accompaniment to coffee or tea.
—Marina Castle Kelley, Canyon Country, CA

Prep: 20 min. • **Bake:** 40 min. + cooling
Makes: 16 servings

- 1 pkg. yellow cake mix (regular size)
- 1 pkg. (3.4 oz.) instant butterscotch pudding mix
- 4 large eggs, room temperature
- 1 cup canned coconut milk
- ¼ cup canola oil
- 1 cup sweetened shredded coconut
- ½ cup butterscotch chips

GLAZE
- ½ cup butterscotch chips
- 2 Tbsp. heavy whipping cream
- ⅓ cup sweetened shredded coconut, toasted

1. Preheat oven to 350°. Grease and flour a 10-in. fluted tube pan.
2. In a large bowl, combine cake mix, pudding mix, eggs, coconut milk and oil; beat on low speed 30 seconds. Beat on medium speed 2 minutes. Stir in coconut and butterscotch chips. Transfer to prepared pan.
3. Bake until a toothpick inserted near center comes out clean, 40-45 minutes. Cool in pan 10 minutes before removing to a wire rack to cool completely. For glaze, in a microwave, melt butterscotch chips and cream; stir until smooth. Drizzle over cake; sprinkle with coconut.
1 slice: 327 cal., 15g fat (10g sat. fat), 49mg chol., 359mg sod., 42g carb. (30g sugars, 1g fiber), 4g pro.

JUMBO BROWNIE COOKIES
Take these deeply fudgy cookies to a party, and you're sure to make a friend. A little espresso powder in the dough makes them over-the-top good.
—Rebecca Cababa, Las Vegas, NV

Prep: 20 min. • **Bake:** 15 min./batch
Makes: about 1½ dozen

- 2⅔ cups 60% cacao bittersweet chocolate baking chips
- ½ cup unsalted butter, cubed
- 4 large eggs, room temperature
- 1½ cups sugar
- 4 tsp. vanilla extract
- 2 tsp. instant espresso powder, optional
- ⅔ cup all-purpose flour
- ½ tsp. baking powder
- ¼ tsp. salt
- 1 pkg. (11½ oz.) semisweet chocolate chunks

1. Preheat oven to 350°. In a large saucepan, melt chocolate chips and butter over low heat, stirring until smooth. Remove from the heat; cool until mixture is warm.
2. In a small bowl, whisk the eggs, sugar, vanilla and, if desired, espresso powder until blended. Whisk into chocolate mixture. In another bowl, mix flour, baking powder and salt; add to chocolate mixture, mixing well. Fold in chocolate chunks; let stand until mixture thickens slightly, about 10 minutes.
3. Drop by ¼ cupfuls 3 in. apart onto parchment-lined baking sheets. Bake until set, 12-14 minutes. Cool on pans 1-2 minutes. Remove to wire racks to cool.
Note: This recipe was tested with Ghirardelli 60% Cacao Bittersweet Chocolate Baking Chips; results may vary when using a different product.
1 cookie: 350 cal., 19g fat (11g sat. fat), 60mg chol., 65mg sod., 48g carb. (40g sugars, 3g fiber), 4g pro.

PEACH COBBLER COOKIES

My sister brought me fresh peaches one year, and we decided to make these fruity cookies. A quick and easy change from pie, they're a fabulously creative way to use fresh peaches.

—Anna Miller, Churdan, IA

- -

Prep: 30 min. • **Bake:** 15 min./batch + cooling
Makes: about 4½ dozen

1	cup butter, softened
1	cup sugar
⅓	cup packed brown sugar
1	large egg, room temperature
1	tsp. vanilla extract
¼	tsp. almond extract
3	cups all-purpose flour
1½	tsp. ground cinnamon
1	tsp. cream of tartar
1	tsp. baking soda
½	tsp. salt
¼	tsp. ground nutmeg
1	cup chopped peeled fresh peaches

1. Preheat oven to 350°. In a large bowl, cream butter and sugars until light and fluffy, 5-7 minutes. Beat in the egg and extracts. In another bowl, whisk flour, cinnamon, cream of tartar, baking soda, salt and nutmeg; gradually beat into creamed mixture. Stir in peaches.
2. Drop dough by tablespoonfuls 2 in. apart onto parchment-lined baking sheets. Bake until set, 14-16 minutes. Cool on pans 2 minutes. Remove to wire racks to cool. Store in airtight container.
1 cookie: 78 cal., 4g fat (2g sat. fat), 12mg chol., 74mg sod., 11g carb. (5g sugars, 0 fiber), 1g pro.

STRAWBERRY JAM CAKE

When I need a delicious cake for a special occasion, this is my go-to recipe because everyone is crazy about it. Every year I make it for a Relay for Life cake raffle we have at work. It has raised a lot of money for a very good cause.

—Tammy Urbina, Warner Robins, GA

- -

Prep: 35 min. • **Bake:** 25 min. + cooling
Makes: 12 servings

1	cup butter, softened
1¾	cups sugar
5	large egg whites, room temperature
2	cups pureed strawberries
½	cup sour cream
1	tsp. strawberry extract
3	cups cake flour
2½	tsp. baking powder
¼	tsp. baking soda
¼	tsp. salt

FROSTING

1	pkg. (8 oz.) cream cheese, softened
¼	cup butter, softened
3¼	cups confectioners' sugar
¼	cup pureed strawberries
½	tsp. strawberry extract
	Red food coloring, optional
1	cup seedless strawberry jam, divided
	Halved fresh strawberries, optional

1. Grease and flour three 9-in. round baking pans; set aside.
2. In a large bowl, cream butter and sugar until light and fluffy, 5-7 minutes. Add egg whites, 1 at a time, beating well after each addition. Beat in the strawberries, sour cream and extract. Combine the flour, baking powder, baking soda and salt; add to the creamed mixture. Transfer batter to prepared pans.
3. Bake at 350° until a toothpick inserted in the center comes out clean, 22-26 minutes. Cool for 10 minutes before removing from pans to wire racks to cool completely.
4. For the frosting, in a large bowl, beat cream cheese and butter until fluffy. Add the confectioners' sugar, strawberries, extract and, if desired, food coloring; beat until smooth.
5. Place bottom cake layer on a serving plate; top with ½ cup jam and ½ cup frosting. Repeat layers. Top with remaining cake layer. Spread remaining frosting over top and sides of cake. Garnish with halved strawberries if desired.
1 slice: 706 cal., 28g fat (17g sat. fat), 78mg chol., 377mg sod., 110g carb. (79g sugars, 1g fiber), 7g pro.

CHOCOLATE AMARETTI

These classic almond paste cookies are like ones you'd find in an Italian bakery. My husband and children are always excited when I include these goodies in my holiday baking lineup.
—Kathy Long, Whitefish Bay, WI

- -

Prep: 15 min. • **Bake:** 20 min./batch
Makes: 2 dozen

1¼ cups almond paste
¾ cup sugar
2 large egg whites, room temperature
½ cup confectioners' sugar
¼ cup baking cocoa

1. Crumble the almond paste into a food processor; add sugar and pulse until evenly combined. Add egg whites and process until incorporated. Transfer mixture to a bowl. Sift together the confectioners' sugar and cocoa; gradually add to almond mixture and mix well.
2. Drop by tablespoonfuls 2 in. apart onto parchment-lined baking sheets. Bake at 350° until tops are cracked, 17-20 minutes. Cool for 1 minute before removing from pans to wire racks. Store in an airtight container.
1 cookie: 92 cal., 3g fat (0 sat. fat), 0 chol., 6mg sod., 15g carb. (13g sugars, 1g fiber), 2g pro. **Diabetic exchanges:** 1 starch, ½ fat.

BUTTERSCOTCH PECAN DESSERT

Light and creamy, this terrific treat never lasts long when I serve it. The fluffy cream cheese layer topped with cool butterscotch pudding is a lip-smacking combination.
—Becky Harrison, Albion, IL

- -

Prep: 15 min. + chilling
Bake: 20 min. + cooling • **Makes:** 20 servings

½ cup cold butter, cubed
1 cup all-purpose flour
¾ cup chopped pecans, divided
1 pkg. (8 oz.) cream cheese, softened
1 cup confectioners' sugar
1 carton (8 oz.) frozen whipped topping, thawed, divided
3½ cups cold 2% milk
2 pkg. (3.4 or 3.5 oz. each) instant butterscotch or vanilla pudding mix

1. Preheat oven to 350°. In a small bowl, cut butter into flour until crumbly; stir in ½ cup pecans. Press into an ungreased 13x9-in. baking dish. Bake until lightly browned, 20 minutes. Cool.
2. In a small bowl, beat cream cheese and sugar until fluffy. Fold in 1 cup whipped topping; spread over crust.
3. In a large bowl, whisk milk and pudding mix for 2 minutes. Let stand for 2 minutes or until soft-set; pour over cream cheese layer. Refrigerate until set, 15-20 minutes. Top with remaining whipped topping and pecans. Refrigerate for 1-2 hours.
1 piece: 242 cal., 14g fat (8g sat. fat), 27mg chol., 247mg sod., 23g carb. (18g sugars, 1g fiber), 3g pro.

EASY FRESH STRAWBERRY PIE

I often use whole fresh strawberries and then arrange them pointed side up in the pastry shell for a different presentation.
—Josh Carter, Birmingham, AL

Prep: 20 min. + cooling
Bake: 15 min. + chilling • **Makes:** 8 servings

- 1 **sheet refrigerated pie crust**
- ¾ **cup sugar**
- 2 **Tbsp. cornstarch**
- 1 **cup water**
- 1 **pkg. (3 oz.) strawberry gelatin**
- 4 **cups sliced fresh strawberries**
  Whipped cream, optional

1. Preheat oven to 450°. Unroll crust into a 9-in. pie plate. Trim edge. Line unpricked crust with a double thickness of heavy-duty foil or parchment. Bake 8 minutes. Remove the foil; bake 5 minutes longer. Cool on a wire rack.

2. In a small saucepan, combine the sugar, cornstarch and water until smooth. Bring to a boil; cook and stir until thickened, about 2 minutes. Remove from the heat; stir in gelatin until dissolved. Refrigerate until slightly cooled, 15-20 minutes.

3. Meanwhile, arrange strawberries in the crust. Pour gelatin mixture over berries. Refrigerate until set. If desired, serve with whipped cream.

1 slice: 264 cal., 7g fat (3g sat. fat), 5mg chol., 125mg sod., 49g carb. (32g sugars, 2g fiber), 2g pro.

TEST KITCHEN TIP
Create a braided crust by cutting a second refrigerated pie crust into ⅜-in. strips. Braid strips, pressing pieces to seal to make braided strip fit the perimeter of the pie crust. Adhere to crust with lightly beaten egg.

CHOCOLATE ECLAIRS

With creamy filling and thick, decadent frosting, these eclairs are extra special. Now you can indulge in classic bakery treats without leaving the house!
—Jessica Campbell, Viola, WI

Prep: 45 min. • **Bake:** 35 min. + cooling
Makes: 9 servings

- 1 cup water
- ½ cup butter, cubed
- ¼ tsp. salt
- 1 cup all-purpose flour
- 4 large eggs, room temperature

FILLING
- 2½ cups cold whole milk
- 1 pkg. (5.1 oz.) instant vanilla pudding mix
- 1 cup heavy whipping cream
- ¼ cup confectioners' sugar
- 1 tsp. vanilla extract

FROSTING
- 2 oz. semisweet chocolate
- 2 Tbsp. butter
- 1¼ cups confectioners' sugar
- 2 to 3 Tbsp. hot water

1. Preheat oven to 400°. In a large saucepan, bring water, butter and salt to a boil. Add flour all at once and stir until a smooth ball forms. Remove from heat; let stand 5 minutes. Add eggs, 1 at a time, beating well after each addition. Continue beating until mixture is smooth and shiny.
2. Using a tablespoon or pastry tube with a #10 or large round tip, form dough into nine 4x1½-in. strips on a greased baking sheet. Bake 35-40 minutes or until puffed and golden. Remove to a wire rack. Immediately split eclairs open; remove tops and set aside. Discard soft dough from inside. Cool eclairs.
3. In a large bowl, beat milk and pudding mix according to package directions. In another bowl, whip cream until soft peaks form. Beat in sugar and vanilla; fold into pudding. Fill eclairs (chill any remaining filling for another use).
4. For the frosting, in a microwave, melt chocolate and butter; stir until smooth. Stir in the sugar and enough hot water to achieve a smooth consistency. Cool slightly. Frost eclairs. Store in refrigerator.

1 serving: 483 cal., 28g fat (17g sat. fat), 174mg chol., 492mg sod., 52g carb. (37g sugars, 1g fiber), 7g pro.

DUTCH APPLE CAKE

My husband and I came to Canada from Holland more than 40 years ago. This traditional Dutch recipe is a family favorite and has frequently gone along with me to potluck suppers and other get-togethers.
—Elizabeth Peters, Martintown, ON

Prep: 15 min. + standing
Bake: 1½ hours + cooling
Makes: 12 servings

- 3 medium tart apples, peeled and cut into ¼-in. slices (3 cups)
- 3 Tbsp. plus 1 cup sugar, divided
- 1 tsp. ground cinnamon
- ⅔ cup butter, softened
- 4 large eggs, room temperature
- 1 tsp. vanilla extract
- 2 cups all-purpose flour
- ⅛ tsp. salt

1. In a large bowl, combine the apples, 3 Tbsp. sugar and cinnamon; let stand for 1 hour.
2. In another bowl, cream butter and remaining sugar until light and fluffy, 5-7 minutes. Add eggs, 1 at a time, beating well after each addition. Add vanilla. Combine flour and salt; gradually add to the creamed mixture and beat until smooth.
3. Transfer to a greased 9x5-in. loaf pan. Push apple slices vertically into batter, placing them close together.
4. Bake at 300° for 1½-1¾ hours or until a toothpick inserted in the center comes out clean. Cool for 10 minutes before removing from pan to a wire rack. Serve cake warm.
1 slice: 282 cal., 12g fat (7g sat. fat), 97mg chol., 120mg sod., 40g carb. (24g sugars, 1g fiber), 4g pro.

CAN'T LEAVE ALONE BARS

I take these quick and easy treats to church meetings, potlucks and housewarming parties. I often make a double batch so we can enjoy some at home.
—Kimberly Biel, Java, SD

Prep: 20 min. • **Bake:** 20 min. + cooling
Makes: 3 dozen

- 1 pkg. white cake mix (regular size)
- 2 large eggs, room temperature
- ⅓ cup canola oil
- 1 can (14 oz.) sweetened condensed milk
- 1 cup semisweet chocolate chips
- ¼ cup butter, cubed

1. Preheat oven to 350°. In a large bowl, combine the cake mix, eggs and oil. Press two-thirds of the mixture into a greased 13x9-in. baking pan. Set remaining cake mixture aside.
2. In a microwave-safe bowl, combine the milk, chocolate chips and butter. Microwave, uncovered, until chips and butter are melted; stir until smooth. Pour over crust.
3. Drop teaspoonfuls of remaining cake mixture over top. Bake until lightly browned, 20-25 minutes. Cool before cutting into bars.
1 bar: 152 cal., 7g fat (3g sat. fat), 19mg chol., 122mg sod., 20g carb. (15g sugars, 0 fiber), 2g pro.

RASPBERRY SWIRL CHEESECAKE PIE

I use jam made from our farm's plentiful wild raspberries to give this pretty dessert its marbled effect. While the cheesecake refrigerates overnight, its flavors blend beautifully.
—Sandy McKenzie, Braham, MN

Prep: 20 min. • **Bake:** 25 min. + chilling
Makes: 8 servings

 Dough for single-crust pie
2 pkg. (8 oz. each) cream cheese, softened
½ cup sugar
½ tsp. vanilla extract
2 large eggs, room temperature
3 Tbsp. raspberry jam
 Optional: Whipped cream and fresh raspberries

1. On a lightly floured surface, roll dough to fit a 9-in. pie plate. Trim; flute edge. Line unpricked crust with a double thickness of heavy-duty foil. Bake at 450° for 5 minutes; remove foil. Bake 5 minutes longer. Remove from the oven; reduce heat to 350°.

2. In a bowl, beat cream cheese, sugar and vanilla until smooth. Add eggs, beating on low speed just until combined. Pour into crust. Stir jam; drizzle over the filling. Cut through filling with a knife to swirl the jam. Bake for 25-30 minutes or until center is almost set. Cool on a wire rack for 1 hour. Refrigerate overnight. Let stand at room temperature for 30 minutes before slicing. If desired, serve with whipped cream and fresh raspberries.

1 slice: 305 cal., 18g fat (10g sat. fat), 89mg chol., 200mg sod., 31g carb. (18g sugars, 0 fiber), 5g pro.

Dough for single-crust pie: Combine 1¼ cups all-purpose flour and ¼ tsp. salt; cut in ½ cup cold butter until crumbly. Gradually add 3-5 Tbsp. ice water, tossing with a fork until dough holds together when pressed. Shape into a disk; wrap and refrigerate 1 hour.

BRING IT

This recipe easily lends itself to multiplication for a crowd. Bake 2 deep-dish frozen pie crusts in foil tins—or 3 regular-size frozen pie crusts—and fill the pie shells with a double batch of the filling recipe. Voila! You now have 2 or 3 pies for the occasion and no pie plates to track down later.

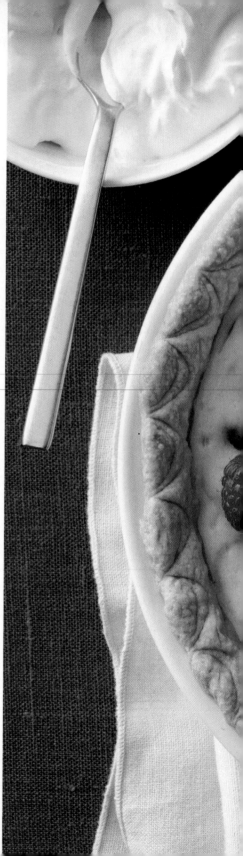

NECTARINE PLUM COBBLER

I live in northern Manitoba, where fresh nectarines and plums are usually available only at summer's end. I make the fruit filling and freeze it for use all winter long. My family really enjoys this recipe, and it's wonderful topped with vanilla ice cream.
—Darlene Jackson, The Pas, MB

Prep: 30 min. • **Bake:** 30 min.
Makes: 12 servings

- 1¼ cups sugar, divided
- 2 Tbsp. cornstarch
- ¾ cup unsweetened apple juice
- 5 cups sliced peeled fresh plums
- 5 cups sliced peeled nectarines or peaches
- 2½ cups all-purpose flour
- 3 tsp. baking powder
- ½ tsp. baking soda
- ½ tsp. salt
- ½ cup cold butter
- 1½ cups buttermilk
  Vanilla ice cream, optional

1. Preheat oven to 375°. In a large saucepan, combine ¾ cup sugar and the cornstarch. Gradually stir in apple juice until smooth. Stir in plums and nectarines. Cook and stir until mixture comes to a boil; cook 1-2 minutes longer or until thickened and bubbly. Reduce heat; simmer, uncovered, for 5 minutes.
2. Remove from heat; cool for 10 minutes. Pour into a greased 13x9-in. baking dish.
3. In a large bowl, whisk flour, baking powder, baking soda, salt and remaining ½ cup sugar. Cut in butter until crumbly. Make a well in center; stir in buttermilk just until a soft dough forms. Drop by tablespoonfuls over fruit mixture. Bake until golden brown, 30-35 minutes. Serve warm, with ice cream if desired.
1 serving: 333 cal., 9g fat (5g sat. fat), 22mg chol., 361mg sod., 61g carb. (36g sugars, 3g fiber), 5g pro.

MAKE AHEAD

PUMPKIN PIE BARS

These bars taste like an amazing cross between pumpkin pie and pecan pie—yum. If you can't find butter cake mix, yellow cake mix works.
—Sue Draheim, Waterford, WI

Prep: 15 min. • **Bake:** 50 min. + chilling
Makes: 16 servings

- 1 can (29 oz.) pumpkin
- 1 can (12 oz.) evaporated milk
- 1½ cups sugar
- 4 large eggs, room temperature
- 2 tsp. ground cinnamon
- 1 tsp. ground ginger
- ½ tsp. ground nutmeg
- 1 pkg. butter recipe golden cake mix (regular size)
- 1 cup butter, melted
- 1 cup chopped pecans
  Whipped topping, optional

1. Preheat oven to 350°. In a large bowl, combine the first 7 ingredients; beat on medium speed until smooth. Pour into an ungreased 13x9-in. baking pan. Sprinkle with dry cake mix. Drizzle butter over top; sprinkle with pecans.
2. Bake 50-60 minutes or until a toothpick inserted in center comes out clean. Cool 1 hour on a wire rack.
3. Refrigerate 3 hours or overnight. Remove from the refrigerator 15 minutes before serving. Cut into bars. If desired, serve with whipped topping.
1 bar: 419 cal., 22g fat (10g sat. fat), 91mg chol., 360mg sod., 53g carb. (38g sugars, 3g fiber), 5g pro.

STRAWBERRY CRUNCH ICE CREAM CAKE

Growing up, I loved treats from the ice cream truck that rolled through my neighborhood. This ice cream cake is inspired by one of those crunchy, strawberry novelties.
—Lisa Kaminski, Wauwatosa, WI

- -

Prep: 20 min. + freezing
Bake: 25 min. + cooling • **Makes:** 9 servings

36 Golden Oreo cookies, divided
 4 Tbsp. butter, melted
 3 cups vanilla ice cream, softened
 5 cups strawberry ice cream, softened
 1 carton (8 oz.) frozen
    whipped topping, thawed
 1 pkg. (1 oz.) freeze-dried
    strawberries, coarsely crushed
    Fresh strawberries, optional

1. Line a 9x9-in. baking pan with parchment. Preheat the oven to 350°. Finely crush 24 cookies. In a small bowl, mix cookie crumbs and butter. Press onto bottom of prepared pan. Bake until firm, 25-30 minutes. Cool on a wire rack.
2. Spread vanilla ice cream onto crust; freeze, covered, until firm. Spread with strawberry ice cream and then whipped topping; freeze, covered, until firm.
3. Coarsely crush the remaining cookies. Combine cookie crumbs and freeze-dried strawberries; sprinkle over the whipped topping. Freeze, covered, until firm, 8 hours or overnight. Remove the cake from freezer 10 minutes before serving. If desired, garnish with fresh strawberries.
1 piece: 584 cal., 30g fat (16g sat. fat), 54mg chol., 280mg sod., 72g carb. (33g sugars, 2g fiber), 6g pro.

CINNAMON BUN COOKIES

I love cinnamon rolls, but working with yeast can be scary. These cookies give you the taste of a cinnamon roll in cookie form—no yeast required! They feel special enough to serve around the holidays.
—Erin Raatjes, New Lenox, IL

- -

Prep: 30 min. + chilling
Bake: 10 min./batch + cooling
Makes: about 4 dozen

 1 cup unsalted butter, softened
 ¾ cup confectioners' sugar
 ⅓ cup sugar
1½ tsp. grated orange zest
 ½ tsp. salt
 1 large egg, room temperature
 1 tsp. vanilla extract
2¼ cups all-purpose flour
FILLING
 5 Tbsp. unsalted butter, softened
 ¼ cup packed brown sugar
1½ tsp. light corn syrup
 ½ tsp. vanilla extract
 2 Tbsp. all-purpose flour
 1 Tbsp. ground cinnamon
 ½ tsp. salt

GLAZE
 1 cup confectioners' sugar
 ¼ cup light corn syrup
 2 tsp. vanilla extract
 1 to 2 tsp. water

1. Cream the first 5 ingredients until light and fluffy, 5-7 minutes. Beat in egg and vanilla. Gradually beat in flour. On a baking sheet, roll dough between 2 sheets of waxed paper into a 12-in. square. Refrigerate for 30 minutes.
2. For filling, beat butter, brown sugar, corn syrup and vanilla. Add flour, cinnamon and salt; mix well. Remove top sheet of waxed paper; spread filling over dough to within ¼ in. of edges. Using waxed paper, roll up tightly jelly-roll style, removing paper as you roll. Cover and freeze until firm, about 30 minutes.
3. Preheat oven to 375°. Uncover and cut dough crosswise into ¼-in. slices. Place 2 in. apart on parchment-lined baking sheets. Bake until the edges are lightly browned, 10-12 minutes. Cool on pans 5 minutes. Remove to wire racks to cool completely.
4. For glaze, mix confectioners' sugar, corn syrup, vanilla and enough water to reach desired consistency. Spread or drizzle over cookies. Let stand until set.
1 cookie: 103 cal., 5g fat (3g sat. fat), 17mg chol., 53mg sod., 13g carb. (8g sugars, 0 fiber), 1g pro.

OLD-FASHIONED WHOOPIE PIES

Who can resist soft chocolate sandwich cookies filled with a layer of fluffy white frosting? Mom has made these for years. They're a treat that never lasted very long with me and my two brothers around.
—Maria Costello, Monroe, NC

Prep: 35 min. + chilling
Bake: 10 min./batch + cooling
Makes: 2 dozen

- ½ cup baking cocoa
- ½ cup hot water
- ½ cup shortening
- 1½ cups sugar
- 2 large eggs, room temperature
- 1 tsp. vanilla extract
- 2⅔ cups all-purpose flour
- 1 tsp. baking powder
- 1 tsp. baking soda
- ¼ tsp. salt
- ½ cup buttermilk

FILLING
- 3 Tbsp. all-purpose flour
-    Dash salt
- 1 cup 2% milk
- ¾ cup shortening
- 1½ cups confectioners' sugar
- 2 tsp. vanilla extract

1. Preheat oven to 350°. In a small bowl, combine the cocoa and water. Cool for 5 minutes. In a large bowl, cream shortening and sugar until light and fluffy, 5-7 minutes. Beat in the eggs, vanilla and cocoa mixture. Combine dry ingredients; gradually add to the creamed mixture alternately with buttermilk, beating well after each addition

2. To form each cookie, drop 2 Tbsp. 2 in. apart onto greased baking sheets. Bake until firm to the touch, 10-12 minutes. Remove to wire racks to cool.

3. For filling, in a small saucepan, combine flour and salt. Gradually whisk in milk until smooth; cook and stir over medium-high heat until thickened, 5-7 minutes. Remove from heat. Cover and refrigerate until completely cool.

4. In a small bowl, cream the shortening, sugar and vanilla until light and fluffy, 5-7 minutes. Add milk mixture; beat until fluffy, 7 minutes. Spread filling on half the cookies; top with remaining cookies. Store in the refrigerator.

Note: To substitute for 1 cup buttermilk, use 1 Tbsp. white vinegar or lemon juice plus enough milk to measure 1 cup. Stir, then let stand 5 min. Or, use 1 cup plain yogurt or 1¾ tsp. cream of tartar plus 1 cup milk.

1 serving: 244 cal., 11g fat (3g sat. fat), 19mg chol., 116mg sod., 33g carb. (20g sugars, 1g fiber), 3g pro.

★ ★ ★ ★ ★ **READER REVIEW**

"Making whoopie pies is fun. Here are 2 tips that make it not so labor-intensive: First, make the filling ahead—if you don't feel like making the cookies, you can refrigerate the filling and make the cookies the next day. Second, use parchment—greatest invention ever!"
CAROL459 TASTEOFHOME.COM

MACAROON CHERRY PIE

In summer, I use homegrown cherries in this amazing pie with a crunchy coconut topping. But canned tart cherries yield a dessert that's almost as delicious. I always bake this pie around Presidents Day or Valentine's Day, but it's popular with my family the whole year through.
—Lori Daniels, Beverly, WV

Prep: 25 min. • **Bake:** 35 min. + chilling
Makes: 8 servings

  Dough for single-crust pie
3 cans (14½ oz. each) pitted
  tart cherries
1 cup sugar
⅓ cup cornstarch
½ tsp. ground cinnamon
¼ tsp. red food coloring, optional
TOPPING
1 large egg, room temperature,
  lightly beaten
2 Tbsp. 2% milk
1 Tbsp. butter, melted
¼ tsp. almond extract
¼ cup sugar
⅛ tsp. salt
1 cup sweetened shredded coconut
½ cup sliced almonds

1. Preheat oven to 400°. On a lightly floured surface, roll dough to a ⅛-in.-thick circle; transfer to a 9-in. cast-iron skillet or deep-dish pie plate. Trim to ½ in. beyond edge of plate; flute edges. Bake 6 minutes; set aside.
2. Drain cherries, reserving 1 cup juice. Set cherries aside. In a large saucepan, combine the sugar and cornstarch; gradually stir in cherry juice until blended. Bring to a boil over medium heat; cook and stir until thickened, 2 minutes.
3. Remove from heat; stir in cinnamon and food coloring if desired. Gently fold in cherries. Pour into crust. Cover edges loosely with foil. Bake at 400° 20 minutes.
4. Meanwhile, in a large bowl, combine the first 6 topping ingredients. Stir in coconut and almonds.

5. Remove foil from pie; spoon topping over pie. Reduce oven to 350°; bake until topping is lightly browned, 15-20 minutes. Cool on a wire rack 1 hour. Chill 4 hours or overnight before cutting.
1 piece: 434 cal., 16g fat (8g sat. fat), 36mg chol., 199mg sod., 70g carb. (48g sugars, 3g fiber), 5g pro.
Dough for single-crust pie: Combine 1¼ cups all-purpose flour and ¼ tsp. salt; cut in ½ cup cold butter until crumbly. Gradually add 3-5 Tbsp. ice water, tossing with a fork until dough holds together when pressed. Shape into a disk; wrap and refrigerate 1 hour.

CRANBERRY FUDGE

This creamy, crunchy fudge is packed with walnuts and cranberries to satisfy all who try it. Though it may seem decadent, each little bite is filled with tons of fabulous, guilt-free flavor.
—Delia Kennedy, Deer Park, WA

Prep: 20 min. + chilling
Makes: 1⅓ lbs. (81 pieces)

2 cups semisweet chocolate chips
¼ cup light corn syrup
½ cup confectioners' sugar
¼ cup reduced-fat evaporated milk
1 tsp. vanilla extract
1 pkg. (5 oz.) dried cranberries
⅓ cup chopped walnuts

1. Line a 9-in. square pan with foil. Coat the foil with cooking spray; set aside.
2. In a heavy saucepan, combine chocolate chips and corn syrup. Cook and stir over low heat until smooth. Remove from the heat. Stir in the confectioners' sugar, milk and vanilla. Beat with a wooden spoon until thickened and glossy, about 5 minutes. Stir in the cranberries and walnuts. Spread into prepared pan; refrigerate until firm.
3. Using foil, lift fudge out of pan; discard foil. Cut fudge into 1-in. squares. Store in an airtight container in the refrigerator.
1 piece: 35 cal., 2g fat (1g sat. fat), 0 chol., 2mg sod., 6g carb. (5g sugars, 0 fiber), 0 pro.

No-Bake Mango
Strawberry Cheesecake
page 252

Trifles & No-Bake Desserts

Keep the kitchen cool and be easily on your way with a luscious no-bake dessert. These simple sweets are recipes you'll turn to time and again.

GRILLED ANGEL FOOD CAKE WITH STRAWBERRIES

One night I goofed, accidentally using the balsamic butter I save for grilling chicken on my pound cake. What a delicious mistake that my entire family loved! For a patriotic look, add a drizzle of blueberry syrup.
—Tammy Hathaway,
Freeman Township, ME

- -

Takes: 15 min. • **Makes:** 8 servings

- 2 cups sliced fresh strawberries
- 2 tsp. sugar
- 3 Tbsp. butter, melted
- 2 Tbsp. balsamic vinegar
- 8 slices angel food cake (about 1 oz. each)
  Optional: Reduced-fat vanilla ice cream and blueberry syrup

1. In a small bowl, toss strawberries with sugar. In another bowl, mix butter and vinegar; brush over cut sides of cake.
2. On a greased rack, grill cake, uncovered, over medium heat until golden brown, 1-2 minutes on each side. Serve cake with strawberries and, if desired, ice cream and blueberry syrup.

1 cake slice with ¼ cup strawberries: 132 cal., 5g fat (3g sat. fat), 11mg chol., 247mg sod., 22g carb. (4g sugars, 1g fiber), 2g pro. **Diabetic exchanges:** 1½ starch, 1 fat.

TEST KITCHEN TIP
The butter and balsamic glaze will lightly caramelize when you grill the cake. If you can't find blueberry syrup, use strawberry or raspberry ice cream topping.

CHOCOLATE-COVERED CHERRIES

Not only is this my family's favorite festive dessert, it makes a delicious present, too. Best of all, you can (and should) prepare these ahead. The candy gets better as it's stored, with the centers becoming even juicier.
—Linda Hammerich, Bonanza, OR

Prep: 25 min. + chilling • **Makes:** 3 dozen

2½ cups confectioners' sugar
¼ cup butter, softened
1 Tbsp. 2% milk
½ tsp. almond extract
2 jars (8 oz. each) maraschino cherries with stems, well drained
2 cups semisweet chocolate chips
2 Tbsp. shortening

1. In a small bowl, combine sugar, butter, milk and extract. Knead until smooth and pliable. Shape into 1-in. balls and flatten each into a 2-in. circle.

2. Wrap 1 circle around each cherry and lightly roll in hands. Place with stems up on a waxed paper-lined baking sheet. Cover loosely and refrigerate 4 hours or overnight.

3. In a microwave, melt chocolate and shortening; stir until smooth. Holding on to the stems, dip cherries into chocolate; allow excess to drip off. Place on waxed paper until set. Store in a covered container. Refrigerate 1-2 weeks before serving.

2 cherries: 206 cal., 10g fat (5g sat. fat), 7mg chol., 28mg sod., 33g carb. (31g sugars, 1g fiber), 1g pro.

MALTED MILK PIES

Malted milk balls provide the delightful flavor in each cool bite of this light dessert. So easy to make, the pies feed a crowd and are a longtime favorite of my family.
—Jann Marie Foster, Minneapolis, MN

- -

Prep: 10 min. + freezing
Makes: 2 pies (8 servings each)

- 1 pkg. (7 oz.) malted milk balls, chopped
- 1 pint vanilla ice cream, softened
- 1 carton (8 oz.) frozen whipped topping, thawed
- 2 chocolate crumb crusts (9 in.)
  Additional whipped topping, optional

1. Set aside ¼ cup malted milk balls for topping. Place ice cream in a large bowl; fold in whipped topping and remaining malted milk balls. Spoon into crusts. Cover and freeze until firm, about 4 hours.
2. Remove from freezer 20 minutes before serving. If desired, garnish with additional whipped topping; top with reserved malted milk balls.

1 piece: 234 cal., 11g fat (7g sat. fat), 7mg chol., 150mg sod., 31g carb. (21g sugars, 1g fiber), 2g pro.

RAINBOW CAKE

From out of the blue this time comes a truly beautiful sight. As soon as folks get a glimpse of it, though, it'll likely disappear fast!
—*Taste of Home* Test Kitchen

- -

Prep: 1 hour • **Makes:** 8 servings

- 1 loaf (10¾ oz.) frozen pound cake, thawed and cut into 1-in. cubes
- ½ cup heavy whipping cream
- 8-oz.pkg. cream cheese, softened
- ¼ cup confectioners' sugar
- 5 tsp. orange juice
- ½ tsp. grated orange zest
- 2 cups fresh raspberries
- 1 cup fresh blueberries
- 15 to 18 large green grapes, halved
- 15-oz. can of mandarin oranges, well drained
- 10 to 15 fresh strawberries, halved

1. Arrange cake cubes in a rainbow arch on a large serving platter. In a small bowl, beat whipping cream until soft peaks form. In another bowl, beat cream cheese, sugar, orange zest and orange juice until smooth; fold in whipped cream.
2. Gently spread cream cheese mixture over cake cubes. Arrange fruit over cream cheese mixture in a rainbow pattern. If desired, garnish with additional whipped cream to create cloud shapes.

1 serving: 395 cal., 24g fat (14g sat. fat), 101mg chol., 208mg sod., 44g carb. (31g sugars, 4g fiber), 5g pro.

★ ★ ★ ★ ★ **READER REVIEW**

"Thanks for the idea. I have a rainbow-shaped tray and this will be perfect for brunch. I plan to use red = raspberries; orange = mandarin oranges; yellow = bananas; green = green grapes; blue = blueberries; indigo = blackberries; violet = blue grapes."

EKALAKA TASTEOFHOME.COM

WATERMELON BOMBE DESSERT

When cut, this sherbet dessert looks like actual watermelon slices—complete with seeds. It is very fun to eat and so refreshing, too.
—Renae Moncur, Burley, ID

- -

Prep: 20 min. + freezing • **Makes:** 8 servings

    About 1 pint lime sherbet
    About 1 pint pineapple sherbet
    About 1½ pints raspberry sherbet
¼ **cup miniature semisweet chocolate chips**

1. Line a 1½-qt. bowl with plastic wrap. Press slightly softened lime sherbet against the bottom and sides of bowl. Freeze, uncovered, until firm. Spread pineapple sherbet evenly over lime sherbet layer. Freeze, uncovered, until firm. (Lime and pineapple sherbet layers should be thin.) Pack raspberry sherbet in center of sherbet-lined bowl. Smooth top to resemble a cut watermelon.

2. Cover and freeze until firm, about 8 hours. Just before serving, uncover bowl of molded sherbet. Place a serving plate on the bowl and invert. Remove bowl and peel off plastic wrap.

3. Cut the bombe into wedges; press a few chocolate chips into the raspberry section of each wedge to resemble seeds.

1 piece: 205 cal., 4g fat (2g sat. fat), 8mg chol., 60mg sod., 43g carb. (35g sugars, 0 fiber), 2g pro.

CIRCUS PEANUT GELATIN

Circus peanuts are one of the most popular candies in my hometown's old-fashioned candy shop. When I saw this circus peanut gelatin recipe, I knew just where to buy them. Kids love the fruity taste, and older folks enjoy the trip down memory lane.
—Ruthanne Mengel, De Motte, IN

- -

Prep: 10 min. + chilling • **Makes:** 15 servings

47 **circus peanut candies, divided**
1 **cup boiling water, divided**
2 **pkg. (3 oz. each) orange gelatin**
2 **cans (8 oz. each) crushed pineapple, undrained**
1 **carton (8 oz.) frozen whipped topping, thawed**

1. Cut 32 candies into small pieces; place in a microwave-safe bowl. Add ¼ cup of boiling water. Cover and microwave on high for 45 seconds; stir. Microwave 45 seconds longer. Stir until smooth. In a large bowl, dissolve gelatin in remaining boiling water. Stir in candy mixture and pineapple. Refrigerate until partially set.

2. Fold in whipped topping. Pour into a greased 13x9-in. dish. Refrigerate until firm. Cut into squares; top each square with a remaining circus peanut.

1 piece: 186 cal., 3g fat (3g sat. fat), 0 chol., 26mg sod., 39g carb. (38g sugars, 0 fiber), 1g pro.

FROZEN PEPPERMINT DELIGHT

If you're looking for a dessert that's festively fun and easy to make, this is the one for you. Drizzled in hot fudge sauce and loaded with pretty peppermint pieces, this tempting treat will have guests asking for seconds.
—Pam Lancaster, Willis, VA

Prep: 25 min. + freezing
Makes: 15 servings

1	pkg. (14.3 oz.) Oreo cookies, crushed
¼	cup butter, melted
2	containers (1½ qt. each) peppermint ice cream, slightly softened
1	carton (12 oz.) frozen whipped topping, thawed
	Hot fudge ice cream topping, warmed
	Crushed peppermint candy

1. In a large bowl, combine cookie crumbs and butter. Press into an ungreased 13x9-in. dish. Spread ice cream over crust; top with whipped topping. Cover and freeze until solid. May be frozen for up to 2 months.
2. Just before serving, drizzle with hot fudge topping and sprinkle with candy.
1 piece: 425 cal., 22g fat (11g sat. fat), 24mg chol., 296mg sod., 52g carb. (35g sugars, 2g fiber), 4g pro.

EASY MINT THINS

My friends often attempt to guess the ingredients in these cookies, but I never tell them how simple they are to make. They taste just like the Girl Scouts cookie!
—Jennifer Setser, Morgantown, IN

Prep: 40 min. + standing • **Makes:** 5 dozen

24	oz. milk or dark chocolate candy coating
1½	tsp. peppermint extract
60	Ritz crackers
2	oz. white candy coating, melted
	Optional decorations: Chopped Andes mint candies, crushed spearmint candies and green colored sugar

1. In a microwave, melt chocolate candy coating; stir until smooth. Stir in extract.
2. Dip crackers in chocolate candy coating; allow excess to drip off. Place on waxed paper; let stand until set.
3. Drizzle tops with white candy coating; decorate as desired. Let stand until set. Store in airtight containers.
1 cookie: 89 cal., 4g fat (2g sat. fat), 0 chol., 34mg sod., 9g carb. (6g sugars, 0 fiber), 1g pro.

TEST KITCHEN TIP
If desired, use a few drops of peppermint or spearmint oil instead of the mint extract.

RED-WHITE-AND-BLUE BERRY DELIGHT

Loaded with fresh strawberries and blueberries, this luscious treat is perfect for any Fourth of July celebration!
—Constance Fennell, Grand Junction, MI

- -

Prep: 25 min. + chilling • **Makes:** 8 servings

- ½ cup sugar
- 2 envelopes unflavored gelatin
- 4 cups white cranberry-peach juice drink, divided
- 1 Tbsp. lemon juice
- 2 cups fresh strawberries, halved
- 2 cups fresh blueberries

CREAM

- ½ cup heavy whipping cream
- 1 Tbsp. sugar
- ¼ tsp. vanilla extract

1. In a large saucepan, combine sugar and gelatin. Add 1 cup cranberry-peach juice; cook and stir over low heat until gelatin is completely dissolved, about 5 minutes. Remove from the heat; stir in lemon juice and remaining cranberry-peach juice.

2. Place halved strawberries in an 8-cup ring mold coated with cooking spray; add 2 cups gelatin mixture. Refrigerate until set but not firm, about 30 minutes. Set aside remaining gelatin mixture.

3. Stir blueberries into remaining gelatin mixture; spoon over strawberry layer. Refrigerate overnight. Unmold onto a serving platter.

4. In a small bowl, beat cream until it begins to thicken. Add sugar and vanilla; beat until stiff peaks form. Serve with gelatin.

Note: If using frozen blueberries, use without thawing to avoid discoloring the batter.

1 piece with 2 Tbsp. whipped cream: 203 cal., 6g fat (3g sat. fat), 20mg chol., 12mg sod., 38g carb. (35g sugars, 2g fiber), 3g pro.

GRANDMA'S ENGLISH TRIFLE

This delicious trifle recipe was my grandmother's. I remember Mother telling me stories from her girlhood—especially how her mother would make an enormous dish of this dessert for Saturday night dinners, when they often had guests. If there were leftovers, they would have that trifle for dessert every night until it was gone! Nowadays, on our dairy farm, this recipe always goes over big with my husband and our six children.
—Ruth Verratti, Gasport, NY

- -

Prep: 30 min. + chilling • **Makes:** 10 servings

- 1 prepared loaf pound cake or 1 pkg. (10¾ oz.) frozen pound cake, thawed
- ¼ to ½ cup raspberry jam
- 1 pkg. (3 to 3½ oz.) regular or instant vanilla pudding mix
- 2½ cups 2% milk
- 1 cup chilled heavy whipping cream
- 3 Tbsp. confectioners' sugar
  Slivered almonds
  Maraschino cherries, halved

Slice pound cake in half horizontally. Spread with jam and replace top of cake. Slice cake into 9 pieces. Line the sides and fill the center of a 2-qt. glass serving bowl with cake pieces. Prepare pudding with milk. Pour over cake. Chill. Beat cream and sugar until soft peaks form; spread over cake and pudding. Chill at least 4 hours. Garnish with almonds and cherries.

1 serving: 292 cal., 16g fat (10g sat. fat), 76mg chol., 176mg sod., 31g carb. (24g sugars, 0 fiber), 4g pro.

WINTER WISHES TRIFLE

I created this light and fluffy trifle for a dear friend who was looking for a stunning dessert. This recipe hit the mark.
—Susan Stetzel, Gainesville, NY

Prep: 20 min. + chilling • **Makes:** 12 servings

- 1   prepared angel food cake (8 to 10 oz.)
- 4   oz. white baking chocolate
- 4   cups heavy whipping cream, divided
- ½   tsp. peppermint extract
- 12 peppermint candies, crushed

1. Place mixer beaters in a large metal bowl; refrigerate 30 minutes. Cut or tear cake into bite-sized pieces; set aside.

2. Break white chocolate into smaller pieces; microwave at 70% power, stirring after 45 seconds. Microwave until melted, about 30 seconds more. Stir until smooth. Let stand 5 minutes; stir ¼ cup heavy cream into white chocolate until smooth.

3. In the chilled bowl, beat remaining heavy cream until soft peaks form. Gently fold two-thirds of whipped cream into white chocolate. Stir extract into remaining whipped cream.

4. In a trifle bowl, layer cake and white chocolate mixture, repeating layers. Top with peppermint-flavored whipped cream. Refrigerate, covered, until serving. Sprinkle with crushed candies.

1 serving: 392 cal., 32g fat (20g sat. fat), 90mg chol., 173mg sod., 25g carb. (12g sugars, 0 fiber), 4g pro.

PISTACHIO CREAM DESSERT

With its crisp crumb crust, frosty filling and crunchy topping, this frozen dessert is a cool end to a hot-weather meal.
—Hazel King, Nacogdoches, TX

Prep: 15 min. + freezing • **Makes:** 8 servings

- 2 **Tbsp. butter**
- ¾ **cup Ritz cracker crumbs**
- ¾ **cup cold milk**
- 1 **pkg. (3.4 oz.) instant pistachio pudding mix**
- 2 **cups vanilla ice cream, softened**
- 1 **carton (8 oz.) frozen whipped topping, thawed**
- 2 **Heath candy bars (1.4 oz. each), crushed**

1. In a microwave-safe 8-in. square dish, melt butter. Stir in cracker crumbs; press mixture onto bottom of dish. In a bowl, whisk milk and pudding mix for 2 minutes. Let stand 2 minutes or until soft-set. Whisk in ice cream. Pour over crust. Cover and freeze for 2 hours.

2. Spread with whipped topping; sprinkle with candy bars. Freeze 1 hour or until firm.

1 piece: 303 cal., 16g fat (10g sat. fat), 26mg chol., 317mg sod., 35g carb. (22g sugars, 0 fiber), 3g pro.

HOW TO MAKE A CRUMB CRUST

To make crumbs, crush crackers with a rolling pin or use a food processor. Then press the crust evenly into the dish using a juice glass or measuring cup.

CHOCOLATE PEANUT BUTTER NO-BAKE COOKIES

These peanut butter and chocolate cookies bring back fond memories of my mom. The no-bake recipe was her favorite, and she always made a batch when she knew company was coming.
—Jacquie McTaggart, Independence, IA

Prep: 20 min. + chilling • **Makes:** 2½ dozen

- 2 **cups sugar**
- ½ **cup butter or margarine, cubed**
- ½ **cup 2% milk**
- 3 **Tbsp. baking cocoa**
  Dash salt
- ½ **cup creamy peanut butter**
- 1 **tsp. vanilla extract**
- 3 **cups old-fashioned oats**

1. In a large saucepan, combine the first 5 ingredients. Bring to a boil, stirring constantly. Cook and stir 3 minutes.

2. Remove from heat; stir in peanut butter and vanilla until blended. Stir in oats. Drop mixture by tablespoonfuls onto waxed paper-lined baking sheets. Refrigerate until set. Store in airtight containers.

1 cookie: 139 cal., 6g fat (3g sat. fat), 8mg chol., 50mg sod., 20g carb. (14g sugars, 1g fiber), 2g pro.

BUTTERSCOTCH-RUM RAISIN TREATS

I love making rum raisin rice pudding around the holidays—and those classic flavors inspired this confection. Crispy rice cereal adds crunch, but nuts, toasted coconut or candied pineapple could do the job, too.
—Crystal Schlueter, Northglenn, CO

Takes: 20 min. • **Makes:** about 4½ dozen

- 1 pkg. (10 to 11 oz.) butterscotch chips
- 1 pkg. (10 to 12 oz.) white baking chips
- ½ tsp. rum extract
- 3 cups Rice Krispies
- 1 cup raisins

1. Line 56 mini-muffin cups with paper liners. In a large bowl, combine butterscotch and white chips. Microwave, uncovered, on high for 30 seconds; stir. Microwave in additional 30-second intervals, stirring until smooth.
2. Stir in extract, Rice Krispies and raisins. Drop by rounded tablespoonfuls into prepared mini-muffin cups. Chill until set.
Freeze option Freeze treats in freezer containers, separating layers with waxed paper. Thaw before serving.
1 treat: 76 cal., 4g fat (3g sat. fat), 1mg chol., 21mg sod., 11g carb. (9g sugars, 0 fiber), 0 pro.

CHERRIMISU

Inspired by the traditional Italian tiramisu, this easy dessert dresses up a prepared angel food cake with a cherry cream filling and frosting. Dust the top with cocoa for a decadent finishing touch.
—Kelly Byler, Goshen, IN

Takes: 25 min. • **Makes:** 12 servings

- 1 jar (10 oz.) maraschino cherries
- ½ cup ricotta cheese
- 4 oz. cream cheese, softened
- 2 Tbsp. confectioners' sugar
- ¼ tsp. cherry extract
- 1½ cups heavy whipping cream
- 1 prepared angel food cake (8 to 10 oz.)
- 1 Tbsp. baking cocoa

1. Drain cherries; reserving ¼ cup juice. In a large bowl, beat ricotta cheese, cream cheese, confectioners' sugar and extract until blended. Gradually beat in cream and reserved cherry juice until stiff peaks form.
2. Using a long serrated knife, cut cake horizontally in half. Place 1 cake layer on a serving plate; spread with 1 cup whipped cream mixture. Arrange cherries over cream layer. Top with remaining cake layer. Frost top and sides of cake with remaining cream mixture. Dust with cocoa.
1 piece: 235 cal., 15g fat (10g sat. fat), 48mg chol., 192mg sod., 23g carb. (12g sugars, 0 fiber), 4g pro.

DIRTY BANANA TRIFLE

What could be better than bananas, cookies and Kahlua? You can adjust this to suit your taste, depending on whether you like a stronger or weaker Kahlua flavor.
—Laurie Handlin, Ocean View, DE

Prep: 40 min. + chilling • **Makes:** 24 servings

- 2 pkg. (8 oz. each) cream cheese, softened, divided
- 2 cans (14 oz. each) sweetened condensed milk, divided
- 1½ cups Kahlua (coffee liqueur), chilled
- 2½ cups cold 2% milk, divided
- 2 pkg. (3.9 oz. each) instant chocolate pudding mix
- 3 cartons (8 oz. each) frozen whipped topping, thawed, divided
- 9 whole chocolate graham crackers, coarsely crushed
- 2 pkg. (3.4 oz. each) instant banana cream pudding mix
- 1½ cups coarsely crushed vanilla wafers (about 45 wafers)
- 5 medium bananas, sliced
  Additional wafers, crushed chocolate graham crackers and sliced bananas

1. In a large bowl, beat 1 package cream cheese and 1 can condensed milk until blended. Beat in Kahlua, ½ cup milk and chocolate pudding mixes until thickened, about 2 minutes. Fold in 1 carton whipped topping, then chocolate graham crackers. Set aside.

2. In another large bowl, beat remaining cream cheese and condensed milk until blended. Beat in remaining 2 cups milk and banana pudding mixes until thickened, about 2 minutes. Fold in 1 carton whipped topping, vanilla wafers and bananas.

3. Spread chocolate pudding mixture in the bottom of a 6- or 7-qt. trifle bowl or glass bowl. Layer with 1½ cups whipped topping and banana pudding mixture; top with remaining 1½ cups whipped topping. Cover and refrigerate overnight.

4. Garnish with additional wafers, crushed chocolate graham crackers and sliced bananas before serving.

1 cup: 381 cal., 16g fat (11g sat. fat), 33mg chol., 326mg sod., 46g carb. (33g sugars, 1g fiber), 5g pro.

PEANUT BUTTER BROWNIE TRIFLE

This rich, tempting trifle feeds a crowd and features the ever-popular combination of chocolate and peanut butter. Try this dessert for your next get-together.
—Nancy Foust, Stoneboro, PA

- -

Prep: 1 hour + chilling
Makes: 20 servings (1 cup each)

- 1   fudge brownie mix (13x9-in. pan size)
- 1   pkg. (10 oz.) peanut butter chips
- 2   pkg. (13 oz. each) miniature peanut butter cups
- 4   cups cold 2% milk
- 2   pkg. (5.1 oz. each) instant vanilla pudding mix
- 1   cup creamy peanut butter
- 4   tsp. vanilla extract
- 3   cartons (8 oz. each) frozen whipped topping, thawed

1. Preheat oven to 350°. Prepare brownie batter according to package directions; stir in peanut butter chips. Bake in a greased 13x9-in. baking pan 20-25 minutes or until a toothpick inserted in the center comes out with moist crumbs (do not overbake). Cool on a wire rack; cut into ¾-in. pieces.
2. Cut peanut butter cups in half; set aside ⅓ cup for garnish. In a large bowl, whisk milk and pudding mixes for 2 minutes (mixture will be thick). Add peanut butter and vanilla; mix well. Fold in 1½ cartons whipped topping.
3. Place a third of the brownies in a 5-qt. glass bowl; top with a third of remaining peanut butter cups. Spoon a third of the pudding mixture over the top. Repeat layers twice. Cover with remaining whipped topping; garnish with reserved peanut butter cups. Refrigerate until chilled.
1 cup: 680 cal., 38g fat (15g sat. fat), 28mg chol., 547mg sod., 73g carb. (54g sugars, 3g fiber), 13g pro.

FLUFFY KEY LIME PIE

For a taste of paradise, try this light and creamy confection. It's low in fat, sugar and fuss. Dessert doesn't get any better than that!
—Frances VanFossan, Warren, MI

- -

Prep: 20 min. + chilling • **Makes:** 8 servings

- ¼   cup boiling water
- 1   pkg. (0.3 oz.) sugar-free lime gelatin
- 2   cartons (6 oz. each) Key lime yogurt
- 1   carton (8 oz.) frozen fat-free whipped topping, thawed
- 1   reduced-fat graham cracker crust (9 in.)

1. In a large bowl, add boiling water to gelatin; stir 2 minutes to completely dissolve. Whisk in yogurt. Fold in whipped topping. Pour into crust.
2. Refrigerate, covered, until set, about 2 hours.
1 piece: 194 cal., 3g fat (1g sat. fat), 2mg chol., 159mg sod., 33g carb. (18g sugars, 0 fiber), 3g pro. **Diabetic exchanges:** 2 starch, ½ fat.

FIVE-MINUTE BLUEBERRY PIE

If you like the taste of fresh blueberries, you'll love this pie. Since it's a breeze to whip up, I make it often, especially in summer.
—Milda Anderson, Osceola, WI

Prep: 15 min. + chilling • **Makes:** 8 servings

- ½ cup sugar
- 2 Tbsp. cornstarch
- ¾ cup water
- 4 cups fresh or frozen blueberries, thawed
- 1 graham cracker crust (9 in.)
  Whipped cream, optional

In a large saucepan, combine sugar and cornstarch. Stir in water until smooth. Bring to a boil over medium heat; cook and stir for 2 minutes. Add blueberries. Cook for 3 minutes, stirring occasionally. Pour into prepared crust. Chill. Garnish with whipped cream if desired.

1 piece: 202 cal., 6g fat (1g sat. fat), 0 chol., 122mg sod., 39g carb. (29g sugars, 2g fiber), 1g pro.

★ ★ ★ ★ ★ **READER REVIEW**

"Delicious and easy. I usually use a regular cooked pastry shell. For an extra special taste, spread the cooled shell with a couple tablespoons of sweetened, softened, plain cream cheese before adding the blueberry mixture."

KNOLLBROOKCOOK TASTEOFHOME.COM

CHOCOLATE-PEANUT BUTTER CRISPY BARS

These chewy peanut butter chocolate bars are the perfect contribution to a potluck or bake sale. I've discovered the trick is to get them into the refrigerator to set up before they disappear!
—Lorri Speer, Centralia, WA

Prep: 30 min. + chilling • **Makes:** 2 dozen

- 1 cup sugar
- 1 cup light corn syrup
- 1 cup peanut butter
- 6 cups Rice Krispies
- 2 cups semisweet chocolate chips, melted

1. In a large saucepan, combine sugar, corn syrup and peanut butter. Cook and stir over medium-low heat until sugar is dissolved. Remove from heat; stir in cereal.
2. Spread into a greased 13x9-in. pan; press lightly. Spread melted chocolate over top; refrigerate until set. Cut into bars.

1 bar: 302 cal., 14g fat (6g sat. fat), 0 chol., 96mg sod., 46g carb. (37g sugars, 2g fiber), 4g pro.

MAKE AHEAD

7-LAYER GELATIN SALAD

My mother makes this colorful gelatin salad to accompany our Christmas dinner each year. Choose different flavors to create special color combinations for particular holidays or gatherings.
—Jan Hemness, Stockton, MO

Prep: 30 min. + chilling • **Makes:** 20 servings

4½ cups boiling water, divided
  7 pkg. (3 oz. each) assorted flavored gelatin
4½ cups cold water, divided
  1 can (12 oz.) evaporated milk, divided
  1 carton (8 oz.) frozen whipped topping, thawed
    Optional: Sliced strawberries and kiwifruit

1. In a small bowl, add ¾ cup boiling water to 1 gelatin package; stir 2 minutes to completely dissolve. Stir in ¾ cup cold water. Pour into a 3-qt. trifle or glass bowl. Refrigerate until set but not firm, about 40 minutes.
2. In a clean bowl, dissolve another gelatin package into ½ cup boiling water. Stir in ½ cup cold water and ½ cup milk. Spoon over the first layer. Refrigerate until set but not firm.
3. Repeat 5 times, alternating plain and creamy gelatin layers. Refrigerate each layer until set but not firm before adding the next layer. Refrigerate, covered, overnight. Serve with whipped topping and, if desired, fruit.

Note: Recipe may also be prepared in a 13x9-in. dish coated with cooking spray; follow recipe as directed. Cut into squares before serving.

1 serving: 163 cal., 3g fat (3g sat. fat), 6mg chol., 85mg sod., 30g carb. (30g sugars, 0 fiber), 4g pro.

EASY KEY LIME PIE TRIFLE

I came up with this easy trifle because I adore Key lime pie in all its forms. It's a refreshing treat on a hot summer day, and since it can be made ahead, it's ideal for entertaining, too. The pie is easier to cut when still a little frozen, but be sure to let the pieces finish thawing before starting the recipe.
—Barbara Moorhead, Gaffney, SC

Prep: 20 min. + chilling • **Makes:** 10 servings

  1 pkg. (8 oz.) cream cheese, softened
1½ cups heavy whipping cream
  ¼ cup sugar
1½ tsp. vanilla extract
  1 frozen key lime pie (36 oz.), cut into 1-in. cubes, thawed
  1 cup sweetened shredded coconut, toasted
  1 cup chopped pecans, toasted

In a large bowl, beat cream cheese, cream, sugar and vanilla until soft peaks form. Place half of the pie pieces in a 3-qt. trifle bowl or glass bowl. Spread with half the cream cheese mixture; top with ½ cup coconut and ½ cup pecans. Repeat the layers. Refrigerate, covered, at least 1 hour before serving.

1 cup: 685 cal., 48g fat (24g sat. fat), 79mg chol., 255mg sod., 58g carb. (46g sugars, 1g fiber), 9g pro.

NO-BAKE MANGO STRAWBERRY CHEESECAKE

Cheesecake is my mom's favorite dessert. I made this especially for her on Mother's Day to thank her for being such an awesome mom. Decorate to your own taste!
—Elizabeth Ding, El Cerrito, CA

Prep: 45 min. + chilling • **Makes:** 12 servings

- 2 cups graham cracker crumbs
- ⅔ cup butter, melted
- ⅓ cup sugar

FILLING
- 1 envelope unflavored gelatin
- 3 Tbsp. cold water
- 2 pkg. (8 oz. each) cream cheese, softened
- 1⅓ cups sugar
- 1 cup heavy whipping cream
- 2 tsp. vanilla extract
- ½ large mango, peeled and cubed (about ¾ cup)
- 4 fresh strawberries, chopped

GLAZE
- 1 envelope unflavored gelatin
- 3 Tbsp. plus ½ cup cold water, divided
- ½ large mango, peeled and cubed (about ¾ cup)
  Optional: Whipped cream, mango pieces and sliced strawberries

1. In a small bowl, mix crumbs, butter and sugar. Press onto bottom and 1 in. up sides of a greased 8-in. springform pan.
2. For filling, in a microwave-safe bowl, sprinkle gelatin over cold water; let stand 1 minute. Microwave mixture on high for 10-20 seconds or just until water is warm but not hot. Stir and let stand until gelatin is completely dissolved, about 1 minute. Cool until partially set.
3. In a large bowl, beat cream cheese and sugar until smooth. Gradually beat in cream, vanilla and gelatin mixture until blended. Fold in mango and strawberries. Pour over crust. Refrigerate while preparing glaze.
4. For glaze, in another microwave-safe bowl, sprinkle gelatin over 3 Tbsp. cold water; let stand 1 minute. Microwave on high 10-20 seconds or until water is warm but not hot. Stir and let stand until gelatin is completely dissolved, about 1 minute. Cool until partially set. Meanwhile, place mango and remaining ½ cup water in a food processor; process until pureed. Stir in gelatin mixture; pour over filling. Refrigerate, loosely covered, overnight.
5. Loosen sides from pan with a knife. Remove rim from pan. If desired garnish with whipped cream, additional mango pieces and strawberry slices.

1 piece: 495 cal., 32g fat (19g sat. fat), 88mg chol., 285mg sod., 48g carb. (38g sugars, 1g fiber), 5g pro.

ORANGE COCONUT BALLS

When my mother first made these slightly sweet morsels years ago, we immediately fell in love with their unique flavor.
—Helen Youngers, Kingman, KS

Takes: 20 min. • **Makes:** 4½ dozen

- 1 pkg. (12 oz.) vanilla wafers, crushed
- ¾ cup confectioners' sugar
- ¾ cup sweetened shredded coconut
- ½ cup finely chopped pecans
- ½ cup thawed orange juice concentrate
  Additional confectioners' sugar

In a large bowl, combine the first 5 ingredients. Roll into 1-in. balls, then roll in confectioners' sugar. Store in the refrigerator. Roll in additional confectioners' sugar before serving.

2 each: 98 cal., 4g fat (1g sat. fat), 1mg chol., 46mg sod., 15g carb. (9g sugars, 1g fiber), 1g pro.

CARAMEL APPLE TRIFLE

Trifles are terrific desserts because they're made in advance and feed a crowd. This caramel apple version appeals to kids of all ages.
—Joanne Wright, Niles, MI

- -

Prep: 40 min. + chilling • **Makes:** 14 servings

- 3 **Tbsp. butter**
- 4 **cups chopped peeled tart apples (about 5 medium)**
- 1 **cup chopped walnuts**
- ½ **cup packed brown sugar**
- 1 **tsp. apple pie spice, divided**
- 1 **pkg. (8 oz.) cream cheese, softened**
- 1 **jar (12¼ oz.) caramel ice cream topping, divided**
- 1 **carton (12 oz.) frozen whipped topping, thawed, divided**
- 2 **loaves (10¾ oz. each) frozen pound cake, thawed and cut into 1-in. cubes**
  Additional apple pie spice, optional

1. In a large skillet, melt butter over medium heat. Add the apples, walnuts, brown sugar and ½ tsp. apple pie spice. Cook and stir for 8-10 minutes or until apples are tender.
2. In a large bowl, beat cream cheese until smooth. Beat in ½ cup caramel topping and remaining apple pie spice. Fold in 2 cups whipped topping.
3. In a 3½-qt. trifle bowl or glass serving bowl, layer a third of the cake cubes, cream cheese mixture and apple mixture. Repeat layers twice. Garnish with the remaining whipped topping and drizzle with remaining caramel topping. Sprinkle with additional pie spice if desired. Cover and refrigerate for at least 1 hour before serving.
1 cup: 472 cal., 25g fat (14g sat. fat), 87mg chol., 313mg sod., 57g carb. (26g sugars, 2g fiber), 6g pro.

BROKEN GLASS DESSERT

This decidedly vintage dessert may sound dangerous, but it's fun to make and to eat. When it's cut, it looks like stained glass windows!
—Kathy Crow, Cordova, AK

- -

Prep: 30 min. + chilling • **Makes:** 15 servings

- 1 **pkg. (3 oz.) lime gelatin**
- 4½ **cups boiling water, divided**
- 1 **pkg. (3 oz.) strawberry gelatin**
- 1 **pkg. (3 oz.) orange gelatin**
- 1½ **cups graham cracker crumbs**
- ½ **cup sugar**
- ½ **cup butter, melted**
- 1 **envelope unflavored gelatin**
- ¼ **cup cold water**
- 1 **cup pineapple juice**
- 1 **carton (8 oz.) frozen whipped topping, thawed**

1. Combine lime gelatin and 1½ cups boiling water; stir until gelatin is dissolved. Pour into a lightly greased 8x4-in. loaf pan; chill until very firm. Repeat to make the strawberry and orange gelatins in sugar and butter; press into a greased 13x9-in. dish. Chill.
2. Meanwhile, in a small bowl, soften unflavored gelatin in cold water for 5 minutes. In a small saucepan, bring pineapple juice to a boil. Stir in unflavored gelatin until dissolved. Transfer to a large bowl; set aside until room temperature, 20-30 minutes.
3. When flavored gelatins are firm, cut into ½-in. cubes. In a large bowl, whisk whipped topping into pineapple juice mixture. Gently fold ⅔ of the cubes into whipped topping mixture. Spoon over crust; top with the remaining cubes. Chill for at least 2 hours.
1 piece: 183 cal., 4g fat (3g sat. fat), 0 chol., 86mg sod., 35g carb. (29g sugars, 0 fiber), 3g pro.

Recipe Index